Lukacs's Road to God

Current Continental Research
is co-published by
The Center for Advanced Research
in Phenomenology
and
University Press of America, Inc.

CURRENT CONTINENTAL RESEARCH 208

Michael Holzman

LUKACS'S ROAD TO GOD

The Early Criticism Against Its Pre-Marxist Background

1985

Center for Advanced Research in Phenomenology
& University Press of America, Washington, D.C.

University Press of America,® Inc.

4720 Boston Way
Lanham, MD 20706

3 Henrietta Street
London WC2E 8LU England

Library of Congress Cataloging in Publication Data

Holzman, Michael.
  Lukacs's road to God.

  (Current continental research ; 208)
  Bibliography: p.
  Includes index.
  1. Lukács, György, 1885-1971. I. Center for
Advanced Research in Phenomenology. II. Title.
III. Series.
B4815.L84H64   1985   199'.439   85-9042
ISBN 0-8191-4719-2 (alk. paper)
ISBN 0-8191-4720-6 (pbk. : alk. paper)

CONTENTS

Acknowledgments

This study began at the suggestion of Claudio Guillén. Jim Rother read an early version of the manuscript. It has also been read and corrected by other, more recent, colleagues, but at this point I begin to run the risk of slighting some who have helped me – or implicating them – so I will conclude these personal acknowledgments with thanks to the anonymous readers of the Center for Advanced Research in Phenomenology: generous, learned, scrupulous beyond all measure.

Two of these essays have been previously published in other forms in **Clio** and **Criticism**. I am grateful to their editors for granting permission to use that material here. Most quotations from **Soul and Form** and **The Theory of the Novel** in English are from The MIT Press editions, which has generously granted permission for their use. (Occasionally, particularly at the beginning of Chapter V, the translations are my own.) The publication of this book has been made possible by a grant from the University of Southern California.

In Memory of Robert C. Elliott

Introduction

There may be, somewhere, an ideal scholarly reader, who, when examining a text, brings to bear upon it simultaneously all that need be known of its place among other, similar texts, its place in the life of its author and the time of its composition, its place, in short, in the overwhelming complexity of history, history construed in the broadest possible sense. There may be such a reader, indeed, from time to time each of us may actually be such a reader, but for the most part we are usually much closer to the common reader – serious, well-informed, but not overly careful to distinguish here and compare there, interested, rather, in finding what interests us in the book that happens to be at hand. Accidents of translation and fashion become much more important than we wish to admit, so that Dostoevsky, say, has a certain Edwardian quality about him for those of us who have no Russian, and the Golden Ages of the Italian and Spanish theater barely exist for those of us who have not taken them as special studies. Another such blank – or dim – area even for many literary scholars is German philosophy in the late nineteenth century. Kant, of course, we would be ashamed to admit not knowing, and Hegel is a great name, connected, somehow, with George Eliot or Emerson. But as for later figures, it is all a fog or a cloud or some other image dismal and damp.

Turning then to the criticism and theory of Georg Lukács, we tend to read him backward. He was a Marxist, after all, the supreme Marxist literary critic. There is the Brecht-Lukács debate, of course, and the question of Stalinism, and that related question of the paradoxically old-fashioned nature of Lukács's taste in literature, so satisfying to contrast to the adventurousness of Walter Benjamin. But, for most of us, he is the typical Marxist literary critic and theorist. His **Theory of the Novel** is very important, particularly to those of us interested in literary theory. It is convenient to have such a thing from a Marxist literary critic. We realize, if we think about it, that Lukács was not a Marxist when he wrote the **The Theory of the Novel,** but we need not think about that often. We can, if we wish, imagine a Marxist Lukács who wrote **The Theory of the Novel** and then interpret the text as if that had actually been the case. Such approaches might worry us more if we realized that the book was meant to be read in the context of a Jewish Messianicism. The present work is partially an attempt to read some of Lukács's pre-Marxist writing front to back, rather than in the currently popular back to front manner, and to read it as situated in the Central Euopean intellectual climate in which it originated.

There is a frequent implication, and often something more than that, in the following pages that the peculiarities of Lukács's spiritualized concept of literary study have parallels in the work of certain scholars in the United States. I have called these peculiarities the ideology of the spirit and attempt to describe them extensively in the instance of the early Lukács in the body of this work and briefly in the concluding section as they appear in some American locales. Generally, the ideology of the spirit is that set of beliefs which claims that the human sciences are valuable chiefly as stepping-stones to "higher things" and that scholars are justified in using the occasion of the study of literature as a platform for the exposition and propagation of their personal values. This is not an uncommon stage in the development of scholarship. Mathematics did not abandon similar views until the seventeenth century and the natural sciences did not do so until the end of the eighteenth or the middle of the nineteenth century. The issue of values was also present at the birth of the modern social sciences. Wilhelm Dilthey and Georg Simmel developed an interpretation of cultural studies based on a doctrine of the reality determining function of the mind. Rickert and Weber attempted to cope with the question of values by defining a methodology for the human sciences that would allow intersubjective validity, "objectivity," in research. I believe that those turn-of-the-century debates may well illuminate our own concerns with the methodology of literary studies.

In order to focus my accounts of philosophical debates on literary matters I have given detailed and systematic readings of Georg Lukács's **Die Seele und die Formen [Soul and Form]** in terms of Simmel's radically subjectivist theory of knowledge and of his **Die Theorie des Romans [The Theory of the Novel]** as exhibiting the influence of that doctrine as modified by the Weberian methodology of ideal types and the pervasive concerns associated with the Life Philosophy of Dilthey. Such readings were chosen for the simple reason that **Soul and Form** was written while Lukács was studying with Simmel while **The Theory of the Novel** shows Lukács coming under the influence of Weber at Heidelberg. I trust that it will be for my readers, as it has been for me, somewhat easier to see how Lukács's literary writings were embedded in the ideological manifestations of his times than it would be to realize similar connections operating in our own work.

All analogical arguments are only illustrative; nonetheless the present study is not merely intended for those few scholars interested in what Claudio Guillén has called Lukács's "blue period," before Lukács's road led him to Marx, but for all those interested in such broader issues as the methodology of the human sciences, and of literary theory, as well as the crisis of criticism which occupies so much attention today. Indeed, there are probably very few readers who would seek such an exhaustive study as this for Lukács's sake alone, and those who would will find little in it that they do not already know from other, more specialized, sources. It is not my primary purpose to contribute more bricks to the great Anglo-American-Hungarian wall of Lukács scholarship, although I hope that a few modest contributions to that worthy project have been made, in passing, as it were. It is, again, an analogical argument.

The methodology of this study is based on Max Weber's theory of ideal-typical construction as an heuristic tool. I have, therefore, "constructed" a Lukács on the basis of a

> one-sided accentuation of one or more points of view and by the synthesis of a great many diffuse, discrete, more or less present and occasionally absent concrete individual phenomena, which are arranged according to those one-sidedly emphasized viewpoints into a unified analytical construct.[1]

I am not claiming that this construction is wholly valid. The omission, for instance, of much in the way of a discussion of the value of Lukács's early work from the point of view of literary research seems to imply a much more severely negative judgment of that work than I believe it to deserve. On the other hand, I am claiming that the result of forming this ideal-typical model of a literary critic has a certain value which is perhaps greater than that to be gained by a traditional "balanced" view of him. This would be the value that Weber sought for all research in the human sciences. In this regard, "there is only one criterion, namely, that of success in revealing concrete cultural phenomena in their interdependence, their causal conditions and their significance. The construction of ideal-types recommends itself not as an end but as a means."[2]

If my attribution of Lukács's literary views to the ideology of the spirit is convincing, then I believe that similar views, in contexts not too dissimilar, would be similarly grounded. As that is apt to be rather controversial, I have done my best to make the arguments à propos of Lukács as convincing and exhaustive as possible. Everything else in this study is subordinated to that end. The accounts of Dilthey and Simmel, for instance, are not meant to do full justice to those great and influential thinkers; rather, I have used them, as I have used Lukács, as, in part, the visible signs of one of the major subterranean currents of thought of our time. Too often critics forget that criticism itself is a means, not an end. I have attempted to elucidate some interesting aspects of the history of ideas, to arrive at an understanding of what Lukács assumed as a basis for his writing, and therefore to better understand the significance of that writing in its period. I believe that many of the puzzling, and most taken for granted, aspects of criticism in late-twentieth-century America can best be

---

[1] Max Weber, "'Objectivity' in Social Science and Social Policy," in **Max Weber's Ideal Type Theory,** ed. Rolf E. Rogers (New York: Philosophical Library, Inc., 1969), p. 17.

[2] Weber, p. 19.

understood by situating them against this particular background.

The Philosophical Background

Georg Lukács was born into a middle class Jewish family in Budapest in 1885. His father was an extraordinarily successful banker, who eventually became the head of the Hungarian General Credit bank, a friend of the Prime Minister and of such German intellectual and cultural figures as Thomas Mann. The elder Lukács was an important member of that German-speaking Jewish middle class of the Dual Monarchy which was influential far beyond its numbers in forming the typical culture of the West in the twentieth century: Wittgenstein, Schoenberg, Buber, Mannheim, Kafka, Bloch, Freud – the list seems endless. Vienna, Budapest, and Prague were ruled by antisemitic German (or Magyar or Czech) aristocrats, and yet the culture formed there in the three-quarters of a century after the failed revolutions of 1848 owes its fame largely to a despised minority from Galicia. Lukács's writings, like those of many members of this culture who came of age between 1890 and 1920, continue to affect us, often in surprising and little noticed ways.

Although he took a law degree, Lukács early decided on a literary and philosophical career. Helping to found the "Thalia" theater at the age of 19, he spent the remaining years before the War working on his Doctorat and writing a series of academic and popular literary studies which included a **History of the Development of Modern Drama** (1908–11), **Soul and Form** (1910–11), and **The Theory of the Novel** (1916), an essay preparatory to his Habilitationsschrift at Heidelberg as a teacher of philosophy.

The War interrupted both this latter work and his ambitions, making him a censor for the Hungarian government (1915), then, with the Revolution, first Deputy Minister of Education, and later Minister of Education (1919), and finally a refugee in Vienna (1919), Moscow (1929), Berlin (1931), and again Moscow (1933). It is as a refugee that he became the famous Lukács, the author of **History and Class Consciousness** (1923), **The Historical Novel** (1937), **The Young Hegel** (1938), and **Studies in European Realism** (1948). Here we are not concerned with that mature – Marxist – literary critic, philosopher and polemicist. We are studying a much younger man than the author of these works, an Impressionist literary critic and searcher after God whose writing has much to tell us about the condition of literary studies in the West in our own time at the other end of the twentieth century. His early career is, as it were, a ready-made ideal typical form, illustrating with exceptional purity the foundations of subjective criticism and its path from Impressionism to mysticism, or further still.

Lukács went through several literary and philosophical phases between 1907 and 1916. We begin with Lukács and his context in his earliest Impressionist phase,[3] that of **Soul and Form.** According to René Wellek, the term "Impressionism" first entered the vocabulary of literary criticism in France in the late 1880's:

> Lemaître apparently transferred the painters' term "impressionism" to literary criticism and argued from a similar subjectivist theory of knowledge. "Works pass by the mirror of our mind; but as the procession is long, the mirror changes, in the meantime, and when by chance the same work returns, it no longer projects the same image." The critic can do no more than "define the impression which, at a given moment, this work of art has made on us where a writer himself has put down the impression which he in turn has received from the world at a particular hour." Criticism is "the representation of a world as personal, as relative, as vain, and hence as interesting as that which other literary genres constitute."[4]

Lemaître, we see, argued that literary criticism is an artistic endeavor because it is an attempt to represent the work of art as part of the world in the same way that the work of art itself was thought to represent the world, or, rather, that both the work of art and literary criticism are attempts to objectify the subjective impression made upon the mind by sense perceptions. This theory of knowledge and of the mind's interactions with the world is, as we shall see, close to that of the Neo-Kantians, and especially to that of Georg Simmel. It lacks only the doctrine of "coherence," which is the touchstone of his system; but, of course, Simmel carried things much further than this, believing, in his despair, that all knowledge was radically subjective.

But if the term "Impressionism" was originally French, the practice of literary Impressionism was predominantly English, originating in certain works of Ruskin, maturing in those of Pater, and achieving an early decadence in the career of Oscar Wilde. Writing of this type of critic, Harold Bloom states that

> his value inheres neither in his accuracy at the direct interpretation of meaning in texts, nor in his judgments of relative eminence of works and authors. Rather, he gives us a vision of art through his own unique sensibility, and so his own writings obscure the supposed distinction

---

[3] See Istvan Meszaros, **Lukacs' Concept of Dialectic** (London: The Merlin Press, 1972), which contains one of the first good outlines of the development of Lukács's ideas.

[4] René Wellek, **A History of Modern Criticism, 1750–1950,** V. 4 (New Haven: Yale University Press, 1965), p. 22.

between criticism and creation. "Supposed," because who can convince us of that distinction? To adapt Shelley's idea of the relation between poetry and the universe, let us say that criticism creates the poem anew, after the poem has been annihilated in our minds by the recurrence of impressions blunted by reiteration. Ruskin's or Pater's criticism tends to create anew not so much a particular work of art but rather the precisely appropriate consciousness of the perceptive reader or viewer.[5]

Lemaître's ideal critic writes about the impression the work of art makes on the mirror of his mind, while Bloom's critic does not necessarily write about the work of art at all, but instead concerns himself with indicating the timeless "precisely appropriate consciousness" for the aesthete. In neither case is the critic concerned with the world, or with the literary work of art, as existing independently of the perceiving subject. Lemaitre's use of the image of the mirror is misleading, as his mirrors are not meant to reflect: they are meant to take impressions, as mystic writing pads or waxed tablets. It is these impressions, no matter how created, that were the objects of knowledge for him, as for Bloom. Representation is not enough. As noted in the first instance by Wellek, both doctrines are based on subjectivist and idealist theories of knowledge.

Lemaître and Bloom (and the argument is probably applicable to all subjectivist critics) abandon the world for the shadow play of Plato's cave. They engage in a search for, or, rather, assume the existence of, a purely psychological theory of knowledge, such as that which had interested Dilthey. These theories are probably a manifestation in the world of ideas of certain conditions in the inter-subjective world of everyday life, conditions which are particularly dominant during periods of great historical stress. (We will trace their development in late-nineteenth-century Central Europe as a reaction to industrialization and the political pressures accompanying the unification of Germany. One can see such ideologies as the secular equivalent of the mysticism of the fourteenth century, which blossomed in a similarly unfortunate age.) As it becomes increasingly clear that individuals are an insignificant part of social forces beyond any individual's control, the elements of ego and class interest unite to seek a theory of knowledge which will nonetheless deny that powerlessness and assuage the psychological wound and class decline caused by it. Clinging to a belief in the world-forming ability of the individual mind, the subjectivist critic, for instance, claims a central role by assimilating to the character of "writer" both critic and artist, a character usually seen as Romantic – and not by accident – as it is just the artist as egoist, as Creator and hero, that is the desired role. Hence Bloom's interest in the English Romantics and the interest of the early Lukács in their German contemporaries.

---

[5] Harold Bloom, "Introduction," **Selected Writings of Walter Pater** (New York: New American Library, 1974), pp. vii-viii.

It was just such a purely psychological or subjectivist theory of knowledge which brought the Life Philosophers of late-nineteenth and early-twentieth-century Central Europe to the conclusion that the only possible basis for life is an act of faith, a conclusion that had as a consequence a variety of religious movements in the twentieth century – such as Buber's mystical Judaism and the Existential Christianity so popular among theologians in the West after the World Wars. Secular consequences of these theories have included not only the semi-Marxist Existentialism of post-War France, but also Italian Fascism and German National Socialism. The seeds for what at first sight seem to be such unexpected and contradictory growths from what was ostensibly a theory of aesthetics were present from the beginning of the movement. If we turn, for instance, to Pater's famous "Conclusion" to **The Renaissance,** we of course find that: "Great passions may give us this quickened sense of life, ecstasy and sorrow of love, the various forms of enthusiastic activity, disinterested or otherwise, which come naturally to many of us."[6] This can easily be taken as a call for a more civilized life, for a devotion of one's time, finally, to the appreciation of art for its own sake. That is, indeed, how it usually is presented. In an earlier version of this passage, Pater had written: "High passions give one this quickened sense of life, ecstasy and sorrow of love, political or religious enthusiasm, or the 'enthusiasm of humanity.'"[7] In that suppressed wording the specific mention of political enthusiasm pointed the path that the Life Philosphy would take – through aesthetics to the bacchanal of modern irrationalism.

The subjectivization of values, the exaltation of "experience," the development of a secular mysticism – all of these are associated with the Impressionist approach to the study of art. The aesthetic studies of the young Lukács were, then, typically incidental to the formation of a philosophy of life. We hear him murmur:

> This is the most profound meaning of form: to lead to a great moment of silence, to mould the directionless, precipitous, many-coloured stream of life as though all its haste were only for the sake of such moments . . . We may say that art becomes possible, and in particular the art of writing came to have a meaning, only because it can give us the great moments we have been speaking about. It is only on account of these moments that art has become a life-value for us.[8]

---

6 Walter Pater, **The Renaissance** (New York: New American Library, 1959), pp. 157–8.

7 Walter Pater, "Poems by William Morris," **Westminster Review,** XC (October 1868), pp. 300–12.

8 Georg Lukács, **Soul and Form,** trans. Anna Bostock (Cambridge, Mass.:

One of the more characteristic phenomena of   nineteenth-century   culture was its obsession with art and the artistic, an obsession, perhaps, only heightened by the general hideousness of the epoch.[9] In England this manifested itself in the writings first of Ruskin, then of Morris, and finally in the general popularization of their concerns in the Arts and Crafts movement and their commercialization in the development of interior decoration shops, such as Morris's own, a tendency as familiar in Vienna as in Hammersmith. As Lukács put it: "An epoch that longs for culture will find its centre only in the arts; the less culture there is and the more intensely it is missed, the stronger the desire for it" (48).

Some of this interest was not at all what we would now call aesthetic, but had to do, rather, with an attempt to provide meaning for the lives of people who more and more felt that individual lives were losing all subjective validity in the on-rushing collectivist tide of capitalist industrialization.[10] An entire class, apparently, took its stand against this tendency by denying the existence of objective reality and exalting the primacy of the individual ego. It is not without significance that this class, exemplified by Pater's Oxford students and Wilde's theater audiences, by Simmel's auditors and George's "circle," were exactly the chief beneficiaries of the process that so horrified them. Fleeing the industrialized cities that their fathers had built, they spent their time on the magic mountain of aesthetic culture, waiting for the War. Table-tapping in darkened rooms, romantic agonies in others more darkened yet, lectures by popular scientistic saviors; these were their pastimes as they prepared themselves for the self-abnegation that was to come. It is not at all mysterious that they finally sought relief in action, any action that promised to free them from the intolerable solitary confinement of subjectivity.[11] The career of Georg Lukács was typical in this regard. As was mentioned earlier, we see him here, and will use this phase of his career, as an ideal type in the true Weberian sense, an heuristic construction which will allow us to examine certain tendencies in literary criticism by referring to a writer whose intellectual descent can be plotted clearly. Impressionism in Lukács's early career was nourished not only by English aesthetic traditions, but by the

---

The MIT Press, 1974). [Page references and translations in the text are from this edition unless otherwise noted.]

[9] E. P. Thompson, **William Morris, Romantic to Revolutionary** (London: Lawrence & Wishart, Ltd., 1955).

[10] Ferdinand Tönnies, **Gemeinschaft und Gesellschaft,** trans. Charles P. Loomis (East Lansing: The Michigan State University Press, 1957).

[11] Thomas Mann, "The Thunderbolt," in **The Magic Mountain,** trans. H. T. Lowe-Porter (London: Penguin Books, 1960), pp. 706-16.

common philosophical viewpoint of Central Europe in his time. This, once known, illuminates Impressionism itself, both in the case of Lukács, and by extension for the Anglo – American tradition. The initial stage of our study will focus on an important aspect of the history of ideas in central Europe during the quarter of a century preceding the First World War – namely that aspect indicated by the concepts of typicality and totality, value and form – seeking to describe the historical development of those concepts and to relate them to their contemporary environment.

If we look back beyond Lukács's teachers to the previous scholarly generation, we find the looming figure of Wilhelm Dilthey, Professor of Philosophy at Berlin, who was born in 1833, received his doctorate in 1864 and lived until 1911. The first half of his life was punctuated by the events that changed Germany from a geographical expression to one of the strongest industrial and military powers of the world: the establishment of the German Zollverein, or customs union in 1833; the war between Prussia and Austria in 1866; and the Franco–Prussian War of 1870. These political events were accompanied by rapid and fundamental changes in the economic and social structure of the country. The decisive date for the political formation of the Reich was 1848, the year of the failure of the bourgeois revolution. That failure, combined with the antithetical successes of 1866 and 1870, produced a Prussianized Germany, increasingly rich, industrialized, and urbanized, but still under the tutelage, as it were, of an anachronistic class, the Junkers.   Dilthey, immersed as he was in the previous era through his work on Schleiermacher and basically a product of pre-Imperial, pre-industrial mid-nineteenth-century Germany, was able to believe in the promise of Positivism – if not in its practice – the promise, that is, of scientific certainty in all studies, including the human sciences. Younger scholars, those who received their doctorates in the 1880's, found such a belief to be untenable. They were to come to maturity – after the unification of the Reich had been accomplished through the use of pure force – in an age when ideals were still to be found in the universities, to be sure, but hardly anywhere else except there, the Church, and the bourgeois household. Theirs was also an age when the Emperor was a mountebank and the Reich was seen more and more as a commercial entity established almost exclusively for the benefit of the banks and the cartels. And to make matters seem even worse, the only serious opposition to this regime was centered in the German Social Democratic Party, an organization as "soulless," vulgar, materialistic, and bureaucratized as the government of the Reich itself.

For the generation of 1885 (Simmel, Tönnies, Weber are the representative names), the modernization of Germany presented itself as a cultural crisis. For

German industrialization, once it accelerated around 1870, was particularly abrupt. The social and cultural strains it engendered were unusually severe, and above all, the German academics reacted to the dislocation with such desperate intensity that the specter of a "soulless" modern age came to haunt everything they said and wrote, no matter what the subject.[12]

These German academics, the "mandarins" of Fritz Ringer's study, tended to center their careers on the examination of precisely that cultural crisis of which they were both the principal instigators and the most sensitive victims. They began those careers as   part of a very small university educated minority.[13] These men came from bourgeois homes and were the children of ministers or politicians or merchants. Each climbed steadily through the elite schools system of the day (a system that reached its apogee in those years), won his doctorate, and then – somehow – slipped: Simmel taught as a private lecturer for the greater part of his career, Tönnies remained in the provinces, Weber suffered a nervous breakdown just after receiving a university chair.

That slippage, in many cases the failure of brilliant scholars to fulfill their early promise, was no mere accident; rather, it was the sign of a fundamental contradiction in the social structures in which they found themselves. For if Weber's breakdown was in part the result of overwhelming emotional pressures arising from a classical Oedipal conflict, it was also, no less certainly, a by-product of the very effort which had raised him to such early eminence, that nearly universal learning which he saw as a task that he had set himself, as he said, "to see how much I can endure."[14] Why did Weber view the accumulation of knowledge as a task necessarily involving the risk of the sacrifice of sanity? And if the failure of Tönnies to progress beyond the confines of such a provincial university as Kiel – to progress, indeed, beyond the intellectual position that he had achieved with his original book – was in a large measure due to his socialistic leanings, those ideas in themselves were not a priori's, but were of the same intellectual order as were the insights embodied in **Gemein-schaft und Gesellschaft** that had made his career possible in the first

---

[12] Fritz K. Ringer, **The Decline of the German Mandarins** (Cambridge, Mass.: Harvard University Press, 1969), p. 3.

[13] "In 1885, when the population of Germany stood near 47 million and around 7.15 million children were attending primary schools, roughly 128,000 were studying at a gymnasium. Attendance had reached 27,000 at the universities . . . For every 10,000 inhabitants of Prussia, 30 students went to a gymnasium, and less than 1.5 received an Abitur." Ringer, p. 39. (In the absence of entrance examinations, the certificate of graduation from a classical high school, the Abitur, virtually ensured admittance to a university.)

[14] H. Stuart Hughes, **Consciousness and Society** (New York: Alfred A. Knopf, 1958), p. 290.

place. Why did Tönnies come to see learning itself, in its academic context, as a Gesellschaft in opposition to his ideal of a Gemeinschaft of thought? And if, finally, Simmel's failure to obtain a university chair prior to 1917 was due in part to the negative influence of such academicians as Dilthey himself, was it not also, quite apart from the antisemitic context and phrasing of such reactions, that Simmel did in fact represent, and present, the very horror of the cultural crisis which was the orienting fear of most mandarins in the human sciences? We find even Ernst Bloch, one of Simmel's own students, writing that: "Simmel, the best head among his contemporaries, is beyond this utterly empty, a man without goals, who wants everything but the truth; he collects his many standpoints which float around the truth without ever wanting or being able to possess it."[15]

Part of the truth of the history of the ideas that we will be examining here, then, is the belated industrial revolution in Germany, the dissolution of community in German society, and the direct effects of that latter process on the thought of the time. Simmel and Weber, particularly, were concerned with those effects and an awareness of this background is essential for the understanding of their thought and its influence on Lukács. But we must turn, now, to our immediate task of tracing the origins of the ideas of typicality and totality in the human sciences, ideas central, also, to the understanding of our own culture.

Wilhelm Dilthey

The mid-nineteenth-century collapse of the great Idealist systems of German philosophy has been interpreted as resulting in the domination of the historical sciences by a crude, unselfconscious positivism, more philosophically primitive than anything prevalent in the contemporary natural sciences, a parody of a layman's view of the procedures of the naturalist. For instance, Jost Hermand has written that as

> a result of this positivistic objectivism, for which only surface facts existed, purely mechanical methods of scholarship, oriented to the natural sciences, necessarily made deep inroads in the humanities. Thus around 1880, in many academic circles, the mere collecting of facts was itself viewed as a scholarly achievement, while any interpretation of the heaps of amassed material was usually postponed to a later day.[16]

---

[15]   Ernst Bloch, "Schulphilosophen heute." **Durch die Wüsste,** trans. Paul Breines (Frankfort, 1964), pp. 91-2.

[16]   Jost Hermand and Evelyn Torton Beck, **Interpretive Synthesis** (New

Here the central negative figure was the historian Leopold von Ranke. If, however, scholars look more closely at the work of Ranke himself, they find that Hermand's strictures are difficult to justify. Fritz Ringer's analysis of Ranke's views is quite at odds with the impression given by Hermand:

> When Ranke made his famous remark about just finding out "how it actually was," he certainly did not mean to urge a complete suspension of interpretive judgment until all the evidence was in and the whole story could be told correctly once and for all. No German historian ever took such a position. Ranke was simply trying to avoid an overly present-minded and unimaginative treatment of the past.[17]

But Ranke did say that the explicit differentiation of facts by means of reference to value should be avoided by the historian. Such a method-ological principle was, for example, implicit in his dictum that "all generations of mankind have equal rights before God, and the historian must see them in this same light."[18] Although Ringer might be correct in stating that no German historian ever took a position such as that criticized by Hermand, it nonetheless was the case that some of Ranke's students did simplify his idealism so as to consign his methodological ideals to the pri-vacy of contemplation, leaving the field of historical research itself to decidedly non-idealist empiricists.[19] Moreover, this process was abetted by the habit (endemic within German intellectual circles) of confusing Idealism as a specific philosophical system (or set of systems) with the moral-ethical category of idealism, in our everyday sense of the term.[20] If one assumes that one is an idealist, in this latter sense, there is a great temptation to leave it at that, and to neglect the practice of Idealism, in the technical sense, in one's approach to research. Ranke himself did not avoid this confusion. Convinced as he was that he examined historical objects without "present-mindedness," he nonetheless repeatedly projected the Christian Royalism of his time into the past. This, in turn, influenced his students to select their research topics with reference to the diplomatic and military history of the unification of the Reich, so that the dreaded "present-mindedness" became formative in the very structure of academic historical research (although appearing to have been avoided at the literal level of the

---

York: Frederick Ungar, 1975), pp. 16-7.

[17] Ringer, p. 98.

[18] Hermand, p. 13.

[19] Hughes, p. 186.

[20] Ringer, p. 95.

individual studies themselves). Thus, the influence of Ranke was such as to make "in this era the ideal of the scholar . . . the directionless, omniscient polyhistor, who lent his immense knowledge to only one carefully selected subject and, with a gesture of renunciation, limited himself to plugging those famous gaps in the towering edifice of learning."[21] This was an empiricism which, as is often the case, implicitly depended on a theory which its practitioners explicitly denied. The ideal of non-interpretive scholarship constituted in itself an interpretation both of history and of the methodology of the human sciences.

Wilhelm Dilthey's intervention at this point was crucial. His primary historical concerns were understanding and interpretation. He taught that

> knowledge in the field of cultural science was derived through some kind of internal process – through living experience and understanding . . . Hence, meaning in history was not fixed, but changed with the situation in time and culture of the historian himself, and with the active decisions he took in his own personal world.[22]

Ranke had also believed that the experiencing subjectivity of the historian is important, that the individual historical epochs are the objects of study of the historian and not somehow absolutely other. But just as that position had decisively changed the methodology of historical research, while remaining also a modification and not a simple rejection of the Hegelian interpretation of history, so Dilthey's views became important as they altered, rather than reversed, the previous trend of thought: "He felt that German historicists such as Ranke had made great strides in freeing the theory of history from metaphysical speculation. But Dilthey also realized that historicism without a new epistemological grounding was exposed to the dangers of relativism."[23] It was not just that Ranke rejected the Hegelian vision of teleological history, nor that Dilthey in his turn rejected Ranke's emphasis on the intrinsic value of the particular historical moment, but that their shifting theoretical accentuations ultimately had the consequence of significantly changing the practice of historical research.

Instead of facing a simple series of binary oppositions, we are dealing with a more dynamic – perhaps Hegelian – process in which each succeeding point of view evokes another, with which it at least partially reacts in order to form a third, if not higher, then at least different, interpretation. The reflexive nature of Dilthey's view of historical research

---

[21]   Hermand, p. 17.

[22]   Hughes, p. 195.

[23]   Rudolf A. Makkreel, **Dilthey, Philosopher of the Human Studies** (Princeton University Press, 1975), p. 4.

thus contributed the possibility of making explicit the presuppositions of the historian, and so avoiding that Germanization of historical studies that was the unintended consequence of Ranke's method. Ranke's precepts had built upon an analysis of an Enlightenment tradition of overtly polemical historical narratives, beginning the effort to write, for instance, histories of specific aspects of Roman civilization, rather than subordinating all details to a theory of decline and fall. (Here it might be noted that it was Weber's teacher Mommsen, rather than Ranke himself, who in seeking to discover rather than to impose an interpretation of historical development reaped the intellectual harvest of this approach.)[24]

The emphasis in Dilthey's writing on the importance of experience as a category came not only from Ranke, but more fundamentally from Dilthey's study of Schleiermacher. Immersing himself in the Romantic era of the older man's life and work, Dilthey caught, as it were, the contagion of the Romantic idealization of lived experience itself, while at the same time appreciating the scholarly importance of reliving, or attempting to relive, the experiences of the research object. Dilthey's historical interests – and these are essential to his philosophy – were Romantic in several senses. It is significant, therefore, to note both how his work complemented that of other German philosophers of his day and how it differed:

> The individuality in which the . . . neo-Kantians were interested is the result of an attitude or approach adopted by the cognitive subject; the historian, they maintained, examines the same realm (i.e., empirical reality) as the natural scientist, but he focuses his attention on the unique and singular, deliberately disregarding the general or common. Dilthey recognized no such distinction in attitude, although he did admit that the Geisteswissenschaften take a particular interest in uniqueness. An individuality, in Dilthey's view, is not constituted as an object for theoretical investigation by some scientist's focusing on certain aspects of reality and ignoring others; rather, it is given as something individual.[25]

But, at just this point, through a kind of intellectual short-circuit, the emphasis of the Romantic category of lived experience was shifted to a purely mental phenomenon. "To him, as to Kant, experience itself was the product of the mind's activity which shapes and structures the data it receives."[26] Similar transformations are common enough in German cultural

---

[24] Carlo Antoni, **From History to Sociology,** trans. Hayden V. White (Detroit: Wayne State University Press, 1959), p. 124.

[25] Theodore Plantinga, **Historical Understanding in the Thought of William Dilthey** (Toronto: University of Toronto Press, 1980), p. 35.

[26] H. P. Rickman, "Introduction," in **W. Dilthey, Selected Writings**

history, that is to say, transformations of processes on the social level to
the philosophical level, transformations that Lukács was to attribute to the
relative social backwardness of the country.[27]

If it is true that Romanticism itself involved such a transformation,
changing the late-eighteenth-century revolutionary emphasis on social
existence to a valorization of the particular circumstances of the individual,
then Dilthey's later move from that vantage point back to a Kantian and
"revolutionary" stress on the mental life (itself perhaps in part a reaction to
the political and social revolutionary impulse in France and elsewhere)
resulted in a theory at once abstract in content and emotional in form. We
arrive, then, at a philosophy which practices an intense internalization, yet
proclaims that it is a "Life Philosophy." This was not merely an attempt at
professional differentiation. "Life," not thought or abstract reason, was
Dilthey's fundamental process:

> Life itself, as something lived . . . contains cohering structures . . .
> which are then explicated in all experience and thinking. And here, now,
> is the decisive point for the entire possibility of knowledge. Only
> because the entire structure that appears in forms, principles and
> categories is contained in life and experience, only because it can be
> demonstrated analytically in life and experience, do we have knowledge
> of reality.[28]

The complicated emotional charge of this seemingly rigorous doctrine
comes through most clearly in Dilthey's discussion of mood.

> Nothing is more fleeting, more fragile or more changeable than man's
> mood vis-a-vis the totality (Zusammenhang) of things in which he finds
> himself or than the ideas about the inner coherence (Zusammenhang) of
> life and the world that arise within him. Sometimes life casts deep
> shadows across our soul, sometimes it imparts life and joy to it . . . Our
> sense of life (Gefühl des Lebens) changes like light and shadow moving
> across a landscape.[29]

(Cambridge: Cambridge University Press, 1976), p. 22. Translations of
Dilthey's writings given in the text are by Rickman unless otherwise
noted. Page numbers in square brackets refer to Rickman.

[27]   As Marcuse did also. See Herbert Marcuse, **Reason and Revolution**
       (Boston: Beacon Press, 1960).

[28]   Plantinga, p. 71.

[29]   Plantinga, p. 74.

Dilthey's concern with mood and experience was a scholar's transplantation of Wilhelm Meister to the study. If it was, thus, a bit pale, at least it was not the fevered and decadent Lebensphilosophie glorified by Dilthey's successors.[30] It was, for him, still an analytical tool, not a substitute for thought. And so we find him asserting that: "The history and theory of literature and art must refer to the composite, fundamental, aesthetic moods of seeing something as beautiful, sublime, funny or ridiculous. Without psychological analysis these moods would remain dark and dead ideas to the literary historian."[31] While the first sentence of this statement would have seemed highly suspect to positivist historians, the second would have seemed equally suspect to the practitioners of Lebensphilosophie who were to claim descent from Dilthey. It was precisely this combination of a desire to find life in the records of the past with his commitment to rational analysis that raised Dilthey to the rank of a major theorist. Even the possibility that the type of literary and historical analysis that he wished for was a mythification of psychology does not alter his exemplary position. Where later philosophers in his tradition succumbed to the temptation of a blind worship of the life force – or of force alone – Dilthey maintained that human reason had, and had to have, some measure of control over the irrational: "The flow of life, in which all is swept away into the past, is overcome by memory, and the contingency of events by the coherence of thought."[32] (We will deal more precisely with the nature of this "overcoming" when we consider the theories of Georg Simmel.)

If Dilthey's ambiguous Kantianism was at least partially responsible for the restrictions of his concept of experience, it was also responsible for his faith in reason, and especially critical reason. In that the most severe judgments pronounced on Hegel and his followers stem from Hegel's supposed validation of the Prussian state as both rational and real, the turn to Kant in the late nineteenth century at the high tide of Christian and Royal Prussianism, was a move of more than academic significance. According to H. A. Hodges, the "heart and soul of [Dilthey's] Kantianism lies in the conception of philosophy as a critique of knowledge. The emergence of the critical movement in the eighteenth-century, and its gradual victory over the traditional idea of philosophy as metaphysics, appear to him as the great turning point in philosophical history."[33] It was by following Kant that Dilthey was able to observe and interpret the division between the natural

---

30   Ringer, pp. 336–40.

31   Wilhelm Dilthey, **Gesammelte Schriften,** V, (Leipzig, 1914), pp. 147–48 [90].

32   H. A. Hodges, **The Philosophy of Wilhelm Dilthey** (London: Routledge & Kegan Paul Ltd., 1952), p. 43.

33   Hodges, p. 1.

and the human sciences that was to be central to the "critique of knowledge" in the period under examination here.

Dilthey's debate with the Neo-Kantians about the divisions in the sciences focussed on the location of psychology. They argued that it was part of the natural sciences; he, that it should be classified with history: "Psychology is fundamental for Dilthey because the differences between the two types of sciences is rooted in a difference within the realm of experience; more specifically, it is rooted in two different modes of givenness, i.e., inner and outer experience."[34] This was a particular instance of Dilthey's claim that "the human studies differ from the [natural] sciences because the latter deal with facts which present themselves to consciousness as external and separate phenomena, while the former deal with the living connections of reality experienced in the mind." From this it follows that the "sciences arrive at connections within nature through inferences by means of a combination of hypotheses while the human sciences are based on directly given mental connections." In the human sciences, inner "experience grasps the processes by which we accomplish something as well as the combination of individual functions of mental life as a whole. The experience of the whole context comes first: only later do we distinguish its individual parts." Dilthey concludes, then, that "the methods of studying mental life, history and society, differ greatly from those used to acquire knowledge of nature."[35]

Heinrich Rickert was to criticize Dilthey for illegitimately extending a logical and formal distinction of methodologies, and it certainly does seem to be the case that Dilthey's psychological distinction between the natural and human sciences was ill-founded. In what way, for instance, are the phenomena of historical study less external (or more internal) than those of physics? Dilthey's position might have been valid if the scholar simply remembered history, as he or she might remember his or her own life, but that is rarely the case. The general situation is that history is studied from records of various sorts, records which are not perceived, in principle, in a manner any different from the way in which the various readings of dials and gauges are perceived by the physicist. And although the analyses that historical phenomena are subjected to are different, perhaps, from those to which natural phenomena are subjected, the analytical process does not itself vary significantly from one context to another. That is, one performs roughly the same type of mental operations in order to comprehend natural facts as one does in order to comprehend historical facts.

---

34 Plantinga, p. 31.

35 Dilthey, **Gesammelte Schriften**, V., p. 144 [89].

Dilthey, of course, claimed that "gifted" historians actually do re-live, and thus, in a sense, "remember" the objects of their research: "Now inasmuch as the exegete tentatively transports his own sense of life into another historical milieu, he is able within that perspective, to strengthen and emphasize certain psychic processes in himself and to minimize others, thus making possible within himself a reconstruction of an alien form of life."[36] (It is difficult to see this claim as anything other than a Romantic assertion, not, say, a philosophical conclusion.)   But this is to anticipate our argument. For the moment it will suffice to locate the probable source of Dilthey's analysis in his reaction against positivistic historicism and toward a mode of historical research   emphasising the re-experiencing of the historical moment under study. While doing this he seems to have believed that some other historians were adherents of that vulgar Positivism, and that scholars in the natural sciences were also.

For the modern reader, Vico looms behind Dilthey's statement that "We explain nature but we understand mental life." It is here that Dilthey's efforts to free himself from the assumptions of Positivism founder, leading him to transfer the positivistic impulse from history to psychology. His hope was to elicit from the new and emerging psychology a scientific methodology of the human sciences, but the new psychology that was coming into being proved of little use in this respect. Far from offering hope for the formula-tion of such a methodology, it would attempt to found a science of the irrational growing out of the study of hysteria and its articulation in dreams. Dilthey himself was occasionally aware that Vico's project must necessarily shipwreck, if not on the fact of the unconscious, then at least on the consciously apprehended knowledge of the irrationality of human beings. Not that he ever lost faith in the worth of the project itself:

> None of the great turning-points in human history can be seen as the inevitable result of preceding circumstances. If man were a rational being, as Hegel assumed, or if he were determined by the succession of his ideas and concepts . . . then we could infer every later stage of human intellectual life from a previous one. Everyone knows from his own experience how little we resemble thinking machines . . . What happened then [at the end of the Middle Ages] was not determined by previous circumstances, nor could it be explained by social conditions. These only precipitate great historical actualities as the rays of the sun make flowers grow. What there is in human nature is revealed by the great turning-points of history. For history alone shows what man is.[37]

---

36   Makkreel, p. 250.

37   Wilhelm Dilthey, **Die Grosse Phantasie Dichtung** (1953), pp. 33-4 [84].

As we have seen, Dilthey's study of Schleiermacher resulted in his exaltation of the category of experience as an approach to history; it also provided him with the concept of the "hermeneutical circle" as a tool of analysis. The latter was a lasting contribution to the methodology of the human sciences, and its revival became immediately significant   historio-logically through its emphasis on the category of totality. "The experience of the whole context comes first: only later do we distinguish its individual parts." If it is not altogether true that such an approach is absent from the practice of the natural sciences, it is nonetheless the case that Dilthey's willingness to allow for the endless circle of the hermeneutical method seemed to open the possibility for his time of eventually grasping the totality of existence, of life. This was not, however, the task of science. He

> assigned to poetry the task of understanding life out of itself. . . . and in his essay on the types of world views we read that the poetic task is "to make life again understandable out of itself" (VIII, 93). In the post-1900 years, this poetic task then becomes the task of philosophy. In **Das Wesen der Philosophie** (1907), Dilthey declares that modern philosophy of life seeks to construct an "interpretation of life." (Lebensdeutung) on the basis of our experience of life and then adds: "life is to be interpreted out of itself - this is the great idea that unites these philosophers with the world's wisdom and with poetry."[38]

That possibility, that hope and ultimately its failure, was to be one of the major forces in the intellectual history of the quarter of a century before the First World War. The young Lukács was haunted by this vision, seeking first in literary criticism or literature itself for such a grasp of the world, then turning to the classical totalizing path of mysticism. (Still later of course, in a period outside the scope of the present study, Lukács was to seek the whole in the point of view of the revolutionary working class.)

Before we return to Dilthey's own use of the concept of totality, it is necessary to consider briefly two more aspects of the "turning-points" quotation given above. First, Dilthey's attack on Hegelian rationalism was also an attack on Marxism, the Marxism of the contemporary German Social Democratic Party, not that of Marx himself. This institutionalized Marxism was a factor which, in the words of H. Stuart Hughes,

> was to figure in the intellectual renovations of the 1890's as an aberrant, and peculiarly insidious, form of the reigning cult of Positivism. It loomed on the cultural horizon as the last and most ambitious of the abstract and pseudo-scientific ideologies that had bewitched European intellectuals since the early eighteenth-century.[39]

---

[38] Plantinga, p. 76.

[39] Hughes, p. 42.

Marxism, then, for many of the philosophers and sociologists of Lukács's generation was a reductionist theory of social determinism. The early Marx was as yet unknown and the canonical texts of the mature Marx were read through the interpretive framework of pronouncements made by the German Social Democratic Party or, at best, by Engels.[40] Another aspect of the "turning-points" quotation to be underlined is Dilthey's statement to the effect that "history alone shows what man is." The ghost of Vico appears to us here as a Wilhelmian philosopher, placing the human sciences firmly within the context of the study of history. This realignment radiates in two directions. First, it validates history as the human science par excellence, and, secondly, it produces that historical and historicizing focus that we have received as our inheritance from the Geisteswissenschaften (although we take it perhaps more seriously as a methodological imperative than Dilthey himself did, given the fact that we view all efforts at understanding as methodologically as well as historically bound.)

Having elevated inner experience to the position of the primary mode of contact between the subject and the world, Dilthey was still left with the problem of how to organize the totality of experience. He resolved it by claiming that the mind of the individual organizes the raw flux of experience in accordance with the broad conceptual schemes of various world views. World views were a methodological touchstone in the human sciences throughout the remainder of the period under discussion, underlying the structure of **The Theory of the Novel,** for instance, which cannot be well understood without an adequate account of Dilthey's theory and its development. We must be careful here to exercise the same caution in regard to Dilthey's thought as we tried to employ earlier in dealing with Ranke's. Their concepts should not be confused with the vulgarizations of their disciples or those who claimed to be their disciples; nor should they be confused with their intellectual ancestors. In Dilthey's case, that identification is most frequently made in connection with the cult of the "wide and deep" thought of the hero or genius common to the Romantics and to the twentieth-century adherents of Geistesgeschichte and the Stefan George circle (which so fascinated the young Lukács). Unlike those writers, Dilthey was not devoted to the personality of the poet. In spite of his emphasis on the importance of psychology, Dilthey thought that

> literary history and criticism are only concerned with what the pattern of words refers to, not – and this is decisive – with the processes in the poet's mind but with a structure created by those processes yet separable from them . . . Thus the primary subject-matter of literary

---

[40] It is interesting here that Dilthey identifies the explanation by social conditions with Hegel's emphasis on man as a rational being, for it was just that return to Hegel that was to be basic to Lukács's renewal of Marxism.

history or criticism is wholly distinct from the mental processes of the poet or his reader.[41]

(As we shall see, this is at once similar to and the exact opposite of the view that the young Lukács first arrived at and used in **Soul and Form**.)

And yet, it is also the case that Dilthey's own Romanticism was such that he could privilege the poet as a receptor of feelings which characterize the world. For Dilthey, firstly, the poet's

> perceptual impressions are more intense, exact, and manifold than usual . . . Secondly the poet can revive memory images possessing unusual "clarity of outline, strength of sense, and energy of projection". . . . Thirdly, Dilthey notes that the energy with which the poet can reproduce psychic states, either his own or those of others, presupposes an unusual intensity of feeling . . . Fourthly, the poet is said to be especially gifted in charging images with life, in finding "satisfaction in intuition saturated with feeling" . . . Finally, the poet distinguishes himself by "freely unfolding images beyond the bounds of reality."[42]

The importance of the poet for Dilthey is not limited to the poet's role as the supreme experiencer of inner life. The aesthetic emotions have a place in Dilthey's thought leading to the concept of value. He claims that value

> is nothing more than the representational expression for the fact which is experienced in feeling . . . In pleasure we in part enjoy the condition of objects – their beauty and meaning (Bedeutung) – and in part the intensification of our own existence – personal states that provide value (Wert) to our own existence.[43]

Here, then, the crucial category of value is identified with feeling, emotion aestheticized by the poet.[44]

---

[41]   Dilthey, **Gesammelte Schriften**, VII, pp. 83–4 [174–5].

[42]   Makkreel, p. 141.

[43]   Makkreel, pp. 118–9.

[44]   Many agreed with Dilthey: "Urged by his students to republish some of his early writings in literary criticism, Dilthey revised and rewrote his essays on Lessing, Goethe, Novalis, and Hölderlin, and brought them together under the title **Das Erlebnis und die Dichtung**. Published in 1906, it was immediately praised for exhibiting both unusual scholarship and sensitivity." Makkreel, p. 143.

This emphasis on the poet may seem excessive to a non-Germanic reader, but as Makkreel points out it is not meant as exclusively aesthetic. With Dilthey, we must always return to Schleiermacher, to the task of understanding Schleiermacher in his own time. The devotion of Dilthey to the power of poetic understanding of life is directly related to the historian's task. It is a search for a method.

> The individual subject was interpreted by Dilthey as the intersection of cultural systems and the external organization of society, and . . . systematic attempts to create a grand socio-historical synthesis for the human studies were criticized for having overlooked the unity of perspective that is possible through psychological analysis. The ability of a poet to unfold a typical point of impression has therefore more than just an aesthetic import. In that the poetic imagination can be seen as a way of focusing on certain images as intersections of the cooperating functions of the acquired psychic nexus, the poetic articulation of inner form can stand as a model for the general process of understanding complex interdependence. Applied to the historian's task, it can help to articulate the particular point of intersection which is constituted by a great individual. To the extent that it is possible for historical understanding to disclose that which is representative of an age in the biographical account of an individual, the power of the poetic imagination to articulate typicality amidst ordinary experience becomes a basic tool for human understanding.[45]

Although for Dilthey the subject matter of literary history is distinct from that of psychology, his methodology for the study of that subject matter is organized around the analysis of psychological categories, the world views, Weltanschauungen These are, as it were, the mean expression of certain points on a continuum: "for every aspect of human expression of life there arises a type of its appropriate execution. This designates a norm lying between the deviations on both sides. Thus a typical expression of life represents an entire class."[46] These may differ, perhaps without limit, in detail, but they do share a common structure: "This structure always takes the form of a system in which questions about the meaning and significance of the world are answered in terms of a conception of the world."[47] This basic concept of the world is in each case a psychological structure peculiar to the individual. Thus, while it makes sense to ask whether "questions about meaning and significance," are consistent within a given conception of the world, for Dilthey it does not make sense to

---

[45]   Makkreel, pp. 201–2.

[46]   Makkreel, p. 241.

[47]   Dilthey, **Gesammelte Schriften**, VIII.

evaluate one such conception, as a whole, against another. There can be better or worse Hegelian or Kantian philosophies, but no one can properly say that the Hegelian is a better or worse world view than the Kantian. All philosophical systems that are internally consistent are in principle incomparable. (This opinion might be contrasted with New Critical doctrines which we will touch on later, which, while superficially similar to Dilthey's, explicitly privilege, in this instance, a Christian world view.)

Dilthey's theory of world views does not claim to explain the world in itself, nor does it claim to explain humanity; rather, it attempts to "describe methodically, on the basis of an analysis of the historical development of religion, poetry and metaphysics . . . the relationship of the human mind to the enigma of the world and of life."[48] This is done through a tripartite typology (perhaps under the influence of Kant's typology of reason, judgment, and emotion), and a reflexive theory of the role of the categories. The first level of a world view is formed from "regular stages of knowing reality . . . a second level of the structure of the world view [then] develops; the conception of the world becomes the basis for the evaluation of life and the understanding of the world . . . [finally] the world view becomes formative; it shapes and remoulds]"[49] "The world view becomes formative; it shapes and remoulds]" What has happened here? The theory which was at first concerned only with the relationship between the mind and the world becomes a theory of how the mind changes . . . what? the world? life? In Dilthey's hands this theory is the sophisticated result of careful attention to the Kantian critique of vulgar Positivism: a world view shapes and remolds whatever conception of the world is held by the thinking subject. But in less sophisticated hands this theory could be made to support the comfortable vulgar Idealist position that changing world views somehow directly change, in an unmediated fashion, the world itself. (This was a danger which the later Lukács was not to entirely avoid.) Even without that degradation, Dilthey's theory of world views, with its emphasis on the primacy of psychological categories, produced an intellectual atmosphere in which it was all too easy for those categories to take on a strange, ghost-like existence of their own.

Dilthey, then, contributed to the intellectual life of his, and our own, time three momentous ideas: that of the paramount importance of the whole, that of experience, and that of world views. An aspect of his concept of world views that became important later had to do with their role in literary studies. Here, again, there is a three part typology, which in this case Dilthey thought generally applicable to all artistic expression:

---

[48]   Dilthey, **Gesammelte Schriften,** V., pp. 405–6 [123].

[49]   Dilthey, **Gesammelte Schriften,** VIII.

materialism, which views physical matter as the only reality and holds that everything in the universe can be explained in terms of physical laws; objective idealism, which accepts nature as ideal or spiritual, but existing independently of any subject; and subjective idealism, which holds that nature has no existence outside the perceiving mind and insists that true reality consists of mental images or ideas.[50]

World views are not limited to individuals. They may be shared by entire communities. As a matter of fact, "community" might be defined by the sharing of a world view. If we are on somewhat tricky ground here, it is in part due to the later development of these concepts, but even Dilthey's position was not clear cut:

> If the psyche is acknowledged to be primarily the logical carrier of consciousness, Dilthey sees no reason why individuals, communities and cultural systems can not also be conceived as the logical carriers of objective spirit. There is then nothing inappropriate about using expressions like Zeitgeist and Volksgeist so long as one does not anthropomorphize them by substituting Seele (soul) for Geist (spirit). The soul of a people (Volksseele) connotes a collective mode of consciousness, but the spirit of a people (Volksgeist) posits no such thing.[51]

Dilthey associated these world views with typical literary representatives (such as Balzac, Schiller, and Goethe) and treated literary history as a cyclical phenomenon, moving from one to another of these ahistorical constructs. (Lukács was to pick up this idea in **The Theory of the Novel**.) The literary application of Dilthey's world view typology became widely known chiefly because of the success of his **Das Erlebnis und die Dichtung:**

> The lasting value of **Das Erlebnis und die Dichtung** can be accounted for by the fine understanding that Dilthey reveals, not only of individual works, but also of the whole attitude or Weltanschauung of a poet and his generation. Its direct influence was manifested in the rise of the so-called Geistesgeschichte school of literary history. Some of its adherents . . . came to interpret the history of literature as one possible way to deal with philosophical problems.[52]

---

50   Hermand, p. 30.

51   Makkreel, p. 313.

52   Makkreel, p. 144.

Another key idea for literary studies contributed by Dilthey was that of Nacherleben, which

> is a creative understanding which may go beyond the original. Its task is to understand a text as an unfolding continuity whereby the fragments of life that an author selects are articulated into a unified theme. The creativity of Nacherleben is specifically what makes it possible to understand an author better than he understood himself.[53]

Nacherleben derived from Schleiermacher's adaptation of the Enlightenment project of attempting to recapture the spirit of a text, be it Biblical, Classical, or folk song. Dilthey's revival of this approach to literary study popularized it among historians and literary critics associated with the Geistesgeschichte school. Thus Lukács, in some of his studies in **Soul and Form** was to use a variety of Nacherleben analysis as a way of analyzing certain literary works.

For a young philosopher like Lukács in the Central Europe of the decade of 1900, Dilthey's thought set the terms of the debate. Dilthey's concerns framed or counterpointed those of his rivals, disciples, and would-be successors. Some of Dilthey's ideas were developed to a sensational extreme by Lukács's teacher, Georg Simmel.

Georg Simmel

Dilthey's work had helped form an intellectual atmosphere rich in subjectivist and idealist nutrients in which philosophical systems even less positivistic than his own could flourish. The logic of Simmel's philosophy, in contrast to that of Dilthey, rests on the concept of life as a process that – although it can be experienced – can never be known. This concept is based on a Kantian identification of a split between content and form. The former, Simmel calls Weltstoff, which he privileges as existing independently of all acts of cognition and in itself in principle ungraspable by the thinking subject. This Weltstoff is a fairly shadowy substance and is immediately subordinated to a version of Erlebnis, inner experience. This had been Dilthey's mental analogy to our usual experience of events in everyday life. It is the mind's experience of its own condition. For Simmel, though, the concept is somewhat more intense; in Erleben, every act "is completely unified. We have a feeling which contains neither a consciousness of an object as such, standing apart from us, nor a consciousness of a self which

---

[53] Makkreel, p. 329.

is distinguished from its present state."[54] Thus Simmel's _Erleben_ is virtually identical with the Freudian concept of primary narcissism: "in which libido and ego-interests dwell together still, united and indistinguishable in the self-sufficient self."[55] This similarity between narcissism and _Erleben_ reinforces the impression of solipsism that most later life Philosophy gives.

Apart from this, Simmel's idea of experience might be contrasted with Dilthey's in that for Simmel experience is an emphatically total emotional experience of the whole person, while for Dilthey it usually seems that experience, no matter how vivid, is still the experiencing subjectivity of the purely mental subject. Admittedly, this is perhaps only a difference of tone, but it was just that disturbing tone of Simmel's thought that both isolated him in the academy – of whose crisis he was so symptomatic – and attracted to him such ardent students as the young Lukács.

For Simmel, then, experience is not merely a category of understanding utilized by the subject, it is, rather, a condition such that in the state of _Erleben_, life is "interwoven with the world of reality, and all of its functions are carried out like the breathing of a sleeper."[56] Everyday experience for Simmel is virtually the sleep of reason. In this context Rudolf Weingartner has pointed out that Simmel opposes "any theory which understands experience as a purely mental activity. It is symbolic of this conception that his preference is for the broader term, _Seele_ (here better translated as 'psyche,' than as 'soul') before _Geist_, which has the narrower meaning of 'mind.'"[57] The connotations of these terms overlap, but one might risk the formulation that it was this emphasis on the lived experience of the soul, rather than that of the mind, that Lukács was to take over from Simmel and which was to lead him down such unusual paths.

Through another logical operation of distinction, one similar to that which separated the _Weltstoff_ from _Erleben_, Simmel separates objective spirit from experience. He discovers a perennial contradiction "between subjective life which is restless but limited and time-bound, and its

---

54 Rudolph H. Weingartner, **Experience and Culture, The Philosophy of Georg Simmel** (Middletown, Conn.: Wesleyan University Press, 1962), p. 42. [Translations from Simmel are by Weingartner unless otherwise noted. Page numbers in square brackets refer to Weingartner.]

55 Sigmund Freud, **A General Introduction to Psychoanalysis,** trans. Joan Riviere (New York: Washington Square Press, Inc., 1960), pp. 422–24.

56 Georg Simmel, **Lebensanschauung: Vier metaphysische Kapitel,** 2nd ed. (Munchen & Leipzig: Duncker & Humblot, 1922), p. 52 [42].

57 Weingartner, pp. 46–7.

contents which once created, are immovable but timelessly valid."[58] We will return, shortly, to those contents which make up the realm of objective spirit, noting here only that as the items of objective spirit become created they are, in principle, graspable (in contrast to the Weltstoff) and also experienceable. But first we will follow Simmel's tracing out of a path of life, beginning with the primary narcissism of Erleben, and progressing through a mirror stage of the creation of the ego to the process of the creation of the mental forms by which objective spirit is grasped. Simmel makes the claim that the objects   of experience have no structure in themselves, but rather that structure is imparted to them by the attempts of the soul, or psyche, to deal with them. In its attempts to cope with the world, the soul utilizes a priori's, not exactly Kantian a priori's, but those functions of the soul which are the building blocks of conceptual thought.

This process whereby the objects of subjective life are formed is wholly in accordance with the conventional Kantian categories of knowledge, judgment, and emotion. At an early stage this formative project results only in relatively primitive proto-forms which, together, amount to what Simmel calls "proto-culture." This is the stage at which the forming process is "for the sake of life." A higher stage is that in which the forming is for the sake of form itself. These forms, properly, act as a "'circumference' within which a particular set of contents 'merges into a unity.' What holds for all cases of unity is merely the feeling of Bundigkeit of coherence, the feeling that this set of contents belongs together."[59] Thus, for Simmel, the objects of thought are never actually reached or understood (in anything other than a special definitional sense of understanding, certainly not in the totalizing sense of understanding used by Dilthey).   Therefore, Simmel is forced to work with a Lucretian concept of understanding as that which occurs when any satisfying account of a circumstance is given. Within this conceptual framework, the objects of subjective consideration can never be fully understood for "only with the understanding of the incalculable possibilities to which it . . . unfolds would its content really be understood."[60] The position that Simmel reaches is that we are faced with a world which may be grasped part by part, but the totality of which constantly escapes us. He holds that we develop methods of thought primarily to defend ourselves against the frustration which results from this by evolving forms of understanding which claim to make the world understandable, form by form,

---

[58]   Lewis A. Coser, "Introduction," **Georg Simmel** (Englewood Cliffs, N.J.: Prentice-Hall, Inc., 1965), p. 21.

[59]   Weingartner, p. 33.

[60]   Georg Simmel, "Vom Wesen des historischen Verstehens," in **Brucke und Tur. Essays des Philosophen zur Geschichte, Religion, Kunst und Gesellschaft**, eds. Michael Landmann and Margarete Susman (Stuttgart: Koehler, 1957), p. 74 [112-3].

without making an overall claim that the sum of the forms is the truth. This is at once similar to and quite different from Dilthey's perception of sets of competing and mutually independent world views which each claim to grasp the totality of the human world. Dilthey thought that one could not decide between the truth claims of the great philosophical systems; Simmel felt that truth in itself was an impossible goal.

Simmel's forms are as much processes as they are a system of categories. The process of forming begins with the synthesis of a plurality of elements from "the stream of life" into some unity. This is a process whereby those particular contents are made meaningful to an individual or the social group. Structure, here, is in the process itself, not in the contents that are formed. Those contents are chaos, an unformed reality (similar to the ancient Greek conception of that great Chaos that existed before the gods). It is a measure of Simmel's despair that for him this chaos is one of human manufacture. We have made it, and in a reversal of Vico's dictum, we cannot understand it. But in our efforts to deal with this chaos (and here Simmel comes closer to agreement with Dilthey's theory of world views), the forms become more than mere tools by which we seek to structure the contents of the human world, they become active and reflexive, "stand forth as autocratic ideas and determine life and its values."[61] Since the only way that we can begin to feel at home in the world is by forming the world ourselves, we cling to the forms that we create and begin to live in accordance with them, as if they comprised something other than an artificial reality. Unfortunately, Simmel's forms do not have the stability or finitude of Dilthey's world views. They are constantly in flux. They are not a small group of philosophical systems that are invented by great philosophers and endlessly recur; rather, they are beliefs which grow in number and change almost from moment to moment as individuals attempt to live in a time-constrained world.

The "world forms" are related hierarchically in Simmel's system to the forms as the forms are related to the a prioris. They are systems that bring all the elements of the world of contents together. Each world form is in itself taken to be adequate to refer to (but not to understand) all possible contents, "since each in its peculiar language already expresses the entire world stuff . . . these worlds are not capable of any mixing, overlapping, crossing."[62] Once again, Simmel's theory appears for a moment to converge with that of Dilthey's world views. These world forms are systems with exterior referents. Like the simpler forms, the world forms, when created, become active, transforming the realm of contents into a world, a system, that can be grasped in principle, if not in fact. Thus, for Simmel a world is the way in which one might look at all that one can look at so as

---

[61]   Georg Simmel, **Lebensanschauung,** p. 93 [55].

[62]   Georg Simmel, **Lebensanschauung,** p. 29 [63].

to grasp it, to understand it in a temporarily satisfying, if ultimately unreal fashion: "A world, in the full sense, is thus a sum of contents in which, from the perspective of the mind, each piece is delivered from its isolated condition and is brought into a unified system, into a form which is capable of encompassing the familiar and the unfamiliar."[63] Occasional philosophical systems, perhaps, and religions would constitute such worlds. Their function is to give us the feeling that we are at home in what Simmel characterizes as a radically alien universe.

Among the many possible worlds, Simmel himself seems to favor that based on historical understanding. But he retracts this preference almost at once by limiting historical understanding to the organization of the contents of the past:

> We understand the experienced moment by means of its past, the historical one by means of its future . . . [It is impossible] to understand the present historically. If that meant a derivation from preceding conditions, it would in principle still be possible. But the present has not yet developed its consequences in an identifiable way and because of this we can not understand it historically.[64]

In other words, our understanding of ourselves, of our own thought, for instance, cannot be the same sort of thing as our understanding of our predecessors. This would have important consequences for all historiological projects, making it in principle impossible to apply to our own procedures those standards we apply to the methods of preceding historians. Simmel further limits the realm of historical understanding by agreeing with Dilthey that the object of historical understanding is mental events, not merely because those were, to him, the most interesting of all possible historical objects, but because he thought that it is a condition of historical understanding that there be present to it an object that can be grasped as a living whole. But once again he introduces a further limitation; there can be no general history even in this special sense of a history of ideas:

> As a matter of fact, there are only special histories: histories of external and internal politics, of religion and fashions, of medicine and art, of world views and technology. In short, there are histories of phenomena which, while of course they are ordered chronologically, are selected for this ordering by means of . . . super-temporal concepts which are logically determined by their content. Instead of developing the totality

63   Georg Simmel, **Lebensanschauung**, pp. 27–8 [62].

64   Georg Simmel, "Die historische Formung," in **Fragmente und Aufsatze aus dem Nachlass und Veröffentlichungen der letzten Jahre**.   ed. Gertrud Kantorowicz (München: Drei Masken, 1923), p. 191 [127].

of events which stretches in all dimensions as if it were a single one, we construct such uni-dimensional lines of special developments which run alongside each other. Only here and there can we draw a diagonal across them, connecting similar traits which were found by means of abstraction.[65]

Even with such specialized histories, Simmel does not allow their narrations to be accounts of "what actually happened." For him, "historical truth is not a mere reproduction, but a mental activity which makes something of its material . . . which it is not yet in itself."[66] Thus, the status of, say, the history of technology would be something quite special and not at all a positivistic catalog of inventions. Such an historical narrative would be an attempt to create an ideal mental construct of technological history.

Simmel's pessimism culminates in his discussion of cultivation and culture, two key terms in the German intellectual tradition. At first, culture seems to provide a way out of the airless world of forms: "Culture is the way that leads from the closed unity through the unfolded multiplicity to the unfolded unity."[67] This is at once the culture that is referred to when a person is said to be "cultured" and the phenomena that are socially created and stabilized in society: high culture. "Human culture is the 'cultivation' of things, but the cultivation of things turns out to be a cultivation of ourselves. The human subject, in terms of his new developing skills and capabilities, is created in the act of creating objects, in the act of the formation of things."[68] This is parallel to the creation of forms and is an echo, perhaps, of the Hegelian theory of the development of civilization out of the master/slave dialectic. The most hopeful moment in the discussion, perhaps in all of Simmel's critique of culture, occurs in his account of the development of the cultivated individual:

A man becomes cultivated only when cultural traits develop that aspect of his soul which exists as its most indigenous drive and as the inner predetermination of its subjective perfection . . . In this context the conditions finally emerge through which culture resolves the subject-object dualism . . . culture comes into being by a meeting of the two

65   Simmel, "Die historische Formung," p. 153 [94].

66   Georg Simmel, **Die Probleme der Geschichtsphilosophie. Eine Erkenntnistheoretische Studie,** 4th ed. (München & Leipzig: Duncker & Humblot, 1922), p. 55 [86].

67   Georg Simmel, "On the Concept and Tragedy of Culture," in **Georg Simmel,** trans. K. Peter Etzkorn (New York: Teachers College Press, 1968), p. 29.

68   Andrew Arato, "Lukács' Path to Marxism," **Telos,** 7(1971), p. 129.

elements, neither of which contain culture by itself: the subjective soul and the objective spiritual product.[69]

The highest point of this process is the work of art. Aesthetics occupies a privileged position in the thought of Simmel, as with Dilthey, and those who shared their concerns, since,

> In addition to all subjective enjoyments by which a work of art enters into us, we recognize as a value of a special kind the fact that the spirit created this vessel for itself. Just as there is at least one line running between the artist's will and the individual property of the work of art, which intertwines his objective evaluation of the work with an enjoyment of his own activity and creative force, we find a similar oriented line in the attitudes of the spectator.[70]

The work of art is thus a unique object, the material manifestation of a form.   And precisely because it is such a manifestation, it can, in its particularity, bridge the gap between the subject (the soul) and a world which is not a mere mental construct but which has an existence beyond the subjectivity of the individual soul. This line of thought is a consolation brought forth again and again by those who find themselves, willingly or not, residing in the asylum of subjective idealism.   Simmel's version of it shines forth to our own time, striking here and there similar sentiments, and revealing them by this light, to be based on a similar epistemology.

But, typically, this "objective spiritual product," emerging as it does at the moment when the tragedy of the subject–object dualism is resolved, eventually leads back to dualism and alienation. As the social forces that brought the cultivated individual and the artist into existence continue to act, the area of objective spirit, the accumulated objects created by culture, grows, until it becomes impossible for an individual to be familiar with it all. Simmel claims that the Greeks, comparatively speaking, had only a few cultural objects – poems, temples, statues – around them.   An individual (free, male) Greek could be familiar with them all.   We, on the other hand, are overwhelmed by the sheer number of our and our predecessor's cultural monuments. This very fact gives rise to feelings of alienation:

> Thus, the typically problematic situation of modern man comes into being: his sense of being surrounded by an immeasurable number of cultural elements which are neither meaningless to him nor, in the final analysis, meaningful. In their mass they depress him, since he is not capable of assimilating them all, nor can he simply reject them, since,

---

[69] Georg Simmel, "On the Concept and Tragedy of Culture," pp. 29–30.

[70] Georg Simmel, "On the Concept and Tragedy of Culture," p. 32.

after all, they do belong potentially within the sphere of his cultural development.[71]

We note the importance of mood here. Alienation is immediately characterized by the way in which it produces a mood: depression. Simmel believes that culture, which develops in response to man's isolation in an inhuman world, produces in the end the isolation of the individual from the human world. Only metaphysics offers a way out of this isolation, and that is hopelessly tainted, made valid, unified "by means of a biased selection of one element from totality, which is then enthroned absolutely. In no way, except by paying the price of such one-sidedness, can our intellect bring about a total unity."[72] There is, for Simmel, nowhere to turn. Neither art nor metaphysics can cure the disease of alienation. Exchanging the realm of the mind for that of the soul, the play of world views for that of forms, Simmel arrives at last in a flux of pure subjectivity, alienated and lost in an unfamiliar chaos. His perceptions soon became those of most of the mandarin class, and, indeed, of most Central Europeans. Although it would be altogether too simple to say that this was a pure reflection of the rapid industrialization of Central Europe in the anachronistic political framework of monarchical bureaucracy, it was nonetheless characteristic of that time and place, and perceived then as being the result of those catastrophic social transformations that had brought most of the population of Germany and of the Dual Monarchy from the eighteenth to the twentieth century in the space of a generation. Simmel managed to live with his despairing philosophy, almost, at times, seemed to enjoy it. The next generation would seize on one solution after another to the problems that he had posed, seeking, almost in a frenzy, any path that offered an escape from an intolerable Dostoevskian world.

---

[71] Georg Simmel, "On the Concept and Tragedy of Culture," p. 44.

[72] Georg Simmel, **Hauptprobleme der Philosophie,** 7th ed. ("Sammlung Goschen," No. 500) (Berlin: de Gruyter, 1950), p. 35 [162].

Heinrich Rickert

Heinrich Rickert was a scholar of the same university generation as Simmel, both receiving their degrees in 1881. His ideas are significant here as representing an aspect of the tradition not followed by Lukács, and as contributing to the Weberian synthesis. While Simmel's career was somewhat eccentric, Rickert was known as a disciple of the orthodox Neo-Kantian philosopher Wilhelm Windelband taking over from his teacher an interest in the logic along with methodology of scholarship and a Neo-Kantian approach such questions. This transfer of concerns from the object of research to its methodology was a significant move away from the complexities of the Life Philosophy toward a line of thought that held some promise for the resolution within the walls of the university of some of the intellectual problems of the time. We shall see later that although that promise was not fulfilled, Rickert was able to clarify the issues in such a way as to escape the despair of the Northern German philosophers of existence. That his proposed solutions were not sufficient is an indication, perhaps, that the matters at issue were not exclusively those of science, but indeed did have deep and far spreading roots in the cultural crisis of the time.

Rickert begins in common with most philosophers of Lukács's teachers'generation with the proposition that although there may be a world outside human consciousness, there is no way to know that world except through ideas, and that knowledge is not knowledge of the physical world directly, but is always knowledge of sensations and ideas. It is as if the act of knowing were an operation performed by one part of the mind on another. In this he was in agreement with both Dilthey and Simmel, indeed with the entire non-Marxist German philosophical tradition. The Southwest Neo-Kantians did not begin to differentiate their approach to the problems that we have been considering until they confronted the distinction between the natural and the human sciences. Then Rickert, following Windelband, asserted that Dilthey was incorrect to make this distinction on the basis of the object of study. Rickert held, rather, that the distinction must be logical, in that the natural sciences are not ultimately characterized as those disciplines which study the physical world, but are rather those which delineate what phenomena have in common: they are nomological. The cultural sciences are occupied, on the other hand, with the elucidation of the individual and unique event or process.[73]

Rickert initiates his argument by stressing the infinite nature of the empirical world. According to Thomas Burger,

---

[73] Thus, both parties to the debate may be taken as defending aestheticism in the human sciences.

The systematic starting point of Rickert's logical reflections is the fact that to the human observer the empirical world represents itself as an infinite multiplicity of qualitatively and quantitatively different concrete phenomena. Rickert calls it a "heterogeneous continuum." Its infinity is encountered on two levels: first, any attempt to merely enumerate all concretely existing objects leads to the recognition of the "extensive" infinity of empirical reality; second, any attempt to describe the component parts of just one concrete object reveals the "intensive" infinity of elements of which any concrete phenomenon consists.[74]

It had been precisely this doubly infinite characteristic of the potential realm of knowledge that had led Simmel to give up all hope of rational knowledge of the world and to adopt an irrationalist theory of concept formation. Rickert, in contrast, staves off the irrationalist moment by continuing to pursue the logical consequences of this insight. He says that we do in fact attempt to understand the world in spite of the infinite nature of the phenomena under consideration and that we do this in two ways, neither of which is arbitrary or necessitates a Simmelian leap into faith. These paths to scientific understanding are the formal criteria, or standards, of knowledge.

One of the standards prescribes the selection of those empirical elements which are common to many concrete phenomena. These elements are considered to be essential, whereas individual differences are neglected. The other standard requires the selection of those component elements of one individual phenomenon which in their combined occurrence constitute the unique features of this phenomenon and distinguish it from all others; everything else is neglected as irrelevant.[75]

The use of the first standard, the law governed type, is Rickert's definition of the natural sciences. It is not meant as a description of the procedures of any actually existing science. Here we might note the common and devastating critique of Rickert's analysis: the natural sciences are in fact not as he defines them, but move between the two modes of selection, as also do the human or cultural sciences (those of the second standard), which are not without their generalizing moments. In Rickert's defense it might be pointed out that he is dealing with the logic of scientific knowledge, attempting to generalize about modes of concept formation, and that even if he himself sometimes seems to believe that he is actually describing, say, physics, that confusion does not serve

---

[74] Thomas Burger, **Max Weber's Theory of Concept Formation** (Durham, N. C.: Duke University Press, 1976), p. 21.

[75] Burger, p. 22.

immediately to invalidate his analysis, but instead serves the useful purpose of helping us to historicize his thought.

Rickert further differs from, say, Simmel, in holding that existence is not something above and outside concept formation, but is part of it:

> There are several forms in which contents are judged to occur, and their totality comprises any form in which man can have knowledge. The form-element is called the "category." "Existence" is one of them . . . Every concrete "fact," therefore, is categorically formed. People refer to such facts when, in the empirical sciences, they speak of "objective reality" or "empirical reality." Concrete reality consists of contents of consciousness which are judged by everybody to be "real." Objective reality in its totality is the subject-matter of science.[76]

By invoking a community of agreement as to the nature of the real, that is, of objective or concrete reality, Rickert avoids the radical relativism of Simmel and its inevitable epistemological problems. Where Simmel has each individual simply asserting, as a matter of faith, that certain forms are "true" or satisfying (assertions that have no binding validity for other individuals), Rickert bases his ordering of reality on a social convention uniting form and content, which is binding for all reasoning individuals.

This idea might be made clearer by citing the following example. When someone says:

> "This is a cat," he asserts something of the notion "cat," namely that it exists. The notion, or idea, of one or more immediate sensations – in this case, "cat" – is called the "content" of knowledge. "Existence," which is asserted of it, is the "form" in which in this case knowledge is had. The combined form-content is what is usually called a concrete-fact.[77]

This is a typical result of Rickert's analysis, taking concepts which were nearly blank signifiers and transforming them into logical elements of a system of analysis. It allows Rickert to go beyond both Simmel and Dilthey to the explication of the methodologies of the sciences. While he agrees with his predecessors that human beings are faced with an undifferentiated continuum of data, he holds that this is not the end of the situation, but the beginning. The process of understanding, of scientific explanation, can continue from the chaotic totality of experience to knowledge through the development of modes of selection from the universe of all possible objects

---

[76]   Burger, p. 16.

[77]   Burger, p. 15.

of thought.[78]

It is interesting to follow how, virtually point by point, Rickert uses the same vocabulary as Dilthey and Simmel to arrive at significantly different conclusions. For Rickert the outcome of the formative process of selection is a concept, while for both Dilthey and Simmel that outcome was a world view. Thus, while for Dilthey and Simmel the forming activity of the mind, more or less in each case, is a process that results in the conclusion that inter subjectivity is difficult if not impossible (or, if possible, then arbitrary), for Rickert this process is precisely that which makes possible the inter subjectivity of objective scientific knowledge.[79] Rickert's effort, then, was to save Idealist philosophy from irrationalist Life Philosophy. The argument that had led Dilthey and Simmel directly to Erlebnis and irrationalism was an escape from that for Rickert, an escape into the possibility of objective scientific knowledge where for Dilthey and Simmel there had been only subjective opinion. There is a line here, one suspects, between a philosophy that embraces irrationalism and one that attempts to cling to reason as long as possible, a line that marks the boundary between ideology and philosophy proper.

And yet Rickert's theories were at best only a hope for a rationalist philosophy, as they hinged on his belief that "'objective knowledge' is knowledge of those selected facts which everybody wants to know. This knowledge is, therefore, inter subjective. 'Science' is the systematic effort to establish this knowledge."[80] How did Rickert know that there are facts that "everybody" wants to know? Clearly this is a hypothesis or a wish rather than scientific knowledge. This "everybody" is an unexamined ideal-typical construction, at best. It is a useful fiction which allows Rickert to work out his theories of the methodologies of the sciences. In any case, he

---

[78] "The process of selection involved in the establishment of scientific knowledge, in Rickert's view, is a formative process. Its end-product, a certain account of empirical reality, thus displays a certain form in which the substantive content appears. This form is called 'concept' by Rickert. In this terminology, then, the formal aspect of scientific investigation is a process of concept formation. Its established outcome is a concept." Burger, p. 19.

[79] "Rickert calls concepts 'methodological forms' as opposed to the categories, which are 'constitutive forms,' since through them objective reality is constituted . . . It is the existence of these forms which makes science possible at all. Without them, humans could not have scientific knowledge, but could only try to grasp the infinite whole of the concrete world through intuition or some other kind of all-embracing inner experience (Erlebnis)." Burger, p. 20.

[80] Burger, p. 18.

quickly retreats from the dangerous vagueness of facts which "everybody"
wants to know to the claim that "it depends on the point of view adopted
by a scientist, i.e., the standard of selection applied by him, whether a fact
is essential or not."[81] Here, again, Rickert seems on the verge of a
Simmelian formulation, one perhaps implying that scientists define reality to
conform to, or to form, a world view. But once more he defers a collapse
into irrationalism by introducing a new concept, which in this case is that
the standard of selection in question is applied not arbitrarily or
eccentrically, but by reference to value.

> Only when in practical life the unique and particular constellation of
> elements of which a phenomenon is composed is valued, is there any
> reason for people to be interested in its individuality. Otherwise it is
> merely treated as an interchangeable instance of a class.[82]

A fact which everybody wants to know is, then, an "essential" fact, a valued
phenomenon. This should be seen against Dilthey's concept of value, that
poetic construct. It might be argued that Rickert's concept of value is in
itself liable to be viewed as an ideological construct, a concept just as
problematic in its way as that of experience, for instance, and just as open
to the possibility of mystification. And yet, it cannot simply be dismissed
with that judgment, for if we follow Rickert's (and, later, Weber's)
discussions on this point, we will see how useful this notion can be
precisely in limiting the need to resort to mystification.

Rickert proceeds with his argument as follows:

> The valuation of phenomena by practical actors . . . is a way of
> overcoming the infinite multiplicity of the empirical world. The extensive
> infinity of reality is overcome since only a limited number of things,
> events, and processes is valued. Its intensive infinity is overcome due
> to the fact that not every concrete component element of a valued
> phenomena is relevant to the value, but only the particular combination
> of a limited number of these elements.[83]

Where Simmel figuratively threw his hands up in despair at the infinite and
unending nature of the world, Rickert notes the unquestionable existence of
science and attempts to show how its modes of knowledge are possible in
an infinite world. Simmel was apparently more concerned with the human
condition than with the logic of science and his theories are quite possibly
accurate representations of the phenomenology of the experience of the

---

[81] Burger, p. 22.

[82] Burger, p. 35.

[83] Burger, p. 35.

average citizen of Berlin, say.[84] Yet his aims were more far-reaching than a mere critique of the experience of everyday life; they brought him ultimately to the construction of a more or less systematic philosophy that attempted to deal in a satisfactory way with the entire human experience of the world while systematically excluding from consideration those aspects of human experience that are concerned explicitly with attempting to grasp the nature of that which is. Rickert, focussing on this area neglected by Simmel was able to extend the domain of the rational, of the intelligible, and thus make possible the lessening of the object's intrinsic otherness.

After having introduced these concepts of selection and value, Rickert returns to his prior distinction between the natural and the cultural sciences, but not through Dilthey's reliance on their different subject matters or our supposed different modes of apprehension. Rickert is able to develop the distinction through the methodological use of value theory.

> Looking at empirical reality, therefore, two classes of objects can be distinguished. One may be called "nature" and comprises all those things which originate and persist without human interference or concern. The other, "culture," comprises whatever is either produced directly by men acting according to valued ends or, if they are already in existence, whatever is at least fostered intentionally for the sake of values considered to be attaching to it. Such values are cultural.[85]

---

[84] A good example of the phenomenology of accumulative alienation is given in "Goodbye to Berlin," in **The Berlin Stories** by Christopher Isherwood (New York: New Directions, n.d.): "The tall tiled stove, gorgeously coloured, like an altar. The washstand like a Gothic shrine. The cupboard also is Gothic, with carved cathedral windows: Bismark faces the King of Prussia in stained glass. My best chair would do for a bishop's throne. In the corner, three sham mediaeval halberds (from a theatrical touring company?) are fastened together to form a hatstand. Frl. Schroeder unscrews them from time to time. They are heavy and sharp enough to kill.

"Everything in the room is like that: unnecessarily solid, abnormally heavy and dangerously sharp. Here, at the writing-table, I am confronted by a phalanx of metal objects – a pair of candlesticks shaped like entwined serpents, an ashtray from which emerges the head of a crocodile, a paper-knife copied from a Florentine dagger, a brass dolphin holding on the end of its tail a small broken clock. What becomes of such things? How could they ever be destroyed? They will probably remain intact for thousands of years: people will treasure them in museums" (p. 2).

For Rickert, then, the natural sciences are not those studies focussing on valueless natural phenomena, but are those centering on the organization of those cultural values that treat of such things. The cultural sciences focus similarly on cultural phenomena, but in this case involve those that are concerned with the organization of other cultural elements. Certainly this is a long way from vulgar Positivism and might be used to "save" Rickert's theories from the charge that his restriction of the natural sciences to pure generalizing theory is at least naive and probably untrue. Unfortunately, Rickert does not follow up on his insight, but continues with his idea that the value selection process is simply part of the generalizing methodology of the natural sciences.

Rickert avoids the potential problem in his value theory of how to discover which phenomena are valued (a question that at first sight can only be dealt with by exhaustive surveys) by making a further stipulation:

> Treating a phenomenon as the expression, or embodiment, of a value – a value which some human individual connects with the phenomenon in question – Rickert calls "relating a phenomenon to a value." Relating an object to a value fulfills the same function as direct valuation, as far as the problem of selection is concerned.[86]

It is an easy move from this position to that of locating values in all phenomena that are potentially related to value by some human being. This saves scientific objectivity; the scientist can investigate any potentially valued phenomenon without being restricted to those that he or she personally values. (Weber was to apply this technique to his sociological and historical studies when he isolated, for instance, those social phenomena which might be valued by a person from the point of view of one or another religious system, points of view not necessarily held by Weber himself.)

Rickert continued the concern with the concepts of totality and form which were the poles of thought of Dilthey, Simmel, and Tönnies, winning those concepts back from the realm of the irrational by presenting the totality of experience as a simple given and not a reflection of the alienation of social man from society and presenting form as a tool of scientific logic and not a purely subjective imposition of order on chaos. But his system was not a solution to the problems delineated by Simmel and Tönnies, the problems which obsessed Lukács, it was simply, perhaps could not be anything more than, a delaying action. The tool that he used to delay his inevitable confrontation with the irrational was value theory, and in the end, his conception of the way in which it might be employed

---

85   Burger, p. 37.

86   Burger, p. 36.

failed to serve the purpose. The failure occurred, most visibly, in Rickert's analysis of historical understanding, which was crucial as the debate about the dichotomy in the sciences had focussed on this area:

> Against the formal sort of dichotomies implied by Windelband, Dilthey had already argued that the two sets of disciplines need not be distinguished according to any sharp division of method. Description and explanation can occur in both the Naturwissenschaften and the Geisteswissenschaften, but their scope and task will differ. In the final analysis, only an epistemological grounding for the Geisteswissenschaften can delimit them. Having denied that any particular method or discipline can be considered foundational, the epistemological delimitation occurs with reference to a conception of a historical world common to all the human studies.[87]

Rickert claimed that "Whoever thinks historically must only assume that the world in its temporal development stands in relation to some absolute values which may be completely unknown to him."[88]

It is difficult to imagine what Rickert means by absolute values, especially in light of his earlier analysis which ties values resolutely to individual human beings or groups of human beings, or possible individuals or groups. In the analysis of understanding and knowledge he carried on up to this point, values were always relative to human beings and objectivity was said to be obtainable through the operations of an observer who did not need to hold the values in question but needed only to be aware of their possibility. The attempt to posit absolute values, without regard to the standpoint of the individual, can only refer to the values of Absolute Mind, a problematic notion.

Rickert is a relatively minor figure in the evolution of the system of ideas that we have been tracing here. Although his work of shifting the ground of the argument from notions of the objects of scientific study to the logic of their methods was to be fundamental to Weber's approach to the crisis, Rickert himself did not seem to realize either the gravity of the issues, nor the fact that they involved more than simply a quarrel over the definition of scientific research. The problem that Dilthey and Simmel had confronted was not merely that of how to define the objects (and methodologies) of the natural and human sciences; it was a problem which encompassed nothing less than the means of defining the entire structure of modern society. But even Rickert, for all his dry epistemological investigations, contributed to the atmosphere of crisis in which Lukács was educated. If these "classical" philosophers assumed, with the Life Philosophers, that

---

[87] Makkreel, p. 304.

[88] Burger, p. 51.

objective knowledge is impossible, that even in the natural sciences values are central to knowledge, then what refuge could there be in a world that was daily and evidently losing all firm values? We read Rickert now to measure the inadequacy of his response to Dilthey against Weber's answers. Before Lukács became acquainted with the the strength of the latter, he had a choice to make. He chose Simmel.

Ferdinand Tonnies and Idealism

In contrast to the almost excessively prolific and versatile Simmel, and in contrast also to the fairly conventional career of Rickert, we must refer, at least briefly, to another influential thinker, Ferdinand Tönnies, who was known as the author of a single book, one might say of a single idea, dramatizing the crisis of values in its sociological aspects. Tönnies compared the cold new society of the Reich with the community of an older, rural culture. As his **Gemeinschaft und Gesellschaft** is more a prolonged cry of anguish than a reasoned argument, its tone might best be conveyed by this typical passage, concerning the state of the "masses" in the new Germany:

> City life and Gesellschaft down the common people to decay and death; in vain they struggle to attain power through their own multitude, and it seems to them that they can use their power only for a revolution if they want to free themselves from their fate. The masses become conscious of this social position through the education in schools and through newspapers. They proceed from class consciousness to class struggle. This class struggle may destroy society and the state which it is its purpose to reform. The entire culture has been transformed into a civilization of state and Gesellschaft, and this transformation means the doom of culture itself if none of its scattered seeds remain alive and again bring forth the essence and idea of Gemeinschaft, thus secretly fostering a new culture amidst the decaying one.[89]

These sentences might be endlessly explicated in terms of their contrasts of community and society, culture and civilization, the people and the masses. That would be superfluous here, as the explication has been performed by history itself. **Gemeinschaft und Gesellschaft** first appeared in 1887. Its author died in 1936.

---

[89] Ferdinand Tönnies, **Community and Society,** trans. and ed. Charles P. Loomis (East Lansing: The Michigan State University Press, 1957), pp. 230–1.

Tönnies seemed to be moving toward a formulation of the ideal-typical methodology later developed by Weber. His lists of <u>Gemeinschaft</u> and <u>Gesellschaft</u> social structures eventually become a limiting process close to the Weberian technique, but restricted to his own localized subject matter. More importantly, his depiction of the overwhelming otherness of the <u>Gesellschaft</u> world that he found in the great industrial cities of the Reich isolated an aspect of the negative connotations of the concept of totality similar to those perceived by Simmel. Where Simmel had described totality from an epistemological point of view and then from the point of view of a critique of culture and of cultural alienation, Tönnies had revealed the new negative totalization of social existence. The young Lukács, along with many of his contemporaries, fled from this negative totalization of social reality into what he thought of as the higher realm of the spirit. The traces of that journey are inscribed in the essays collected in **Soul and Form.**

The varieties of philosophical Idealism presented in this chapter were primary components in the intellectual atmosphere of central Europe in the quarter of a century before the First World War. This way of looking at the world, in which it is assumed that the idea, say of a desk, is more important than any particular desk, is not an easy position for most people brought up in the Anglo-American tradition to sympathize with. We tend to value the practical, to talk, for instance, of practical criticism, and to assume that we are free of the theoretical presuppositions of idealism. But, as we will eventually indicate, it has been just that practical criticism, the concentration on the literary object, which has been most firmly based on Idealism. The Neo-Kantian philosophers and their colleagues formulated the questions that had arisen in Central European life after the collapse of Hegelianism and the beginnings of modern social organization. The world had suddenly expanded – telescopes were not powerful enough to search its infinite extension, microscopes not powerful enough to probe its infinite intensity – the village had become the city, community had given way to society. Issues which had seemed abstractly philosophical became urgently emotional. Is nothing certain? Is the sense of certainty reconcilable with reason? Science, in those final years of classical physics, seemed to offer definite knowledge, but what of the human sciences? Would it be possible to place these on a firm foundation, rational and definite? Lukács's work in the first two decades of the twentieth century was rooted in this problematic, commented on it, reacted to it. The combination of epistemological anguish and social alienation felt also as emotional deprivation formed a consciousness that sought satisfactions in art that could not be found in life. The philosophical background became vivid enough generally in Central Europe at this time, contributing as it did to a fashionable despair which mocked reason itself. We will see how for a young man as intensely scholarly as Lukács, it was inextricably involved with his writing and personal evolution as he worked first to introduce his native country to the artistic manifestations of this <u>Zeitgeist</u> then as he sought – and failed – to capture it in a Neo-Hegelian dialectic.

SOUL AND FORM

Between 1907, when he was baptized in the Lutheran Church, and 1911 Lukács established himself in Budapest as a literary figure, an Impressionist, by writing a number of essays, some of which were collected first in **A lélék és a formák (Kisérletek),** and then in German translation, with additions, as **Die Seele und die Formen.** The first collection was published in Budapest in 1910, the second in Berlin the following year. At least eight of the ten essays that were eventually used in the latter volume had originally been published in the Hungarian.[90] These writings, translated as **Soul and Form,** comprise a selection of his work as a contributor to the leading oppositional Hungarian literary periodicals of the day, **Nyugat** and **A Szellem,** and to the German periodicals **Logos** and **Die neu Rundschau.**

The first essay of the collections, the essay on the essay itself (which will be considered at length below), opens with a meditation on the means by which such a collection might be unified. It is probable that both the motivation for this line of reasoning and the solution that it arrives at were Neo-Kantian in origin. In addition to the unities of the book cited in the essay on the essay, much was achieved through the simple and effective

---

90 "Novalis" was originally published with the subtitle "Jegyzetek a romantihus eletfilozofiaröl." In the Berlin edition it became "Zur romantischen Lebenphilosophie: Novalis." "Stefan George" became "Die neue einsamkeit und ihre Lyrik: Stefan George." "Rudolf Kassner" became "Platonismus, Poesie und die Formen: Rudolf Kassner." "Richard Beer-Hofmann was translated as "Der Augenblick und die Formen: Richard Beer-Hofmann." "Sören Kierkegaard és Regine Olsen," became Das Zerschellen der Formam Leben: Sören Kierkegaard und Regine Olsen." The three previously unpublished essays included in **A lélék és a formák** ("Levél a 'Kisértröl'," "Theodor Storm," and "Beszélgetés Laurence Sternéröl") became "Über Wesen und Form des Essays: Ein Brief an Leo Popper," "Burgerlichkeit und l'art pour l'art: Theodor Storm," and "Reichtum, Chaos und Form: Ein Zwiegesprach über Lawrence Sterne" in the Berlin edition. **Die Seele und die Formen** also included "Metaphysik der Tragodie: Paul Ernst," which had been published in German in **Logos** and in Hungarian in **A Szellem** in 1911 as "A tragedia metafizikaja," and "Sehnsucht und Form: Charles-Louis Philippe," which had first been published in German that same year as "Über Sehnsucht und Form" in **Die neue Rundschau** and in Hungarian in **Renaissance.**

device of imposing a common theme on the essays, that of form itself, by renaming some of the essays so that their titles included the word "form." This seems an arbitrary device, but it is precisely because of this, as we have seen, that this naming becomes typical of the Simmelian philosophy, a philosophy that demanded only coherence and which held that any order, no matter how arbitrary, was better than none at all. Lukács's studies with Georg Simmel in Berlin (1909–1910) occurred while he was writing the essays included in **Soul and Form**. If there is any term that was central to Simmel's cultural and aesthetic teaching that term, as we have seen, is "form," not in its usual generic sense (such as the stanza form of a lyric poem), but in the sense of a coherence that is imposed on the chaos of the object world by the thinking subject. It is, therefore, significant that in the process of having his essays translated from Hungarian to German and adding some new works to the collection, Lukács changed many of their titles so that six of the ten contained the crucial word "form," already to be found in the title of the book's Hungarian edition. The term is, then, among other things, an emblem of his regard for Simmel at that time. A consequence of this attempt at coherence through naming that Lukács imposed on his essays was the confusion that arose between various senses of the word "form" used within them. In some, the word is used to denote genre, while in others it takes on the specific Simmelian and Neo-Kantian connotations of an activity within the mind of a critic or artist that creates a world. There are even passages in the book where Lukács shifts from one meaning to the other within a single sentence.

It is best, then, to consider **Soul and Form** not as a unified work of art (the very concept of the unified work of art is itself a manifestation of the contemporary philosophical background sketched above), but rather as the record of the phase through which Lukács was passing during the years in which he wrote its essays. As Lukács was born in 1885, received his law degreee in 1906, and had just won his Doctorat in 1909, it is not at all surprising that these essays reveal his thought in an unstable period of experimentation. This process can best be traced by giving an account of the individual essays, not in their order as presented in either the Hungarian or German volumes, but in the order of their composition. It is fitting that the first of these essays by an author who was then, if brilliant, still quite young, was on Romanticism.

On the Romantic Philosophy of Life

Romanticism has dominated the intellectual life of the West for two hundred years and shows no signs of loosening its grip on the imagination of our culture. One would have to look to the Orient for a parallel to this extraordinary phenomenon – the influence of Zen on Japan, say – and still be at a loss, for Romanticism is not, strictly, a religious matter. It is perhaps most easily grasped for our present purposes as a wide-spread psychological condition, the psychologization of sociological despair. One might apply some of Auerbach's remarks on Fortuna, the worship of which that scholar took to be the institutionalization of insecurity in the classical world. This would supply a certain context in which one could see Dilthey's thought, for instance, as essentially a revival of Romanticism in philosophy. Readers of his 1906 publication **Das Erlebnis und die Dichtung** and those who remembered his dictum that "The poet is a seer who intuits the sense of life," would have had no trouble with the earliest of the essays collected in **Soul and Form,** a meditation focussed on Novalis. Characteristically, the first three of its five short sections are not specifically about Novalis at all; rather, they are concerned with a general overview of the Jena Romantics, especially in regard to the relationship of the Romantics with Goethe.

Lukács portrays the Romantics as anti-rationalist heirs of the eighteenth century, a small, isolated group attempting to create "a new, harmonious, all embracing culture out of the chaos" (42) ("aus diesem Chaos eine neue, harmonische, alles umfassende Kultur zu schaffen"), that is, a type of world view.[91] The particular "chaos" in question here is not only the ontological or epistemological chaos of the Neo-Kantians, but a subjective perception of a specific sociological situation involving what we might now call an underdeveloped country with a small cosmopolitan intelligentsia whose attention is focussed mainly on its own alienation from the larger national life. The Jena Romantics, according to Lukács, thought that the solution to the problem of their alienation could be found in a new "all embracing culture," perhaps seeing models for such a solution in the new bourgeois French culture that had been suddenly revealed by the great Revolution. But Lukács points out that there could not have been a political revolution in Germany at that time.

> For Germany, there was only one way to culture: the inner way, the way of revolution of the spirit; no one could seriously envisage a real revolution. Men destined for action had to fall silent and wither away, or else they became mere utopians and played games with bold possibilities in the mind; men who, on the other side of the Rhine, would have become tragic heroes, in Germany, lived out their destinies only in poetic works. (43)

---

[91] Georg Lukács, **Die Seele und die Formen** (Neuwied und Berlin: Hermann Luchterhand Verlag GmbH, 1971), p. 64.

Here we see the typicality of, say, **Wilhelm Meister's Apprenticeship,** where that apprenticeship is served in the theater itself, as if even for Goethe the world of real action had been sealed off within a zone forbidden to the bourgeoisie, leaving Wilhelm Meister only the theater, and his creator only Weimar.

The desperation of the Romantics' situation, as depicted by Lukács, was apparent in their choice of a path to follow in hope of escaping from their isolation. They thought, he wrote, that the German alternative to political revolution might be found in poetry. It is certainly not now an obvious idea that a nation could be transformed socially if only certain poems of a highly aesthetic nature were to be written. (It is true that the cultural revolutions of the nineteenth and twentieth centuries have often been nationalist movements aimed against multi-national empires. Operating as centers, for example, of Magyar resistance to Habsburg domination, or of Irish resistance to the English, they have worked against forces that were at once economically, administratively, and culturally dominant.) However, Herder had popularized the founding of nationalism in culture, and Lukács, writing of Herder's successors, easily picked up the idea. But what did it mean in Jena at the end of the eighteenth century to attempt to construct a new culture? The bourgeoisie was there opposed to its own incredibly belated domination by the feudal and fragmented Holy Roman Empire, but that opposition could not crystallize. Novalis himself was a von Hardenberg, a member of that small nobility which was not culturally distinguished from the bourgeoisie. The ideals of the intelligentsia of both groups were virtually identical, and were, if anything, more influenced by the antiquarian dreams of the great nobility than the emerging commercial ethos of the middle class.

The isolation of the Jena Romantics was to a considerable extent simply geographical. The lack of a capital for the North German states was so palpable an absence that the resulting desire for unity was confused with the desire for social revolution, and, consequently, the mere concentration of intellectuals at Jena was taken for a national cultural movement. Perhaps it is not aesthetic culture that transforms geographical or even political expressions into nations (the history of the Weimar Republic testifies to the vanity of that hope). It is a common everyday culture among the masses of the people, and, perhaps, linguistic nationalism or exactly that glorification of provinciality that the cosmopolitan intellectuals of Jena hated most, which brings nations into being. Only in France, the nation par excellence, did the revolution precede the phase of cultural nationalism, and that exception demonstrates the rule, as it has been (for these two hundred years) precisely French culture which has been the cosmopolitan culture of the modern West: it is exactly in Paris that there is to be found that intelligence which is the expression of the most advanced thought of the West and at the same time the most isolated and closed provinciality. The efforts of the Jena Romantics were too limited, too isolated, and too premature, to have the effect which superficially similar groups were later to have. And therefore, in Jena, instead of there emerging a consciously nationalistic group, there were only a "few steeply rising trajectories" (44), crossing briefly.

Lukács's argument runs that in general, because of the lack of a bourgeois national culture, the elite culture of the Jena group was bound to remain isolated and could only lead to further isolation of the individuals who made up the movement. For them, he declared, "the only path led still higher, towards a deadly solitude" (43). Lukács introduced the issue of the attitude of the Romantics toward Goethe as exemplary of their situation.

> The truest way of speaking of the early Romantics would surely be to describe in the utmost detail what Goethe meant to each of them at each moment of their lives. Then one would see jubilant victory and speechless tragedy, great hopes, daring adventures, long voyages, and would hear two war-cries merging into a single shout of battle: to reach him] to surpass him] (44)

Lukács claimed that Goethe had reached the goal toward which the Romantics were striving. What could he have meant by such a claim?

Having just asserted that the goal of the Romantics was to produce a German culture, could he be saying that Goethe had, by himself (or in himself), succeeded in doing so? No; what his remarks suggest is that in his oeuvre Goethe had achieved an alternative to the creation of a national culture. Novalis, Lukács wrote,

> was the one who most clearly saw Goethe's superiority to himself and his friends: he saw that everything which remained mere method and idea with them, was turned into action by Goethe; that in trying to cope with their own problems, they could only produce reflections which were in turn problematic, whereas Goethe actually transcended his; they sought to create a new world where the genius, the poet of that world, might find a home, whereas Goethe found his home in the life of his own time. (46)

In other words, Goethe saw that the broader Romantic effort was impossible and was satisfied with his role as poet and sage in a provincial court. "An epoch that longs for culture will find its centre only in the arts; the less culture there is and the more intensely it is missed, the stronger the desire for it" (48). Goethe, by remaining an individual artist, was able both to fulfill himself and to serve a useful cultural function in his society. (After all, Dilthey had used Goethe as the typical exponent of one of his world views.) The Romantics, by wishing to create a culture, had difficulty succeeding as artists. One thinks here of their most characteristic forms: the fragment, the epigram.

In the fourth section of his essay, when Lukács seems at last to be turning to Novalis himself, we find that he is still writing about the Romantics in general, or about Romanticism.

> In Novalis the tendencies of Romanticism find their most intense expression. Romanticism always consciously refused to recognize tragedy as a form of life (though not, of course, as a literary creation). The highest aspiration of Romanticism was to make tragedy disappear completely from the world, to resolve tragic situations in an untragic way. (51)

Lukács gives an account of his impressions of Novalis' life, a description which succeeds in conveying the tone of that life while providing very little in the way of biographical information about this poet and hardly mentioning his work at all. Romanticism (for Lukács, as for many of the Romantics themselves) was as much an attitude toward life as a literary school. This is so obvious, such a traditional approach to the study of Romanticism, that it may seem unnecessary to point it out. Surely an "attitude toward life" is something similar to what Dilthey meant by a "world view," or what Goldmann, a half-century later, would mean by an "ideology." It would appear, then, that Lukács's study of Novalis is like Goldmann's **The Hidden God,** a study not of the world view of a class, but that of a group, which like the Jansenist nobility of the robe, never became a class and yet, for a time, glowed brilliantly in its historical deadend.[92]

> The tragedy of Romanticism was that only Novalis' life could turn to poetry. His victory is a death sentence passed on the Romantic school as a whole. Everything the Romantics wanted to conquer sufficed for no more than a beautiful death. Their life-philosophy was one of death; their art of living, an art of dying. They strove to embrace the world, and this made them the slaves of fate. Perhaps Novalis seems so great and so complete to us today only because he became the slave of an unconquerable master. (54)

The title of the Novalis essay was restructured in the German translation so that the defining statement, "On the Romantic Philosophy of Life," took precedence over the particularity of the name of the poet. This was quite proper, as the essay, in the tradition of Dilthey, was much more concerned with the Romantic philosophy or world view than with either the life of Novalis or his work. Otherwise, the essay remained unchanged in substance between the Hungarian and the German editions (except for the revision of one paragraph). Lukács's concept of literary criticism at this time (he was twenty-two or twenty-three years old), as exemplified in this essay, was

----

[92] Lucien Goldmann, **The Hidden God**, trans. Philip Thody (London: Routledge & Kegan Paul, 1968).

that of Impressionism, but, as befitted an educated Central European in those years, the factors to be appreciated were intellectual and historical rather than narrowly aesthetic. He was indeed attempting to "create anew not so much a particular work of art but rather the precisely appropriate consciousness of the perceptive reader . . . " Having read these reflections "On the Romantic Philosophy of Life," the reader of **Nyugat** could then turn to the poems of Novalis and find in them that Romantic world view which Lukács had indicated, a perspective quite sympathetic for a member of an isolated intelligentsia struggling to create a new culture, that of Jena in the early nineteenth century, or that of Budapest in 1908. Lukács was introducing his still quite provincial Hungarian audience to the practice of contemporary German Life Philosophy, that of the reliving of the spirit of the past as a mode of understanding – a mode of understanding the past, a mode of enduring the present.

Platonism, Poetry and Form

Lukács's next essay for **Nyugat** was concerned with the critic Rudolf Kassner.   Kassner was an Austrian who specialized in studies of such writers as Gide and Hofmannstahl. Lukács's admiration of him is evident at the very outset when he makes a point of affirming that: "In the company of those alive today he is the only active critic. . ." (19).   The aspect of Kassner's work that most appealed to Lukács is that his subject matter is often not art but the artist.   "Two types of men occur in his writings, the two principal types of all those who live in art: the creative writer and the critic, or – to employ Kassner's terminology – the poet and the Platonist" (20).   This distinction has little to do with the usual meanings of those terms except that, as a first approximation, it is a distinction between those writing in verse and those writing in prose. But this is immediately taken as implying a difference in world views, the one law governed and severe, the other open and ambiguous.   The dichotomy is a reversal of the usual cliche: "The poet says either 'Yes' or 'No,' the Platonist believes and doubts all at once, at the same moment" (21).

The object of knowledge for the poet is the formal structure of verse, and the structure of that knowledge is a "restricted totality." "The true type of poet has no thoughts – that is to say, when he has thoughts they are merely raw materials, a mere occasion for rhythm . . . The poet can learn nothing because his vision is always rounded and complete" (21).   The Platonist, on the other hand, longs for form.   "For him, too, a thought is only raw material, only a road which he travels . . . yet never reaches any goal" (21).   (These images of the rounded and complete life and vision, as well as of the road of life, recur throughout **Soul and Form,** and may also be noted in the prelude to **The Theory of the Novel** where they appear as emblems of states of perfection.) The poet, according to Kassner (and Lukács) always writes about himself; the Platonist (the critic) writes about others in order to come "closer to his own self." (It must be observed that these are not in any formal sense definitions of the practice of poets or essayists, but are, rather, samples of the Neo-Kantian rhetorical art, or instances of the privileging of the "seer" and "thinker" whose subjectivity constitutes a world view.)

These categories of poet and critic are opposites only when the pure types are considered. Usually one piece of writing or author appears as poetic or Platonic by way of contrast to another. For instance, Euripides is Platonic in opposition to Aeschylus; it is practically Schiller's distinction between naive and sentimental poetry. A life fully expressed in art is the goal, the unresolved dialectic between poetry and criticism is the problematic. The resolution of this problematic is to be found in form itself.

> The road of every problematic human being leads to form because it is that unity which can combine within itself the largest number of divergent forces, and therefore at the end of that road there stands the man who can create form: the artist, in whose created form poet and Platonist become equal. (22)

Here form is at once aesthetic form (especially innovative aesthetic form such as Browning's closet dramas) and something very different from it – an attitude, a world view, a forming of life by thought. The goal for Kassner's and Lukács's problematic human being is, then, to do away with the accidental; to live a life that expresses in every particular the desperate essence of a unified existence. (Kierkegaard is the great totemic hero for those who seek this goal.) Thus, in Lukács's essay, we find that where formal perfection is at first defined as an attribute of the rules of verse and strictly in the realm of the poet, it ends by being possible only for the critic. "Only in the artist's form can a balance be achieved between the Platonist's heavy-footed hesitations and the poet's weightless arrow-flight . . . Platonism introduces the many-coloured richness of lived life into the divine unison of the poet's songs" (23). Formal perfection, in Lukács's view, is now to be transformed into an unrestricted (an inclusive) rather than a restricted totality.

The essay ends with the supposition that each critic is suited to a particular poet or type, that the most visionary of critics, like Kassner, are best suited to write about such visionary poets as Shelley. Certainly in our own time we have seen such affinities, Bloom's for his "visionary company" of the English Romantics, for instance, or Eliot's for the Metaphysical poets. But having said that, what have we discovered? It is not in such empirical findings that the richness of Lukács's early manner is apparent, but in the displacement of these essays from art to existence, in the longing for some approach to life that would fuse the shattered <u>Gesellschaft</u> of the world of 1900 into a sensible whole. What we see here, in Kassner's work no less

than in Lukács's own, parallels the latter's description of the early
Romantics: "men who, on the other side of the Rhine, would have become
tragic heroes could, in Germany, live out their destinies only in poetic
works." But this emphasis – indeed, this over–emphasis – on the
importance to life of the poetic robs the latter of its peculiar function at the
same time as it is a manifestation of the impoverished possibilities of life in
that age and place.

As with the essay on Novalis, this on Kassner looks at literary production
itself through a lens clouded by longing. Hoping to find in writing all that is
lacking in life, Lukács finds, and creates, world views that finally refuse to
look at the world. After having read these two essays, what do we know
about the writings of Novalis and Kassner? Very little beyond that which we
took to them in the beginning. And yet, if we remember that they were
written for that isolated bourgeois intelligentsia of turn–of–the–century
Budapest, we can discover their value as signposts to that greater Germanic
world of culture to which Lukács himself was to journey and as inner–
worldly consolations for the restriction of Hungarian political and intellectual
life. They bring to bear on the subject matter of the occasional essay the
entire force of Dilthey's emphasis on poetics, of Simmel's concern with
giving coherence to the world. The invocation of Novalis would stand as a
declaration of loyalty to the Life Philosophers, as a nostalgic reference to a
"heroic" cultural period, while the essay on Kassner aligned the young critic
with a more properly literary, and local, tradition than that represented by
Dilthey and Simmel. For years he would cherish the privileging of Platonist
over poet, the possibility of a valued life for the critic longing to be a poet,
or a mystic.

The New Solitude and Its Poetry

Lukács published three essays in 1908 on Hungarian literary topics in
Huszadik Század and five on topics from other European, especially
Germanic, writers in **Nyugat**. "Weg ins Freie: Arthur Schnitzler's Novel," and
"Books on Ibsen" were the two **Nyugat** essays of that year which were not
collected in **Soul and Form**. The collection does include, as we have seen,
"Novalis" and "Rudolf Kassner," as well as "Stefan George." In the Hungarian
edition of **Soul and Form,** the latter piece had only the poet's name for its
title; when it was translated into German, however, the title was expanded
to include the phrase "The New Solitude and Its Poetry." This essay, like
that on Novalis, is more about the philosophy of art than about particular
poems or even particular groups of poems. In both the Novalis and the
George essays we are given elegant discourses on the occasion of a
certain cultural stimulus rather than analytical studies of anything or anyone
in particular. Lukács was to come into contact with George in the

Heidelberg circle of Max Weber, but even at this earlier date, even without a
personal encounter with the "magnetic aura" of the poet, he was prepared
to accept George's work as ranking among the best of the age. Indeed, he
goes further than that, beginning his essay with a comparison of George's
lyrics to those of his culture heroes Goethe, Tasso, Keats, and Mallarme.

Writing somewhat ambiguously, Lukács characterizes George's poetry as
"cold," "far from life," in a word, alienated from common understanding, and
then claims that it is just this alienation that is the mark of greatness in
poetic achievement. This distance from life of great lyric poetry is not
absolute. In Lukács's terms it is not a distance between Life and Poetry, but
a distance between the understanding of the common reader and that
which is truly poetic in art.

> What happens, I believe, is that the reader compares his own feelings
> about life with what the poet (as the reader thinks) feels about his
> self-created world. This attempt of identification reveals certain
> differences of temperature, and the reader projects those differences
> into the poet. (80)

In other words, "the reader" does not see what Dilthey saw, that the poet's
perceptions are privileged. Lukács claims that the common reader finds the
poetry to be out of step with the age. This is not, however, a question of
aesthetics; it is one of the sociology of art. The acceptance of a work of art
by the public "does not touch upon the value of the work, but rather, upon
its situation in society" (80). Therefore, those critiques of George's poetry
which emphasize its "coldness," its distance from life, are irrelevant to a
discussion of its poetic merit beyond the fact that they establish the place
of that work in that sphere of misunderstood writing which is the location
of Romantic greatness. Having embraced the designation of "coldness" as a
sure indicator of quality, Lukács then proceeds to demolish the negative
connotations of this reading of George's poetry. In much the same way that
the defenders of Modernism would later claim that the alleged difficulty of
Joyce and Eliot was a reflection on the reader rather than the writers,
Lukács here states that: "George's coldness . . . is due to the contemporary
reader's not knowing how to read," and not knowing what George is writing
about (80). But if, as Lukács presupposed, all great poetry is premature, how,
then, can it be possible for the poet's contemporaries to know how to read
it? Here Lukács introduces a distinction: "There are writers whose isolation
in their time is only a matter of content, and there are aesthetes; or, to be
more precise, there is a sociological and a psychological variety of art for
art's sake" (81).

George's poetic "coldness" is not merely a matter of misunderstood
content, for he is placed in the aesthetic camp; it is a matter of George
having attempted, and succeeded, in inventing new "forms" for poetry. "He
must find within himself the form for poetry today" (81). The time-lag in
understanding a great poet is a function of what is meant by great poetry.

It is precisely the timeliness of such work, its refusal to use old bottles for new vintages, that distances it from the merely contemporary. It is, though, difficult to discover exactly what Lukács meant by his use of the word "form" in these observations on the poetry of George. One obvious thing about its usage is that he does not seem to be referring to poetic structure: George did not look into himself and find a seventeen-line sonnet. Perhaps Lukács's sense of "form" here is closer to the current popular use of the terms "voice" or "vision." We write of "a new poetic voice," or "a new vision of poetry," meaning in either case something more than just a new poet. We mean by this a new way of looking at the world even though conventional poetic forms might be stylistically involved. In other words, for both the late-twentieth-century critic and for Lukács, much of what is important in the novelty of a new poet may be attributed to his having introduced a more fittingly contemporary world view. Thus, form in the above statements would approximate the world-forming world views of Dilthey and Simmel. George's contemporaries could not read his poetry, could not understand his forms, because their own world views were not contemporary, were not adequate to the task of forming a reality out of the chaos of contemporary impressions. Lukács followed Dilthey in   believing that the task of a great poet is the creation of such an adequate world view.   This poetization of philosophy, the transfer of a task traditionally performed by epistemology or ontology to the poetic realm, was, as we have seen, typical of the Life Philosophers. (The question is always whether the poetic can bear that responsibility and whether philosophy can do without it.)

The second section of the essay begins with an assertion that

> Stefan George's songs are songs of travel, stations on a long, apparently endless road which pursues a definite goal yet, perhaps, leads nowhere. All of them together form a great cycle, a great novel, supplementing one another, explaining one another, reinforcing, modifying, emphasizing, refining one another. Yet none of this is intentional. (81-2)

Here, amid the imagery of roads and travel, which we return to again and again in these pages, we find one of the key ideas of the Life Philosophers, one that reveals their paternity. This idea is that George's work, that the work of any great artist, must necessarily be unified, and that that unity itself is positively valorized, even when pointless. The desire for unity for unity's sake arises on the one hand from the Kantian impulse to seek everywhere for rule-governed unities as mainstays of reason, and, on the other, from the somewhat less rational impulse of the Neo-Kantians to embrace order, any order, as the only possible response by the "cultured" to the chaos of the natural and the human world. George's poems are true manifestations of their time, they are unified, but "lead nowhere." The world can be structured, for instance by art, but it still makes no sense, and, in any case, artistic structures are "unintentional." This philosophy is the architectonic of despair; its proponents were clinging to the chambered nautilus of the structure of the Kantian enterprise long after that structure had lost its living core.

A clue to that which had brought the young Lukács to this desperate point might be found in the phrase he used as a sub-title to this essay: "the new solitude." This new loneliness of the individual in the midst of the swarming populations of the great industrial cities was a favorite theme of the time, for philosophers as well as for artists. We have already noted its most thorough explication in the work of Tönnies. In the writing of Dilthey and Simmel this concern comes close to the denial of the very possibility of intersubjective knowledge. They believed, for one thing, that despite appearances, human beings are necessarily solitary; no person can ever be sure that he lives in the same world as his fellows, even when crowded shoulder to shoulder in a streetcar or a lecture hall. Lukács finds such paradigmatic solitude expressed in George's poetic dialectic of the experiential and the typical, which is the opposite of the classical practice.

> In the past . . . the experience was concrete and the poem typified it . .
> . The experience was palpable, its representation typical, the event
> individual, the adjectives and metaphors general. George typifies the
> experience before there is any question of making poetry . . . George's
> technique is the impressionism of the typical. (83)

In classical poetry, which is to say, in early capitalist or pre-capitalist culture, it was possible to grasp the individual, actual, experience as concrete, as real, and to make poetry through a process of typification always reversible. In George's late capitalist society, only the typical remains; we can never return through the poetry to the concrete lived experience. Lukács calls this typification the "music" of the new poetry, by analogy with lieder.

> Whatever we may perhaps feel to be lacking in a poem by Heine or
> Morike has been added by Schubert and Schumann, Brahms and Wolf:
> what has been added is the metaphysically great universality of the
> experience, everything that is typical about it and that goes beyond the
> purely personal. The essential nature of the new poetry is to render this
> accompanying music unnecessary . . . (85)

Although George's poetry is only typical, dividing the sensible manifold from the subject, leaving the reader isolated, "a generation sealed," it still gives us music, music, according to Lukács, particularly appropriate for our time. He contrasts this with the old poetry as literally combined with music:

> The quality of these songs was such that it could move many hundreds
> of people in a concert hall at the same time; today we feel nothing at
> the same time as anyone else, and if something does touch many of us
> simultaneously, it touches only a large number of isolated beings . . .

The new songs were, in the ideal sense, written for just one person, and only one person can read them, withdrawn and alone. (86)

The music of typicality is the new form for poetry invented by George, a form appropriate to the time, turning to advantage the very isolation of the individual which is the theme of its tragic songs. If "today we feel nothing at the same time as anyone else," George, and Lukács, will then trade fellowship for intimacy and celebrate this new music of alienation. This poetry is "cold" because it is appropriate to the reality of its life-world, and it is incomprehensible to the average reader, because the average reader does not want to hear the harsh music of his or her own time in poetry, preferring to escape into the Gemeinschaftlich lullabies of the past.

As in his piece on Novalis, Lukács attempts in this essay to create in his readers "the precisely appropriate consciousness" for the reading of the text at hand. That consciousness is not one that approaches the poet, much less the poetry, in a critical manner. It is an attitude that accepts the poet's interpretation of his role and status, that accepts, indeed, that very alienation of which the poetry of Stefan George is a symptom. Instead of helping us to understand this poetry, and thus extend somewhat the area covered by reason and understanding, Lukács works with the poet to intoxicate us into giving up yet more of our knowledge and ability to reason about human creations. George's poetry of solitude might well be understandable as a reaction to the situation in which the poet found himself. Alienated from the mass culture of his time no less than from his fellow human beings – in large measure because of the general breakdown of social existence – George chose to embrace that loneliness, to turn it upside down and make it a central value. Yet, in spite of this, we still know that it is unnatural for people to live "withdrawn and alone." Lukács's admiration for George's cold poetry was in part, at least, a justification for his own coldness, his own isolation. The Greeks believed that such a condition was either the punishment of fate or the immoral preference of a tyrant.[93] The solitude and alienation of large numbers of people of George's generation was a major historical tragedy, and the inversion of values which made that condition seem somehow noble, something to be achieved, was one of the many distortions of German culture which led, as a matter of fact, to a quite definite goal.

Although it would be foolish to blame the catastrophe of Central European civilization on a poet, or a critic, or even on an entire group such as the academic intelligentsia, one cannot dispute that the glorification of certain attitudes tends to reinforce those attitudes. The poems of Stefan George form a section of the road followed by German culture from 1870 to 1934. The beauty of their music, no matter how appropriate to the times,

---

[93] Marc Shell, **The Economy of Literature** (Baltimore: Johns Hopkins University Press, 1978).

fails to compensate for the harm that they did in their function as marching songs for that new barbarism. If the student of literature is to play the character of the critic, it is particularly apparent in this case that the role that Lukács, in 1908, saw as fitting for that character was deeply flawed. To praise and sympathize is not enough; the critic, before all else, must understand cultural phenomena and then prepare a critique of culture. For what is a critic, if not a judge? The failure of the ethical sense in the critic, as cultural judge, puts the critic on the other side of the bench, as it were, a defendant at the bar of history.

Lukács's thoughts on George, like George's poetry itself, promotes a masochism of the intellect, a passionate embrace of what had seemed to Lukács's teachers as a philosophical crisis, a collapse of order. If the world has become senseless and alienating, one can try all the harder to understand it, to change it, or one can revel in that irrationality, wallow in that alienation. The links between epistemology and psychology grow close at such times, the lecture hall is near the bedroom, and both overlook the military parade ground.

The Moment and Form

In 1909 Lukács published four essays in **Nyugat:** "Richard Beer-Hofmann," "Notes on Margit Szelpal," "Thomas Mann's New Novel," and "Anzengruber." In addition to these, he published six articles in **Huszadik Szazad** and one in **Budapesti Szemle,** as well as a book, **A drama formaja** (The Form of Drama). Of these only "Richard Beer-Hofmann" was collected in **Soul and Form.** This essay (which was written in 1908) begins with a rhetorical imitation of a typical opening of a Beer-Hofmann short story: "Someone has died. What is left to the survivor, and what this thing that is left makes of him, is the subject of Beer-Hofmann's few short stories" (109). Typically, Lukács writes very little about any particular story of Beer-Hofmann's; rather, he concentrates on the underlying world view expressed in Beer-Hofmann's work as a whole. The introductory section of the essay, placing the writer in his Viennese milieu, is filled with evocative musical similes: "Beer-Hofmann's writings grow from the same soil [as Schnitzler's and Hofmannsthal's], but his strings are more taut and the sounds he plucks from them are soft and deep where, with any other writer, they would be broken long ago" (110). This is followed by a general characterization of Beer-Hofmann's protagonists:

> Beer-Hofmann's aesthetes are . . . more courageous and more sophisticated, more frivolous and more complex than all others, they connect with everything else (the mood of the moment being the sole fixed central point of their world); but when the great experience comes

and destroys the connections, it destroys only the contents, leaving the form intact. The experience detaches the form from the content, it relieves his heroes from being the starting point for all the rest, it gives reality to the outside world and to all those who live in it and puts an end to the delusion that their "I" is something fixed and solid at the center of the world; it seizes hold of them and throws them into the midst of life, where everything is really connected with everything else. (111)

We will be reading more about "great experiences" later. These meditations on Beer-Hofmann's stories, meditations that themselves seem a bit lacking in content, move steadily down a road that we will note Lukács following for the next eight years. It led from aestheticism to religion, from Impressionism to what Lukács will call "destiny."

This, then, is the new world, the way that leads out of aestheticism: a deep, religious sense of everything being connected with everything else. The sense that I can do nothing without striking a thousand resonances everywhere, most of which I do not and cannot know, so that each action of mine – whether I am aware of it or not – is the consequence of many thousands of waves which have met in me and will flow from me to others. That everything truly happens inside me, but that what happens inside me is the All; that unknown forces are my destiny, but that my fleeting moments may likewise be the unknowable destinies of men I shall never know. Thus the accidental becomes necessary; the accidental, the momentary, the never-recurrent is transformed into a universal law, and ceases to be accidental or momentary. It is the metaphysic of Impressionism. (112)

This may be the beginning of Lukács's religious phase. "Everything truly happens inside me." The phrase is the exact crossroad of the psychologistic philosophy of Dilthey and of mysticism. Here the attack on metaphysics is turned against itself, or fulfills itself in the affirmation of the primacy of the irrational. The "metaphysic of Impressionism" is not the same thing as Impressionism. With the essay on Beer-Hofmann Lukács changes his essayistic purpose from the Impressionist one of conveying his feelings on the occasion of certain literary works appearing, or of preparing his readers for the appreciation of those works and their world views, to that of writing obliquely about mysticism under the guise of writing about literature. But this change in his approach was not a complete one. There are later essays in **Soul and Form**, as well as other parts of the Beer-Hofmann essay itself, which are Impressionist or world view criticism much like the essays on Novalis, Kassner, and George. However, the main line of Lukács's interest has definitely moved from book-reviewing to an implicit advocacy of his own emerging world view, that of mystical religion. He has, in other words, taken his own reading of Kassner seriously and assimilated the critic to the Platonist.

The major part of the Beer-Hofmann essay, the second section, has little directly to do with Beer-Hofmann and his work. It begins with a typically fin de siècle thesis that the goal of life is death. "Every written work leads toward great moments in which we can suddenly glimpse the dark abysses into whose depths we must fall one day; and the desire to fall into them is the hidden content of our lives" (113). Part of that which is somewhat indistinctly being claimed here is an equation of aesthetic with religious emotions. It is not at all unusual in our culture to make these equations; the common metaphysical equation of sexual passion with a lusting after death is well known, and it is possible to unravel these tangled skeins of signifiers from one highly charged location of meaning to the other. There is, though, a certain over-simplification in Lukács's account of this, an almost Parisian casualness with regard to logic, rigor, and proof. Is it actually "every written work" which leads us into this doubtful territory? Suspending such questions for the moment, we find Lukács changing his definition of form, or, rather, his definition of the effect of form, from that which he used in the essay on George, form as world view, to that of form as the principle which transforms life into a continuum of religious emotions. "This is the most profound meaning of form; to lead to a great moment of silence, to mould the directionless, precipitous, many-coloured stream of life as though all its haste were only for the sake of such moments" (114).

One might argue that Lukács's assertion does not preclude an interest in generic form, an interest that would distinguish among forms on the basis of their relative power to "lead to a great moment of silence," so that one might be able to say, then, that the lyric is superior to the romance, or the romance to the realistic novel. One might so argue, but even then it would be obvious that Lukács's interest in this was not primarily aesthetic, that, in fact, the aesthetic had become for him simply a means to an end. Not that there is anything intrinsically wrong with such an approach to the study of literature; it should, though, be clear to the reader of "Beer-Hofmann" and some of the other early essays of Lukács that this is the case, that they are formulations of values; they are an ideology and not just analyses derived from one. Although it is impossible for anyone to examine cultural materials from a point of view not informed and restricted by a system of beliefs, whether consciously held or not, it is possible to perform such an examination for the sake of the materials themselves, once a set of preconceptions is granted. This was not Lukács's project.

Lukács was, perhaps, working toward an eschatological Neo-Kantian theory of knowledge, wherein Simmel's arbitrary world-molding forms are given purpose.

> We can say that art becomes possible, and in particular the art of writing came to have meaning, only because it can give us the great moments we have been speaking about. It is only on account of these moments that art has become a life-value for us, just as woods and mountains and men are life-values – but the life-value of art is more

complex, deeper, closer and yet more distant than any of these, more
coldly objective towards our life and yet fitting more firmly into its
external melody. (114)

However much this still seems to echo Pater's "Conclusion" of the
Renaissance, it is, at the most, a distant and distorted echo. A few lines
further we find Lukács writing of form as "an unstifled scream," a
"convulsive movement" shared by the poet and the public. Where Pater
looked to art for an enhancement of life, Lukács believed that modern art, at
least, is a welcome path to death, or to the equivalent religious emotion.

Lukács finds a problem, that of Schiller's sentimental art, in the
contemporary appreciation of poetry. Some of the poets whom he studies
arrive at once at "the goal of form," the awareness of death, without
passing through the "richness of life" as had their naive predecessors. This
is, however, unsatisfying: "a goal is satisfying only when it represents an
arrival, the long-awaited end of a long, hard road" (115). Others write only
of life, abandoning form (that is, the bringing into awareness of death) for
the road itself. Lukács believes that the proper function of the
contemporary writer is to bring the reader to an awareness of death
through an account of the richness of life. He finds greatness in those
writings that represent that same renunciation of life, of pleasure, that Freud
was to diagnose, a few years later, as the effect of civilization itself; yet he
is puzzled by the very binary oppositions that he has evoked: either the
cold perfection of the death inspired poetry of Stefan George or the vulgar
aimlessness of life enhancing works. He believes that the problem has its
origin in the particular formal properties of inherited artistic genres. These
no longer adequately convey the richness of life and the appropriate
awareness of death, since they were created to carry out those functions
for the quite different conditions of other epochs. It is a matter of creating
new forms to articulate the contents of modern life, forms as suited to the
expression of that life (and that death) as were those of classical Greece or
of the Quattrocento to theirs. He ends the section with a question: "Is it
possible to grasp the innermost essence of our time, the essence that even
we ourselves may not know?" (116). Lukács's answer to this question had
already been given in his essay on Stefan George; the essence of his time
was death, the rush to death of a civilization grown, as they said at the
time, "bored with peace" and with civilization itself.

The third part of the essay on Beer-Hofmann begins: "Beer-Hofmann
and forms . . . ," as if Lukács were reminding himself and his readers of the
subject of the essay. He limits his discussion of Beer-Hofmann's forms to
two, those of the short story and the tragedy. "Beer-Hofmann's short
stories are about the development of a human being after an accidental
disaster. . ." (117). This brings us back to the beginning of the essay with
its refrain: "Someone has died." We quickly learn that Lukács has a theory
of prose genre, which presupposes that Beer-Hofmann's stories cannot be
successful because they are about the development of a human being,

which is not a proper subject for a short story: "The subject of the short story is the isolated happening, the subject of the novel is the whole of life" (117). This allows Lukács to move rapidly to his judgment of Beer–Hofmann's prose works: the stories "fall apart; seen from the perspective of the beginning, the end is weak, while from the viewpoint of the end, the basis appears arbitrary – as does the line of development. Thus whatever is fine in these short stories can only be purely lyrical in character" (118). In Lukács's estimation, Beer–Hofmann had made a genre mistake: he had chosen to write on the subject matter of the novel in the form of the short story, and, thus, in accordance with Lukács's rules of generic distinction, his stories must necessarily fail.

Turning to the genre of tragedy, Lukács believes that Beer–Hofmann was successful with his play **The Count of Charolais,** with its formalized action and verse dialogue. (The play is a typical Viennese account of a meaningless seduction.) There is no need for character development in the play; there are only "intense moments." Although it may be just a matter of the difference between short stories and dramas on the one hand and novels and epics on the other, it does seem that at this point in his career Lukács believed that artistic success, the creation of a beautiful literary work, could only be possible through stylization and isolation of incident, as if time itself must stop if we are to achieve aesthetic satisfaction. The still perfection which Lukács attributes to the drama of Beer–Hofmann, like that of the prose of the young Gide so much admired by Kassner, was the negation of that turbulence of life and values characteristic of those pre–War years.

We have seen that in his essay on Beer–Hofmann Lukács's critical method changed from the Impressionism of his earlier essays, which had been concerned mainly with literary aspects of typical world views, to a loose meditative approach to literary themes as a basis for religious speculation. This change was accompanied by a parallel shift in his use of the word "form." In the earlier essays the meaning of this term was most often "world view," while in the essay on Beer–Hofmann it is usually that which leads "to a great moment of silence," although this use is occasionally replaced by an Aristotelian one based on a hierarchy of genres, each with their fit subject matter, a usage which gradually disappears in the later essays of **Soul and Form** as Lukács's solution to the epistemological crisis of Life Philosophy and Neo-Kantianism becomes more and more overtly religious.

The Foundering of Form Against Life

Lukács published four more essays in **Nyugat** in 1910: "The Roads Have Divided," "Sören Kierkegaard and Regine Olsen," "Lajos Fulep on Nietzsche," "On the So-called Obscurity: Answer to Mihaly Babits." He published "Aesthetic Culture," "Charles-Louis Philippe," and "They Are Afraid of Health" in **Renaissance,** and "Die Gedichte von Béla Balázs" in **Pester Lloyd.** During the same year two of his books came out in Budapest: **Megjegyzések as irodalomtörténet elméletéhez** (Observations on the Theory of Literary History), and **A lélék és a formák,** the first version of **The Soul and the Forms.** The latter included just one of the articles from 1910, "Sören Kierkegaard and Regine Olsen."

"Sören Kierkegaard and Regine Olsen" is dated 1909, as "Richard Beer-Hofmann" was dated 1908, although the first was published in 1910 and the second in 1909. 1909 was the year that Lukacs received his "Dr. Phil." at Budapest University, the year that he met Endre Ady (considered by many to be the best Hungarian poet of the twentieth century), Bela Balazs, and Ernst Bloch. It was late in this year that he again went to Berlin to study with Simmel. In addition to the development of these intellectual friendships and influences, the year was notable for Lukács in that his unsettling relationship with Irma Seidler and Balazs occurred at this time. Recent studies by Congdon and others demonstrate that this essay had a central position for Lukács, emotionally, as he identified himself with Kierkegaard, Irma Seidler with Regine Olsen, and sought to justify his Georgian coldness toward Seidler by the tradition of renunciation exemplified in Kierkegaard's work and life. Lukács at this time seems to have suffered from a particularly intense atrophy of the emotions which was at once abstracted in his work and abstracted from it, so that the sociological situation of the thinker became the psychological anguish of the would-be lover.

The essay is not about any specific work of Kierkegaard's, nor is it written to give one an impression of Kierkegaard's work in general. Rather, it is focussed on a single question: "What is the life-value of a gesture?" The gesture referred to is Kierkegaard's gesture of renunciation when he gave up hope of marrying his fiancee Regine Olsen: "that unique leap by which the absolute is transformed, in life, into the possible" (29). It is possible that the Kierkegaard essay bears some connection with Lukács's own gesture, his renunciation of Seidler, whose love he had shared with Balazs. Lukács's interest was moving from the structure of art to that of life and it is just this pre-occupation with the Kierkegaardian aesthetic that is the mark of that shift. "Art . . . seeks to . . . construct . . . a bridge of forms between men" (28), Lukács wrote during this period. With such a view of the purpose of art, it is easy to move to a concern not with the forms themselves, but with the intersubjective relationships they attempt to bridge.

The unique gesture, the autonomous action, these break the glass wall between art and the aesthetic and everyday life. Trapped by a virtually solipsistic epistemology, the young philosophers of Lukács's generation could not think their way out of their desperate isolation. This situation was that of the anomie of thought, and its cure was a transformation of thought into a different mode, into action, to alter Pater's slogan, for action's sake. It was not an accident that their path led from the purest aestheticism to such an apparently diametrically opposed ideal. These were two sides of the same coin, two equally possible reactions to the fin de siècle collapse of values. The failure of aestheticism in the necessary passivity of its adherents brought them, perhaps not inevitably, but just as surely in fact, to the "philosophy of the gesture." That philosophy had within itself the seeds for strange growth which were not apparent at the time. In 1909/10 it still seemed a promising intellectual position, and such thinkers as Lukacs sought justification for it in that branch of Hegelianism of which Kierkegaard was the imputed father. Therefore, five years before the War, and eight before the Revolution, Lukács carefully examined the prototypical intimate gestures of the Danish theologian. It is curious to note, in the light of the extremely odd uses to which, in this century, the Kierkegaardian dialectic has been put, that that first action, so carefully studied, was the highly personal erotic gesture of the lover posing as a seducer. Yet upon reflection this seems reasonable. The intolerable alienation produced by modern society is felt on all levels of social experience, from the intimately erotic or religious to the political and economic. Lukács himself pointed out these connections.

And so there are some major, typical cycles of possibilities in life, or stages to use Kierkegaard's language: the aesthetic, the ethical, the religious stage. Each is distinct from the other with a sharpness that allows of no nuances, and the connection between each is the miracle, the leap, the sudden metamorphosis of the entire being of a man. (32)

Lukács analyzes Kierkegaard's abandonment of Regine Olsen in the terms of the stages of the soul's journey to God, seeing it as necessary for the philosopher's spiritual development and having finally little to do with the woman (who turned from Kierkegaard to a contented married life with someone less – or more – self-absorbed than the author of the **Diary of a Seducer**). Lukács observes that "even the deeply beloved woman was only a means, only a way towards the great, the only absolute love, the love of God" (36). Near the end of this essay, which focuses so steadily on the autonomous gesture of Kierkegaard's renunciation of his fiancee, while merely touching on his struggle with the Church, Lukács comments that "Kierkegaard's heroism was that he wanted to create forms from life" (40). It is the possibility for action that Kierkegaard's meditations pointed towards which was important to Lukács at this time, and to "create forms from life" was to merge the transcendental aspects of art with the lived moment. For such a young bourgeois aesthete as Lukács had been until that time, the crucial need was finally to proclaim the importance of lived experience, of action, any action, over thought itself.

And so, although the essay on Kierkegaard and Regine Olsen is uncharacteristically detailed in its account of "the occasion for the essay," the gesture, that detailing is done with one hand, as it were, for it is not Kierkegaard's particular situation that interested Lukács, nor his status as a writer and philosopher, but his example: his staking of everything on the decisive act itself. In an intellectual tradition which held the publication of **The Critique of Pure Reason** to have been a more important event than the French Revolution, where the development of modern society was parodied, as it was said in the revolutions of Idealist philosophy, the importance of Lukács's essay on Kierkegaard is to be found in just this emphasis on action, just this putting to one side the philosophy of the thinker in favor of the memorialization of that single gesture of the man. "There are stages in life: the aesthetic, the ethical, the religious. . . ."

The Bourgeois Way of Life and Art for Art's Sake

A lélek és a formák included three essays that had not been previously published: "On the Nature and Form of the Essay," "Theodor Storm," and "A Dialogue Concerning Laurence Sterne." Lukács begins his essay on Storm (later entitled "The Bourgeois Way of Life and Art for Art's Sake") with an invocation of the Golden Age, similar in sentiment, if not in rhetorical richness, to that with which he would begin **The Theory of the Novel:**

> As for the notion that art is enclosed within itself and follows no laws but its own, once this was not the consequence of a violent refusal of reality. Art was there for its own sake just as any other kind of work, honestly done, was there for its own sake; because the interests of the totality, which were the justification and the root of everything, demanded that work should be done as though it had no other purpose but itself – that it should exist only for the sake of a perfection enclosed within itself. (55)

We have already explored the social conditions which give rise to that "violent refusal of reality" which now Lukács himself acknowledges. His invocation of the naive condition of the totality (Gesamtheit) and the perfections of closure here echo the intensity of such contemporary social theorists as Tönnies (a friend of Storm's), while referring to the earlier aesthetic theories of Schiller. The paragraph is in many ways a foreshadowing of his diagnosis of the ills of the "Dostoevskian world," a diagnosis that would be developed in his other works of the War and immediate pre-War years.

Lukács goes on from this introduction to describe this norm of naive cultural health.

> Today we look back upon those times with nostalgia, the hysterical nostalgia, doomed from the start to remain unsatisfied, of sophisticated men. We look back with impotent nostalgia upon a time when one did not have to be a genius in order to approach perfection even from afar, since perfection was a natural thing and its opposite was simply ignored, even as a possibility: when the perfection of a work of art was a life-form, and works of art differed from one another only by the degree of their perfection. This nostalgia is the Rousseauism of the artistic consciousness – a Romantic longing for the unattainable blue flower, glimpsed in dreams, insubstantially fashioned from visions of form; a longing for the great, holy simplicity, the natural, holy perfection to be born out of the birthpangs of an ever-growing awareness, to be forced into life by the ultimate, gasping energy of a sick nervous system. (55)

It was the "natural" perfection of Homeric art that Lukács, following Schiller, held up as the conscious goal of the "sick" artists of his time. There is something a bit strange in this, since Schiller had taught that civilized art was sentimental: sophisticated and self-conscious. In other words, Lukács believed that the aesthetic movement was an unnatural, a perverse, attempt to produce artificially naive art in a sentimental age. He finds, however, that there are certain instances, determined by unusual social circumstances, in which naive art could be created in times which ordinarily would demand more sentimental productions. His case in point is the work of Theodor Storm, and the unusual circumstances were those of the survival of the original bourgeois way of life in certain remote rural areas.

> The bourgeois way of life, which consists in cutting down the conduct of one's life to a strictly and narrowly bourgeois measure, is simply a way of coming closer to such perfection. It is a form of asceticism, a renunciation of all brilliance in life so that all the brilliance, all the splendour may be transferred elsewhere: into the work of art . . . This bourgeois way of life is the whip that drives the life-denying man to work without cease. The bourgeois way of life is merely a mask that hides the bitter, useless pain of a failed and ruined life, the life-pain of a Romantic born too late. (55-6)

We will turn, then, for a time, from the overwhelming primacy of life-values, to the consideration of the art that can be obtained from the denial of those values, under certain restricted and special circumstances only, to be sure. Given the impossibility of a rounded, natural life in modern times, a life that would organically give rise to perfect art, one type of artist sacrifices life to art and adopts precisely the most restricted, artificial mode of life in order to produce art of an organic wholeness and perfection as if in compensation for abandoned dreams.

Lukács analyzes the bourgeois way of life as a mode of being in the world that is a mere negative, "a denial of everything that is beautiful, everything that appears to be desirable, everything the life-instinct longs for" (56). The necessary precondition for such a mode of existence is a bourgeois profession and the trivialization of a person's concerns to the point that just these trivia become the focus of his consciousness. "For the true bourgeois, his bourgeois profession is not an occupation but a life-form [which] in consequence of the mysterious interaction of life-forms [Lebensformen] and typical lived experience [Erlebnisse], must penetrate deeply into all creative activity" (56-7). This sudden appearance of the technical vocabulary of Dilthey's and Simmel's analysis of existential being is a clue to the metamorphosis occurring at that time in Lukács's methodological concerns and personal viewpoint. We have already seen how he moved from Impressionism in his earliest essays to the mysticism evident in the essay on Beer-Hofmann and the beginnings of a concern with Life Philosophy in the piece on Kierkegaard. Without abandoning either the Impressionism or the msyticism, he begins a meditation on the problems peculiar to the philosophical schools of Dilthey, Simmel, and Rickert, a broad tradition that continues, through Husserl, Heidegger, Sartre, and Derrida down to our own day. If we do not find Lukács using the method of the transcendental reduction, we do find him already intent on the ethical, as well as the epistemological, complications of being-in-the-world. Philosophizing about life becomes, in this instance, Life Philosophy itself.

Lukács's investigation of the bourgeois profession as a life-form leads him to conclude that this life-form is, firstly, ethical and law-governed: the will and moods of the individual are subjected to the social rules of order. The bourgeois works for the sake of the work process itself. Lukács believes this to be a virtue, the virtue of community. For whereas the idealist, the mystic, is dedicated to something beyond humanity, the bourgeois is dedicated to the production of the alien object, a "work-product" which, once produced, has as little or as much to do with the producing individual as it has to do with other individuals. (If a person makes a chair, that chair is a chair to every other person, also; but if a person has a vision of the Unity of God, that vision cannot normally be used or shared by others.) In other words, the bourgeois way of life allows communal interests to develop and is therefore similar in function to that of Simmel's ideal of the work of art as the vessel of objective spirit. "Ethics forces a sense of community upon all men – if in no other way, at least through the recognition of immediate and calculable utility, of work done, however small it may be" (57). Thus, in the bourgeois life-form work becomes the purpose and the meaning of life; the center of gravity in the life of the artist, for instance, shifts outward.

Where the Romantic subjectivist is always on unstable ground, if sometimes on an ecstatic peak, at other times in deepest melancholy, the bourgeois finds permanent validity in the shared ethical concerns expressed by the made object. Here Lukács again arrives at a division between art and life, a division quite different from that drawn in the essays of the two previous years. In those earlier essays Lukács seemed to be arguing that art is the essence of life, while here we find that, at least in the case of the bourgeois writer, life and art are two different things: that which is lived, and that which is produced through that way of life. Storm and Keller, "the country judge of Husum and the government clerk of Zurich," are presented as models of the unity of life through a social form, not as problematic or tragic individuals. Storm, for instance, worked at a legal career all his life, never seeing a conflict between the demands of bourgeois life and those of art or "spirit." (Lukács here defines tragedy as "where what is life-destructive has become as much of an indispensable necessity as that which is unquestionably good and useful" (59). This can be taken as referring back to his discussion of "great moments" and the death-centered mysticism described above.)

Lukács categorizes Storm, Keller, and Fontane as naive craftsmen of perfect literary objects, in contrast, say, to Flaubert's heroic sentimentality. Where the German provincial realists worked as the literary equivalent of goldsmiths or woodcarvers, Flaubert had lost that innocence.

The goal of the former [the flaubertian aesthetes] was to approach ideal perfection through superhuman effort, that of the latter [Storm, et al.] was to achieve the consciousness of honest work well done – the consciousness that they had done everything in their power to create a perfect thing. For the former the accent was on work, for the latter on life; for the former, life was only a means of attaining the artistic ideal, for the latter perfection of work was only a symbol, only the surest and finest way of exploiting every possibility offered to them by life; a symbol of the fact that the bourgeois ideal – consciousness of work well done – had indeed been achieved. (61)

Lukács explains this difference between French and German realism through a quasi-historical argument, following Dilthey. "Poetry, more than any other art, is influenced by the spirit of the age" (62). He points out that the economic development of Germany was backward in relation to Western countries, so that, especially in the outlying areas, a type of bourgeoisie lingered into the nineteenth century which had been extinguished almost everywhere else in the eighteenth. This patrician mercantile bourgeoisie was Gemeinschaftlich rather than Gesellschaftlich, rooted in the slow life tempos of their home provinces (such as Storm's Schleswig), opposed to the alienating changes of the industrialization process. "These writers sprang from the womb of that bourgeoisie, they are its true and great representatives" (62). (A later Lukács might have said that the craftsmanship of their writing was itself ideological, a sign, as it were, of their loss and its consciousness.)

It was not only the fact that they were provincial that shaped the works of these writers, according to Lukács: there were, after all, many provincials. "No, the decisive experience of these writers, and most particularly Keller and Storm, was their bourgeois way of life" (63). The determining fact in this case, even for the pre-Marxist Lukács, was not that of language, nor of genre, nor of nationality. It was that of class as lived experience. The writerly virtues of these realists are, for Lukács, their presentation of everyday life in such a way as to clearly reveal their class viewpoint.

The essay, in its second section, reverts to Lukács's Impressionist manner in an appreciation of Storm's short stories and poems. He paints word pictures, of the type found in Storm's own work, of their landscapes, interiors, characters, and situations. All this is generalized in the Impressionist manner without any explicit references to specific poems or short stories, except the quotation of a few lines of poetry. The third and concluding section of the essay deals with Storm's use of the genres of short story and lyric poem. Storm's short stories are placed by Lukács in opposition to the essence of the genre: "The nature of the short story form is, briefly, a human life expressed through the infinitely sensual force of a fateful hour" (73). This definition is but a slight modification of that which he had used in the essay on Beer-Hofmann, and he puts it to the same use, classifying Storm's works in the genre as novelistic. The novel

> gives us the totality of life by its very contents, by inserting its hero and his destiny in the full richness of an entire world, whereas the short story does this only formally, by giving form to an episode in the hero's life in such a strongly sensual way that it renders all other parts of his life superfluous. (73)

Lukács criticizes those modern short stories that lack the requisite concentration and attempt novelistic depths and subtlety. In the short story, form is all, and here for once Lukács means by form simply the structure of the piece. And yet, though Storm's short stories do not adhere to the classical norms of the genre, they do avoid the common modern pitfalls, and thus manage to be, in themselves, a new and satisfactory form for the depiction of Storm's subject matter. "Storm achieved unity of tone through unity of delivery, epic form through the use of direct narration, that most ancient form of the epic which defines its very condition of existence" (74). Storm usually uses a framing narrative, one which allows an approach to the oral tradition of story-telling and to the form of that ur-genre, the ballad itself. "These vividly seen pictures fit together with perfect harmony because the narrator remembers only those aspects of the events which united them into a whole – only what has become the center of the structure" (75). Those pictorial elements, with the rigid suppression of connective and analytical discourse, render Storm's stories glowingly symbolic. Because his provincial bourgeois world and point of view were not yet decadent, Lukács found Storm to be the last of the "great German bourgeois" writers. After him, naivete gives way to sentiment and irony and we arrive at **Buddenbrooks**.

Turning to Storm's lyric poetry, Lukács finds that, if anything, more perfectly achieved than the short stories. Availing himself of the classic folk tradition of the lyric, Storm transparently conveyed his views of provincial life.

> The essential factor of Storm's lyrical form is that it makes full use of all the great values of the past: extreme economy of expression an almost impressionistic reduction of images and metaphors to the barest essentials, the barest hint; a narrowly limited vocabulary with sudden sensual highlights; and, most especially, an extraordinarily subtle, deep and unerring musical quality. (77)

Lukács celebrates Storm as the last lyric poet of a tradition, and concludes his essay with the equivocal statement: "A courageous, resigned, austere life-mood: such is the poetry of the last poet of the bourgeoisie, great after his own fashion" (78).

This essay is among the most satisfactory in **Soul and Form** from the point of view of literary historical studies. Lukács's placing of Storm in his social and historical context, the derivation from that situation of the particular qualities of Storm's work, and the clear discussion of form as genre result in a brilliant and orderly discussion both of bourgeois realism in general and of the short stories and lyrics of Storm in particular. Lukács had, for the moment, put aside most of his Neo-Kantian and mystical concerns, concentrating on presenting his readers not only with an approach to the appreciation of Storm's works, but also with a path to the understanding of that author's enterprise. Lukács was to remain sympathetic to bourgeois realism throughout his career, most notably in connection with Thomas Mann; here that sympathy brought him, at an early date, close to an analysis of artistic production that could be classified as part of literary scholarship, a calm moment amid the emotional, epistemological, and spiritual tempests of **Soul and Form**.

A Dialogue Concerning Laurence Sterne

"A Dialogue Concerning Laurence Sterne" is, by contrast, a very close approximation to that odd genre developed by Walter Pater, the imaginary essay. "Laurence Sterne" is more a short story about student life and, perhaps, about Lukács's emotional situation at the time, than a critical essay on Sterne or any of his works. (It is probably no accident that Sterne, rather than Kassner or George, inspired Lukács to write a closet drama.) The dialogue is set in an "inorganically" decorated middle class young woman's room where the furnishings and paintings are in that mixture of historical styles typical of the urban bourgeois taste of the time. The young woman herself (referred to throughout the dialogue as "the girl" or "she") is about twenty years old. She receives a visit from a young man, Vincent, who is a student of modern languages. They are school-mates and he is in love with her. They begin to talk about their school work, "the young woman" feeding Vincent's self-esteem while he modestly claims to be a dilettante. After a few minutes of this, he shows her a "fine illustrated edition" of Sterne that he has brought with him. They admire the binding and the engravings. He begins to read to her from that author's **A Sentimental Journey:**

> The way in which he is reading suggests that the text is nothing important to him: just something, among the many beautiful things that have come his way, that has happened to please him, and even the manner in which it pleases him is a question of mood, of taking pleasure in his own moods. (125)

Their reading is interrupted by the entrance of Joachim, a serious, less well-to-do student. He, too, is in love with the young woman and thus sees their reading as a preliminary, in the traditional manner, to some more intimate activity. Joachim and Vincent, therefore, begin to quarrel, ostensibly about Sterne, but actually over the young woman. This device could be seen inverted, as it were, as a way of discussing Sterne while appearing to be giving an account of student life. Given Lukács's concerns at this point, however, it seems more likely that this is an essay about "life" and not, primarily, about "art."

Lukács has provided the young woman with a volume of Goethe's aphorisms so that Joachim can use it as a pretext for his quarrel with Vincent. Joachim attacks Sterne as a formless writer. The young woman begins and Vincent continues a defense of Sterne on the basis of "richness," calling on Goethe's well-known love of variety in support of this line. He then extends this to a defense, not of Sterne in Goethean terms, but of variety and enrichment themselves as against pedantry: life as against "mere" truth. "If we experience something even a little strongly, the very intensity of the experience refutes any theory imposed from the outside" (128). Vincent goes on to claim that experience is a category of such importance that it overrides all other considerations; that to experience impressions strongly, even when they contradict one another, is the important thing, the contradiction being a merely theoretical category that does not really matter.

> There is no a priori in face of possibilities, and once the possibilities have stopped being possibilities – once they have been realized – there is no criticism that can be addressed to them. Unity means being together and staying together, and the fact of being together is the sole applicable criterion of truth. (128)

Lucien Goldmann would later see this sort of statement as an anticipation of Existentialism, but it is probably more profitable to place such statements within the context of Lukács's own time, viewing them as instances of the Simmelian doctrine of coherence. Within that framework, as we have seen, the real is that which seems properly unified, even when that unity is achieved arbitrarily. In the dialogue, Joachim objects that such a line of thinking leads to "complete anarchy." Vincent counters this objection by once again invoking life against theory: "The limit and the contradiction are only inside ourselves, just as the possibility of unity is inside ourselves" (128). Joachim, rather surprisingly, agrees, but wishes to invoke an internal moral order against the arbitrary doctrines of Neo-Kantian coherence theory. Vincent sneers at this and returns to Sterne as the exemplar of his doctrine. He claims that if Joachim's theory of self-discipline excludes Sterne's work, which is all richness and life, then it is not the true doctrine of experience, at which point he launches into a long speech in praise of Sterne's **Tristram Shandy** at the expense of **Don Quixote** and other less life-like works. Vincent and the young woman are portrayed by Lukács as being quite swept away by his enthusiasm. Joachim's claim is that Sterne's novel would have been quite beautiful if it were as his friend described it, but that, as a matter of fact, Sterne's characters are not at all life-like, their features being but masks of the psychology of humors elaborated by Ben Jonson, and the novel is, therefore, allegorical and not at all realistic.

This argument is met by Vincent's own, which claims that Sterne's novel is dialectical, continually turning about between realism and masque. Joachim replies that if that is the case, then the novel lacks a consistent point of view, and so its lack of form is not really a breakthrough to a new genre but rather simply a manifestation of artistic failure. The only answer that Vincent can make to this is that form does not matter, that is, form as rationality, and that all that is important is the expression of a world view: "All romantic irony is a world view. And its content is always the sense of self, intensified into a mystical sense of the All" (139).[94] One occasionally suspects that most varieties of the doctrine of world views have the same content of romantic irony. Lukács has Vincent continue as follows: "All things are important, certainly, for the all-creating self can make something out of anything; but, for the same reason, because the self can create something out of anything, nothing is really important" (140). This view leaves the subject alone in a world of shadows, shadows not even representing objective reality, but the mere playthings of individual fantasy.

Joachim then objects that the justification for such a philosophy of pure subjectivity can only be found in its utility as a means of reaching the truth, but that it is not truth itself. Truth, reality, is the world that is reflected by

---

[94] This sense of the self which is equated with the All calls to mind one of the forms of Freud's theory of narcissism, the oceanic feeling which Freud claimed to be the basis of religion.

subjectivity: "The self is the mirror that reflects the world's rays for us . . . The highest power of subjectivity is that it alone can communicate real life-contents" (141-2). Joachim takes the position that Sterne's "mirror" is one that gives us an incomplete view of the world. For him, it is the whole which matters, and Sterne's vision is fragmentary "because he couldn't distinguish between value and non-value anywhere. . . " (143). This seems crushing enough, but even then Vincent feels that he can defend Sterne on the issue of form: "form is the essence of whatever has to be said, condensed to a point where we are conscious only of the condensation and scarcely of what it is a condensation of" (144). In other words, form is the world view itself, as ideology. Then in a Kantian phrase, he calls form "the eternal a priori of all content" (144). Therefore, Sterne's work is great because it portrays the world as the pure form of the "endless melody" in all its "richness" and "many-coloured" variety. Again we have the implicit contrast of life with thought, at the cost of a considerable confusion of terminology.

Joachim's response is to condemn chaos, which he contrasts with law. "That which creates order springs from roots in the soul just as deep as chaos, and therefore only a soul in which both – chaos and order, life and abstraction, man and destiny, mood and ethic – are present in equally powerful degrees can be complete and for that reason rich" (148). His concluding statement (after a clever phrase about Sterne's "dirty window" on life) is to challenge Vincent's Neo-Kantian concept of form as a subjective entity ("form, unlike the moment and the mood, is an ideal outside the self" (149)), with the result that Sterne is yet again condemned on moral grounds for living without values.

> Only the ability to apportion value gives a man strength to grow and develop – only the ability to create order, to make a beginning and an end; for only an end can be the beginning of something new, and only by constant beginnings can we grow to greatness. In episodes, however, there is neither beginning nor end, and a mass of disordered episodes is not richness but a lumber-room. And the impressionism which produces them is not a strength but incapacity (149-50).

Lukács awards the victory in the debate to Joachim, but has him leave the stage to Vincent and the young woman, who read a little more of Sterne and then begin making love. "How sterile any discussion must seem compared with the living beauty of life." (150)

On one level the debate between Vincent and Joachim represents a debate within the Neo-Kantian movement, a debate which would bring it from Simmel's disregard for questions of value to the value-centered (if methodologically value-free) position of Max Weber. Joachim's condemnation of Sterne sounds much like Lukács's friend Ernst Bloch's condemnation of Simmel, written a few years after this essay, and quoted above. On another level "Laurence Sterne" can be grouped with the piece on Kierkegaard and the later dialogue "On the Poverty of the Soul," as arising from Lukács's personal situation at the time. The Kierkegaard essay is about the virtue of renouncing an intimate relationship, the Sterne essay is about the conflict between two male friends for the affection of a woman (the less intelligent of the two winning her), and "On the Poverty of the Soul" is about the loss of a loved one after similar vicissitudes.[95]

On the Nature and Form of the Essay

In addition to those that we have already considered, **A lélek és a formák** contained one other chapter, that "On the Nature and Form of the Essay." This takes the quasi-intimate form of a prefatory letter addressed to Leo Popper, the great friend of Lukács's youth. It is dated "Florence, October 1910," a month or so after the suicide of Irma Seidler, who had, apparently, chosen that solution to the Lukácsian problematic. The first paragraph of the "letter" to Popper is filled with the technical vocabulary of Neo-Kantianism and Life Philosophy:

My friend,

The essays intended for inclusion in this book lie before me and I ask myself whether one is entitled to publish such works – whether such works can give rise to a new unity, a book. For the point at issue for us now is not what these essays can offer as "studies in literary history", but whether there is something in them that makes a new literary form of its own, and whether the principle that makes them such is the same in each one. What is this unity – if unity there is? I make no attempt to formulate it because it is not I nor my book that should be the subject under discussion here. The question before us is a more important, more general one. It is the question whether such a unity is possible. To what extent have the really great writings which belong to this category been given literary form, and to what extent is this form of theirs an independent one? To what extent do the standpoint of such a work and the form given to this standpoint lift it out of the sphere of science and place it at the side of the arts, yet without blurring the frontiers of either? To what extent do they endow the work with the force necessary for a conceptual re-ordering of life, and yet distinguish it from the icy, final perfection of philosophy? That is the only profound apology to be made for such writings, as well as the only profound

---

95 This entire aspect of Lukács's life and work has been clarified by Lee Congdon's excellent book, **The Young Lukacs** (Chapel Hill and London: The University of North Carolina Press, 1983).

criticism to be addressed to them; for they are measured first and foremost by the yardstick of these questions, and the determining of such an objective will be the first step towards showing how far they fall short of attaining it. (1)

The initial question is somewhat surprising, since we have seen that, far from being a unified work, **Soul and Form** is a mixed collection of about one-third of Lukács's essays to that date. The principle of selection appears to have been to exclude those essays relating exclusively to Hungarian literature, concentrating further on articles that had originally appeared in **Nyugat.** There is no evidence that in the years 1908 to 1910 he had intended these particular essays to be chapters within a unified work, and much of what has been noted about them above would indicate quite the opposite, that they are precisely, if anything, "studies in literary history," focussing, from our point of view, on the history of Lukács's own development as a literary critic and essayist, with a sub-text of personal anguish. Lukács, however, quickly brushes aside the issue of unity as it applies to this collection: "I make no attempt to formulate it because it is not I nor my book that should be the subject under discussion here." The subject under discussion, it turns out, is the same as that in the earlier essay "Platonism, Poetry and Form" namely, the genre of the essay itself. His approach to this subject is governed by three questions: first, is there an historical genre of the essay? Secondly, is the "standpoint" of the essay that of a science or that of an art? And finally, in his own words, "Do the great essays have the force of a world forming point of view?" In other words, do they produce a Weltanschauung?

The first question is philological, the second Neo-Kantian in the tradition of Dilthey, the last, Simmelian. Lukacs jumps immediately to a discussion of the second: Is the essay a work of art or is it a scientific medium? He attributes to Wilde (in an acknowledgment of the English roots of Impressionism) and Kerr the popularization of "a truth that was already known to the German Romantics, a truth whose ultimate meaning the Greeks and the Romans felt, quite unconsciously, to be self-evident: that criticism is an art and not a science" (1). Lukács here equates criticism with the essay form itself, an act which from the first may have predetermined his conclusions. He goes on to reason that if everyone "knows" that criticism is an art, they very clearly have not considered the questions "What is an essay?" and "What is its intended form of expression and what are the ways and means whereby this expression is accomplished?" (1-2). He sets out to define the essay or critique. In so doing he writes out some ideas that are still timely.

It has been argued that the essay can be stylistically of equal value to a work of the imagination, and that, for this reason, it is unjust to speak of value differences at all . . . "Whatever is well written is a work of art." Is a well-written advertisement or news item a work of art? Here I can see what so disturbs you about such a view of criticism: it is

anarchy, the denial of form in order that an intellect which believes
itself to be sovereign may have free play with possibilities of every
kind. (1-2)

Lukács now explicitly rejects the position that literary criticism is a
variety of imaginative literature. Style alone, whether it is the self-
consciously playful style of Paris or the more ponderous imitation of that as
practiced in certain lecture halls in the United States, does not constitute
art. Lukács had by this time matured to the point of holding that even if
criticism is spoken of as an art form, it is only so spoken of in order more
firmly to establish its difference from, say, fiction. "Let us not, therefore,
speak of the essay's similarities with works of literary imagination, but of
what divides it from them. Let any resemblance serve here merely as a
backdrop against which the differences stand out all the more sharply. . ."
(2). An essay, then, may be well-written, but it is not therefore a species of
imaginative literature. It does not, on the other hand, merely give us
"information, facts and 'relationships.'" We read some essays for instruction,
to be sure, but others, the essays of Lessing, for instance, are read in spite
of our disagreement with their content. "Science affects us by its contents,
art by its forms; science offers us facts and the relationships between facts,
but art offers us souls and destinies" (3).

The distinction that Lukács is drawing here is subtle and has often been
misunderstood. There is science and the written expression of science,
where content reigns supreme (which is not to say that scientific writing
need be bad); there is art where form is the primary matter; and there is a
variety of essay-writing where the surplus value, as it were, of good writing
in the exposition of content remains after the value of the content itself has
disappeared. The word "essay" has many meanings for Lukacs. In this
particular piece he is using it to point to the literary essays of the
Enlightenment. The essay in this sense is neither concerned primarily with
facts nor constituted strictly as a work of art, but insofar as it is more the
latter than the former (from the point of view of our values as students of
literature), it is concerned with "souls and destinies."

At the next stage of his argument Lukács posits that there are "primitive,
as yet undifferentiated epochs" in which "science and art [and religion,
ethics and politics] are integrated," but that as soon as a science becomes
independent, all pre-scientific thought in that realm loses its value. He is,
perhaps, thinking of the relationship between alchemy and chemistry, or
astrology and astronomy, or the literary criticism of the Enlightenment and
modern philology. Lukács would agree with the Logical Positivists in
thinking of mature science as consisting entirely of statements of fact, of
contents. On the other hand, the mature art that emerges from the
"primitive, as yet undifferentiated epochs" is pure form and spirit. The study
of this process, whether as philology or art history, is itself a science of the
arts, "but there is also an entirely different kind of expression of the human

temperament, which usually takes the form of writing about the arts," which sometimes deals directly with "the same life-problems . . . raised . . . in the writings which call themselves criticism" (3). In this category are the works of Plato, of the mystics, of Montaigne, of Kierkegaard, in other words, the Platonists of the essay on Kassner.

We have, then, a continuum of prose writings from scientific reports (including those on literature), through literary criticism which adds aesthetic form to those contents (as in the essays of Lessing) and the non-literary essay (belles lettres), to imaginative literature such as "The Confession of a Beautiful Soul," or the last act of Euripides' **Heracles.** The mention of Euripides leads Lukács to an excursus on drama: "the true dramatist . . . will see a life as being so rich and so intense that almost imperceptibly it becomes life" (4). This in turn leads him to make a general distinction between the particular and the general, between "das Leben" and "das Leben," between Realism and Nominalism, between image and significance. Lukács claims that "for one there exists only things, for the other only the relationships between them, only concepts and values" (5). The first is represented by "imagist" poetry, the second by "the writings which most resolutely reject the image, which reach out most passionately for what lies behind the image . . . the writings of the critics, the Platonists, and the mystics" (6). Here Lukács shifts to a definition of criticism which has nothing to do with the study of literature, which might, or might not take literary works as occasions for writing an essay, but which is primarily concerned with higher spiritual issues. Yet one must be careful not to confuse this sense of "criticism" with one denoting a science of the arts or having reference to the classical essay.

This particular kind of criticism arises from a feeling which "calls for an art form of its own," because "everything in a work must be fashioned from the same material, each of its parts must be visibly ordered from a single point" (6). This is not a theory enabling studies in literary history, it is a judgment based on the aesthetic implications of Simmel's doctrine of coherence. Since the concerns that are met by that doctrine are not literary but sociological, we know at this point that Lukács has definitely left the world of conventional literary criticism (not to mention literary history) and is entering that of sociology and philosophy which will be his home for much of the rest of his life. Within what is at this point a Simmelian framework, the way in which art forms are distinguished is not formal. It has to do, rather, with their spiritual content, their world view. "We are speaking of the fundamental principles which separate forms from one another – of the material from which the whole is constructed, of the standpoint, the world view which gives unity to the entire work" (7). Lukács can, therefore, say that the essay, as an art form, is the instrument for the expression of certain kinds of experiences.

From all that has been said you will know what experiences I mean and of what kind they are. I mean intellectuality, conceptuality as sensed experience, as immediate reality, as spontaneous principle of existence; the world view in its undisguised purity as an event in the soul, as the motive force of life. (7)

These are, for the most part, Kantian concepts. Lukács is referring, within the Critical framework, to the Critical enterprise itself: the reflection of the mind on its own processes of understanding. The investigation of thought has become charged with an experiential urgency. Lukács, perhaps under the influence of personal tragedy, perhaps under the influence of the general angst of pre-War Europe, uses his Kantian methods and phrases to attempt a solution, or an approach to a solution, not to the problem of knowledge, but to the problem of life in the modern world.

The question is posed immediately: what is life, what is man, what is destiny? But posed as a question only: for the answer here, does not supply a "solution" like one of the answers of science, or, at purer heights, those of philosophy. Rather, as in poetry of every kind, it is symbol, destiny and tragedy. (7)

This is an exaggeration of even Dilthey's concern to ground philosophy in life.

Lukács goes on to generalize the claim that the essay is "symbol, destiny and tragedy:" "All writings represent the world in symbolic terms of destiny-relationship; everywhere, the problem of destiny determines the problem of form" (7). The way in which destiny is apparent in writings varies: "form in poetry appears always only as destiny; but in the works of the essayists form becomes destiny, it is the destiny creating principle" (7). But what is destiny? The closest Lukács comes to defining this term is to write about its effects when he remarks that "destiny lifts things up outside the world of things, accentuating the essential ones and eliminating the inessential. . ." (7). One might hazard a guess that Lukács is here working another transformation on Kantian terminology like the one involving mind and spirit noted above. "Destiny" might be the equivalent of the Kantian "concept": "Form sets limits round a substance which otherwise would dissolve like air in the All. In other words, destiny comes from the same source as everything else, it is a thing among things, whereas form – seen as something finished, i.e. seen from outside – defines the limits of the immaterial" (7). This may be an attempted solution to the puzzle of the origin of concepts. If the concept of, say, finch, is something in the world, how is it that we know a new finch to be a finch? We must have a purely mental concept, finch, to which we refer candidates from the world of things. But what is the origin of that mental entity? Lukács appears to be splitting the idea of a concept, defining the worldly part of it as destiny and the purely mental part as form. As with the transformation of mind into soul, this is not merely a logical or intellectual move; rather, it is a rhetorical strategy which charges these ideas with strong emotional overtones. "Because the destiny which orders things is flesh of their flesh and blood of their blood, destiny is not to be found in the writings of the essayists" (7). The tone of this would be quite different had Lukács used some neutral term for this aspect of concept rather than the portentous word "destiny."

Lukács then claims that since critics are not poets – as they do not write about things – they must write about forms and not about destiny. "This form, which springs from a symbolic contemplation of life–symbols, acquires a life of its own through the power of that experience. It becomes a world view, a standpoint, an attitude vis à vis the life from which it sprang: a possibility of reshaping it, of creating it anew" (8). This is reminiscent of a moment in Simmel's dialectic: "the forms stand forth as autocratic ideas and determine life and its values."[96] Lukács is very close to Simmel's theory of forms in these passages. But he still clings to Kant in accepting the reality of the world "out there," even if somewhat ambivalently and in language that is none too clear. "The critic's moment of destiny, therefore, is that moment at which things become forms – the moment when all feelings and experiences on the near or the far side of form receive form, are melted down and condensed into form. It is the mystical moment of union between the outer and the inner, between soul and form" (8). What was for Kant an epistemological problem had become, for Lukács and his generation, a spiritual, a religious issue. Lukács's studies were moving, at this time, from Kierkegaard toward the German mystical tradition, Meister Eckhart in particular, and this essay was in part an expression of that move.

Lukács now traces the path by which the critic goes from the study of literature and the other arts, the classical location of form, in the aesthetic sense, and its contemplation, to a more general object. "For the essayist needs form only as lived experience and he needs only its life, only the living soul–reality it contains. But this reality is to be found in every immediate sensual expression of life, it can be read out of and read into every such experience. . ." (8). The essayist can find in life itself the object of his study, but instead usually writes about art, since there the forms (both aesthetic and Neo–Kantian) are more obvious. The result of this displacement is irony.

> And the irony I mean consists in the critic always speaking about the ultimate problems of life, but in a tone which implies that he is only discussing books and pictures, only the inessential and pretty ornaments of real life – and even then not their innermost substance but only their beautiful and useless surface. (9)

---

[96] Georg Simmel, **Lebensanchauung. Vier metaphysische Kapital,** 2nd ed., (München & Leipzig: Duncher & Humblot, 1922), p. 52.

This is precisely what Lukacs himself had been doing in the later essays collected in the Hungarian edition of **Soul and Form**. While seeming to discuss Beer-Hofmann, Kierkegaard, or Sterne, he was actually discussing the ultimate questions. (This was a change from the earlier essays, where he was arguably just discussing Novalis (or Romanticism) and George, while seeming to do so.) Here it is perhaps sufficient to merely mention the drastic devaluation of the study of literature and art implicit in the passage just cited. Philosophy, for those who agree with such formulations of the essayist's task, threatens like Cronos to swallow its own children, the sciences. This position is also one that devalues Simmel's view of the importance of the arts and is one more sign of Lukác's transformation from a world centered Impressionist to a metaphysician.

Lukács enlarges on his point through a discussion of portraiture, following his argument that art takes its motifs from life while the essayist takes his or hers from art. Lukács claims that the painter paints a "likeness," not in the sense that the painting is really like someone, but in the sense that it creates the impression of verisimilitude to a possible person or landscape at a possible moment. Thus there could be, say, thousands of portraits of Lukács, all essentially alike.

> And that, you see, is more or less how I imagine the truth of the essay
> to be . . . Therefore, two essays can never contradict one another: each
> creates a different world, and even when, in order to achieve a higher
> universality, it goes beyond that created world, it still remains inside by
> its tone, colour and accent, that is to say, it leaves that world only in
> the inessential sense. (11)

This is a statement of the more extreme Life Philosophy position with regard to the reality-endowing properties of subjective considerations. It is part of a radical theory that Lukács proceeds to make more concrete with an example drawn from literary criticism proper: "It is simply not true that there exists an objective, external criterion of life and truth, e.g. that the truth of Grimm's, Dilthey's or Schlegel's Goethe can be tested against the 'real' Goethe" (11). What is important, for Lukács, is the degree of verisimilitude of each of these "Goethes," how life-like every one of them seems. That is, it is not a question of how adequately they can as a group be related to some inter-subjective concept of Goethe, but whether they have "that vital breath which would give them autonomous life" (12). In other words, it is a question of how artistically they are drawn. The Impressionist critic, we remember, can do no more than "defines the impression which, at a given moment, this work of art has made on us where a writer himself has put down the impression which he in turn has received from the world at a particular hour."[97] Lukács seemingly has combined Impres-

---

97   Wellek, p. 22.

sionism with Life Philosophy, attemting to elevate a technique for reviewing books to the status of an epistemology.

But as soon as we might begin to believe that Lukács is wavering in his spiritual quest and is merely calling for a more artistic Impressionism, we find that is not at all what he is interested in. He has returned to examples drawn from the world of literary criticism only to illustrate his point that the essayist creates a world. The Impressionist literary critic is, therefore, a kind of essayist, but Lukács believes that in addition to this, the best literary critics, the best essayists, have quite another end in view. The appreciation of literary art, or even its study, is more or less secondary. Lukács's essayist is a mystic on the path leading toward the vision of the One. The essayist, like the mystic, might "ironically" claim otherwise, might claim, for instance, that he or she is only a humble member of the monastic community trying to follow the Rule, but it is not clean refectory floors that truly matter.   "It is true that the essay strives for truth: but just as Saul went out to look for his father's she—asses and found a kingdom, so the essayist who is really capable of looking for the truth will find at the end of his road the goal he was looking for: life" (12). Lukács's essayists are the mystics of everyday life. This might seem to be a peculiar idea until one remembers that it is precisely everyday life that is the locus of anomie for the bourgeois. Life, the people, these were the signifiers for the dream of happiness that animated Lukács's contemporaries. This emphasis was clearest, in the preceding generation, in the work of Tönnies, while in Lukács's own circle, for instance, his friend Ernst Bloch devoted his entire life to the explication of the principle of hope. And so it is little wonder that Erlebnis stood in the place of the mystic vision for Lukács at this time. It is one more transposition of the myth of the Golden Age, the embodiment of narcissistic nostalgia, but here the Kingdom of God is neither in the past nor in the future, but, once more, within ourselves.

Lukács's special definition of the essayist brings him to make the statement that "We want poets and critics to give us life—symbols and to mould the still—living myths and legends in the form of our questions" (12). Criticism, therefore, is equated with poetry, poetry of a specific kind; the "deep" symbolic poetry of Stefan George. And then, almost immediately, Lukács acknowledges that, on the other hand, "there is a science of the arts: there has to be one" (13). As a matter of fact, it seems that even the mystical essayists use this science: "The essay form has not yet today, travelled . . . the road of development from a primitive, undifferentiated unity with science, ethics and art" (13).   This qualification allows us to resolve the apparent contradictions we have so far met in this discussion regarding the essay form itself. It is an art form, as Impressionism, and it is a science, but it is most characteristically for Lukács a sort of ethics, the path which brings us to mysticism. Such development in the genre as has taken place, Lukács writes, took place, for the most part, at the beginning, with Plato, who

met Socrates and was able to give form to the myth of Socrates to use
Socrates' destiny as a vehicle for the questions he, Plato wanted to
address to life about destiny. The life of Socrates is the typical life for
the essay form as typical as hardly any other life is for any literary
form – with the sole exception of Oedipus' life for tragedy. Socrates
always lived in the ultimate questions. . . . (13)

Striving for the typical moment so as to grasp the essence of his idea of
the essay, Lukács finds the Socratic. (And seems to forget his technical use
of "destiny," but, of course, these technical terms are meant essayistically,
evocatively, and not scientifically. They come and go as terms of art
because of the "primitive" "undifferentiated" nature of Lukács's own use of
the essay form at this time.)

The discussion of Socrates brings in, once more, Schiller's idea of the
naive Greek life as whole and unalienated: "The Greeks felt each of the
forms available to them as a reality, as a living thing and not as an
abstraction" (14). While we, according to the Neo-Kantians, must cling to
abstractions and we cannot reach life itself. Socrates, for Lukács (as for
Nietzsche and Heidegger), marks the Fall from the Greek state of grace; he

expressed the eternal ideal of men of his kind, an ideal which neither
those whose way of feeling remains tied to the purely human nor those
who are poets in their innermost being will ever understand: that
tragedies and comedies should be written by the same man: that
"tragic" and "comic" is entirely a matter of the chosen standpoint. In
saying this, the critic expressed his deepest life-sense: the primacy of
the standpoint, the concept, over feeling; and in saying this he
formulated the profoundest anti-Greek thought. (14–5)

This version of "On the Nature and Form of the Essay" continues, or, rather,
concludes from this that although Plato, as an essayist, was a critic also, he
assumed that role ironically, while later critics, having no Socrates to
emulate, mistook the artistic occasion for the true subject matter of the
essay. As a result criticism became either scientific, clinging to writing, or it
became ethereal, pure ironic belles lettres.

Lukács wonders if the true form of the essay, that of Plato, Montaigne,
the medieval mystics, will ever reappear. "One worries that there will
always be too few men, whose conceptual experiences are strong enough
for their writings to be their intellectual poems.[98] For, he believes, it is at

---

[98] Georg Lukacs, **A lélék és a formák (Kisérletek)** (Budapest: Franklin
Tarsulat Nyomda, 1910), pp. 27–29. The following is a translation of the
Hungarian text:

You see: there is "criticism" in Plato, even if this criticism is only an

least in part due to the times that these forms do not appear: Is "an epoch imaginable whose deepest experiences would demand Plato's dialectic as a form"? Now we have only Paters, Kierkegaards, and Kassners and hardly understand them. Although these are not great essayists, they, with Weinanger, Schlegel, Schleiermacher, Nietzsche, and Ruskin give Lukács hope. There is also the ideal of the "feminine," glowing "in as pure a light – as anywhere else." Humanity has fallen to the point where the essay, which should be the expression of transcendental reality, is degraded to journalism. Lukács hopes that it can rise again to higher goals: Is "it really the case that all literary writings are literature bound? . . . and is it really the case that all literary writings are literature?" He is looking for something more than literature to come out of the work of contemporary essayists. "I believe that our experiences are constantly becoming more and more conceptual." This gives him hope for a new form to supplement the poetic, a form which would be the pure Platonic essay.

The 1910 "On the Nature and Form of the Essay" concludes on a note of mystical striving:

> Why did I feel that I had to tell you all this, in order to justify my having collected these few "experiments" and make a book of them? Perhaps because I feel that we have to give an account only of strivings; of the fact that the road is where one goes along, but of this one must give an account, both to oneself and to others. And one must not be preoccupied, not even for a moment, with how far along one got

---

occasional and ironical mood, as is everything else. Critics of later epochs related only to this, talked only about literature and art, and did not meet with the Socrates in whose fate they could have encompassed everything.

Because of this, criticism clung to the written word and to matter, it became scientific, yielding results and in this way, together with the death of its results, became mortal, dying. Or it became so airy, never touching the ground – not for a second – so that its final questions do not even have a chance for expression. They are ironically despised occasions, even though without them there is not a chance for expression, or are they perhaps despised because they are essential, because these are the essentials?

Will there ever be a true form from these essays, as it was with Plato or Montaigne, or with a few mystics of antiquity and the middle ages? One worries that there will always be too few men whose conceptual experiences would be strong enough for their writings to be their intellectual poems, as Schlegel said of Hemsterhuys. We know that it is not certain men who bring about a form, but the necessity of the times. Is an epoch imaginable whose deepest experiences would

on this road; only to keep on going, going, going . . .

These were the conclusions or, perhaps, this was the point at which Lukács had arrived, when he collected his essays for the Hungarian edition of **Soul and Form**. Irma Seidler was already dead, Leo Popper would soon be dead also. If there is a clear definition of the essay in this version of "On the Nature and Form of the Essay," it is extremely difficult to locate. It seems more convincing to argue that Lukács was expressing many different ways of considering essayistic writing (as well he should, considering the mixture of approaches in **Soul and Form)** and that the one that seemed most attractive to him at this time was the last that he had produced, the essay, the practice of writing essays, as a road to a more ideal way of life. The careful Impressionist introductions of German poetry and literary criticism to his Budapest audience that he had included as the earliest of the essays in **Soul and Form** had given way to a more meditative style of writing. His road, from Impressionism to mysticism, demonstrates a clear and broad, a quite slippery path, that the Impressionist critic might follow. Such sub-jective literary studies are based on an equally subjectivist theory of knowledge, the belief that ideas themselves are world forming, that reality resides within ourselves. This is a comforting doctrine in a world growing steadily more uncomfortable, as the rapidly industrializing world of Central Europe had been for a generation by 1910. On the other hand, it leaves its adherents in a radically isolated position: all-powerful subjective intelligences without a God, without companions. It was not, after all, a road. It was a dead end.

---

demand Plato's dialectic as form, as did the tragedies of great epochs? Who knows? The great critics, up until now, lived in isolation and were not understood – to the depths of their being – and our times are only able to produce Walter Paters, Kierkegaards and Kassners, hardly understanding them.

It does not matter. If I think in what a cowardly manner – now fleeing into a novel, now hidden in literary criticism – the first new voices in Schlegel and in Schleiermarcher appeared, and how it already found self-consciously courageous and rich forms – drawn with secure hands – in Pater's Marius or Kierkegaard's Johannes, then it is hardly possible to despair or doubt. And Kierkegaard and Weininger placed great new Eros-concepts alongside Plato's (these are the great love tragedies of critics), and Schopenhauer created ahead of his time the conceptual equivalents of new poetic tragedy and musical tragedy, and Nietzsche wrote the Platonic Faust and Hamlet and Ruskin sounded his Rousseau-ian voice. And in the words of Hofmannstahl's Lord Chandos – who wrote letters to Bacon about why he did not produce anything, why every thought dissolves into thin air – all of today's upheavals are perhaps more clearly expressed than in any tragedy. And today's feminine ideal glows in as pure a light as anywhere else. And who

When Lukács's essays from the Hungarian edition of **Soul and Form** were translated into German, it was done without making significant changes in any except "On the Nature and Form of the Essay." In this essay the German text diverges from the original at the point where post–Platonic critics are said to be underprivileged for never having met a Socrates. From there until the end of the new version the tone of the piece has been considerably altered. The mystic exaltation of the original has been erased.

> Later on, criticism became its own content; critics spoke only of poetry and art, and they never had the good fortune to meet a Socrates whose life might have served them as a spring board to the ultimate. But Socrates was the first to condemn such critics. "It seems to me," he said to Protagoras, "that to make a poem the subject of a conversation is too reminiscent of those banquets which uneducated and vulgar people give in their houses." (15)

In this version Lukács does not ask whether the essayist is bound to literature; he assumes that is not the case. "The modern essay does not always have to speak of books or poets . . ." and so the essayist has a great deal of freedom (15). But this freedom brings with it its own difficulties. The modern essay "stands too high, it sees and connects too many things to be the simple exposition or explanation of a work; the title of every essay is preceded in invisible letters by the words 'Thoughts occasioned by . . .'" (15). This is a problem for the essayist because he or

---

knows where Kassner's new style – freed from all literary binds – will lead when it is ready and self–contained?

> PROBLEM: And is it really the case that all literary writings are literature?

> Is not Goethe's deepest experience the division of art into imitation of nature, manner, and style; or Schiller's experience grouping, separating, the naive from the sentimental? Or are Emerson's light gratia and Kassner's many, nightmare ridden human types only "literature"? I believe that our experiences are constantly becoming more and more conceptual. Today's poetry has suffered enough from it up until now, but perhaps from this form of experience the form of essay will be born, the supplement to the poetic form and its equivalent.

> Why did I feel that I had to tell you all this, in order to justify my having collected these few "essays" and make a book of them? Perhaps because I feel that we have to give an account only of strivings; of the fact that the road is where one goes along, but of this one must give an account, both to himself and to others. And one must not be

she must stand between two roles, that of the mystic and that of the student of literature. "The modern essay has lost that backdrop of life which gave Plato and the mystics their strength; nor does it any longer possess a naive faith in the value of books and what can be said about them" (15). Whereas in the preceding year Lukács had been confident that the duty of the essayist is to record his or her strivings along the path to the Platonic ideal, the mystic vision, now he presents a different task. The essayist must accentuate the "problematic" of the essay and so free it from its scientific residue. The essayist must seek the poetic in literature. "Poetry is older and greater – a larger, more important thing – than all the works of poetry: that was once the mood with which critics approached literature, but in our time it has had to become a conscious attitude" (16). Decadent, or merely sentimental, we must consciously seek those things which came as a matter of course to our naive ancestors. Lukács, in some of his earlier essays such as the one on George, had already written about the poetic rather than about the poem. The essay at hand thus evolves as a defense of Lukács's literary practice, rather than calling for a new way of life, as the essay had in the earlier version. He now felt that the essayist should seek out the idea behind the occasional words of literary subject matter, rather than the Idea behind the world.

By what right, Lukács asks, does the essayist seek those poetic ideas, make those judgments? He concludes that the essayist does so in the right of a "John the Baptist" for the aesthetician. It is that "one who is always about to arrive, the one who is never quite yet there," who justifies, in retrospect, the essayist's efforts at finding that which is behind the text (16). "The essay can calmly and proudly set its fragmentariness against the petty completeness of scientific exactitude or impressionistic freshness but its pure fulfillment, its most vigorous accomplishment becomes powerless once the great aesthetic comes" (17). One is somewhat surprised to find the previous year's mysticism replaced by aesthetic eschatology. Where before the value of the essay was located in its recording of the strivings of the essayist, we now find that the essay is an approach to aesthetics. We seem, therefore, to have lost the Platonic essay, the essay as something completely apart from the study of art. Lukács states that we must, however, distinguish between what the essay does, in preparing for the great aesthetic, and what it is, longing. It is, to be sure, longing for the great aesthetic, but it is, nonetheless, the pure expression of longing: "but this longing is more than just something waiting for fulfillment, it is a fact of the soul with a value and existence of its own: an original and deep-

_____

preoccupied, not even for a moment, with how far along one got on this road; only to keep on going, going, going . . .

(Translation by Marianne Esztergar and the author.)

rooted attitude towards the whole of life, a final, irreducible category of possibilities, of experience" (17). The essay as a form gives form to longing. It is, therefore, "a judgment, but the essential, the value-determining thing about it is not the verdict . . . but the process of judging" (18). After working out this distinction, Lukács can provide yet another justification for making a book of his essays. They are now unified for him by their being individual journeys along a road (once more), a road perhaps leading to the great aesthetic, but its terminus is not particularly important:

> The point at issue was only the possibility, only the question of whether the road upon which this book attempts to travel is really a road; it was not a question of who has already travelled it or how — nor, least of all, the distance this particular book has travelled along it. The critique of this book is continued, in all possible sharpness and entirety, in the very approach from which it sprang. (18)

This is a repetition, in another key as it were, of the final paragraph of the original. But where in the Hungarian original, the going and striving on the road was for a mystical experience or for experience itself, the journey now is toward aesthetics. It is easy to agree with Lukács that his book is indeed an account of an aesthetic journey, that, moreover, it shows us his development as a critic over three crucial years. But somehow the original conclusion of the essay, by revealing more fully the place to which he had come in 1910, revealed more about the character of that journey. The new conclusion of "On the Nature and Form of the Essay," written for a German audience, sticks more closely to literary-critical consideration than did the Hungarian original; thus it served to introduce Lukács himself to his new audience in a more familiar guise than that of a follower of Meister Eckhart seeking transcendental reality through the contemplation of the poetic rather than the Mystery of the Incarnation. Nevertheless, the original conclusion to the essay seems the truer, more revealing one, showing, as that which is repressed often shows us, the bare motive under the cultural decorations.[99]

---

[99] See Geoffrey Hartman, "Crossing Over: Literary Commentary as Literature," **Comparative Literature** (28: 257–76). Hartman has much of interest to say on the occasion of the German text of this essay. See also T. W. Adorno, "Der Essay als Form" in **Noten zur Literatur,** I (Frankfurt, 1958).

Longing and Form

In addition to the altered conclusion of "On the Nature and Form of the Essay," the Hungarian and German editions of **Soul and Form** differ in other respects. The German version contains two additional essays: "Longing and Form: Charles–Louis Philippe," and "The Metaphysics of Tragedy: Paul Ernst." The former had first appeared (in Hungarian) as "Charles–Louis Philippe" in **Renaissance** (Budapest, 1910) and was translated as "Über Sehnsucht und Form," for **Die neue Rundschau** in 1911; the latter was apparently first published in 1911, in German, as "Metaphysik der Tragödie," in **Logos**. "Charles–Louis Philippe" continues the elaboration of the theme of longing from the German conclusion to "On the Nature and Form of the Essay." Its first words are: "Longing and Form. They always say that Germany is the land of . . . longing. . ." (91).

This longing, although non-specific, is so strong that it destroys all form and reduces one to stammering. Longing, then, is formless. The relationship between it and form may, according to Lukács, be illustrated with a comparison between German and Tuscan landscape. The German is comfortable, yielding and formless; the Tuscan hard and composed, formed.

> Our relationship to a composition . . . is clear and unambiguous, even if it is enigmatic and difficult to explain: it is that feeling of being both near and far which comes with great understanding, that profound sense of union which yet is eternally a being-separate, a standing-outside. It is a state of longing. (91-2)

The argument so far is that Germany is the country of longing, longing is formless, our relationship to form is itself a state of longing. At this point, Lukács turns to the **Symposium**. In the **Symposium** we are told, "Longing and love are the search for one's own lost other half" (92). But this is "the small, the fulfillable longing." The great longing is for another, for the other: "longing makes a link between those who are unlike one another, but at the same time it destroys every hope of their becoming one; becoming one is coming home, and true longing has never had a home" (92). Longing is a virtue for the Platonic Socrates, as it betters the person preoccupied with it. Longing is always nostalgia for a lost Golden Age, a glorified past that never was, projected into a future too good ever to come into being. But the quest, the road traveled by the one who longs, is in itself a good thing, leaving one no nearer the end, but further along, toward the good. (This line of thought, first discernible in the revised conclusion to "On the Nature and Form of the Essay," was to be followed by Lukács into **The Theory of the Novel**.)

Longing has other virtues. "Longing soars higher than itself; great love always has something ascetic about it" (94). "Great love" for Lukács is intimately connected with mysticism. This, then, gives us three levels of love or longing: the love of the mystics for their God, which is religion; the love of heroes for their destiny, which is tragedy; and the love of human beings for one another. This last he divides into the love of men for women and the love of women for men. The love of women for men "is always practical. Only a man sometimes knows real longing, and only in men is longing often completely dominated by love" (94). (One wonders what Irma Seidler would have thought of this idea, an idea which, even if rather old, is hardly respectable.) Lukács's distinction between longing and love is apparently identical to that between carnal and spiritual love, a distinction which he applies to the themes of Philippe's novels. The novels are characteristically about a conflict between two men, one sensual and one spiritual, over a woman who combines these traits. The sensual man always wins. This resolution is presented as a tragedy.

Lukács also finds another form of longing in Philippe's novels: "The people he writes about long to get out of their poverty. . ." (99). Philippe "is the poet of the poverty of the small-town petty bourgeois." It would seem difficult to poeticize poverty, in 1910, but Lukács procedes to undertake this task in a peculiarly "spiritual" manner.

> For the poverty of these people is not external [only]; they are not poor [only] because they were born poor or have been impoverished, but because their soul is predestined for poverty. Poverty is a way of seeing the world: a confused longing, expressed in clear words, for something different, and a much deeper love of what one would like to leave behind . . . (99)

Philippe's heroes flee their small town poverty, only to eventually return to it out of nostalgia. "But their going back is circular: the home they find again has meanwhile become different. They are no longer at one with it. . ." (99). Here Lukács's phraseology links poverty with the naive organic unity of Schiller's Golden Age, which can be imitated but never regained. He sees Philippe as a Christian writer: "It is a genuine and profound Christianity; here, Christianity has returned to its true beginnings and has become an art of living for the poor" (99). Philippe's heroes are born into a state of grace – i.e., poverty, and progress through their longing for a better life into the anomie of the modern. Even though they return to objective poverty, subjectively they have been cursed by their lapse from naivete; thus they remain modern and alienated in the midst of their old way of life. But Philippe's minor characters never leave their village or whorehouse poverty. Lukács describes such lives as taking the form of an idyll, and, because Philippe's sympathies are primarily with the "weak" who cannot win a place in the hard bourgeois world, Lukács classifies him as an idyllist.

The concluding section of the essay begins with a definition and a question: "Longing is always sentimental – but is there such a thing as a sentimental form?" (102) He argues that a priori form is that which is achieved and, insofar as sentimentality is longing, it must be formless. But since poetry is a temporal art, and is therefore not an achievement but a becoming, so in poetry, paradoxically, sentimental forms can exist. The chief of these is the lyric, which is pure longing, while its opposite is the idyll. "In the idyll, all longing should be reduced to silence; it should be the final, unequivocal and complete cancellation of longing" (103). In classical aesthetics, according to Lukács, there is a continuum: epic, elegy, lyric. In the modern period there is a form which emerges between the epic and the idyll. He calls this the lyric novel and places the work of Charles-Louis Philippe in that category. And so he is able to conclude that "Philippe's longing truly dissolved itself in form" (106).

Lukács has it that Philippe wrote lyrical novels about longing, the longing of people for one another, the longing of others for the poverty of the spirit, which, in Christian terms, is another word for love. Since he believed, at the time, that the sole purpose of the essay was to express longing, Philippe's work is a fitting topic to "occasion" the meditations on longing and form that Lukacs has included in this piece.

The essay might be said to have failed in an interesting way: it tells us too much about the novels of Philippe, while succeeding too well in the Impressionist task of preparing the reader to properly appreciate literary works of art. This distracts us from its main concern, the discourse on longing and love. But, of course, that is exactly the point; Lukács had already told us that the essayist is an ironist,

> And the irony I mean consists in the critic always speaking about the ultimate problems of life, but in a tone which implies that he is only discussing books and pictures, only the inessential and pretty ornaments of real life – and even then not their innermost substance but only their beautiful and useless surface. (9)

There is some irony, also, in the thought of a critic, at the age of twenty-six, "always speaking about the ultimate problems of life," but as Marianna Weber noticed when she met him the following year, even this still quite young Lukacs had travelled some distance from his earlier adherence to Stefan George's cult of beauty.

> These young philosophers were moved by eschatological hopes of a new emissary of the transcendent God, and they saw the basis of salvation in a socialist social order created by a brotherhood. For Lukács the splendor of inner-worldly culture, particularly its esthetic side, meant the Anti-Christ, the "Luciferian" competition with God's effectiveness. But there was to be a full development of this realm, for the individual's choice between it and the transcendent must not be facilitated. The final struggle between God and Lucifer is still to come and depends on the decision of mankind. The ultimate goal is salvation

from the world, not, as for George and his circle, fulfillment in it.[100]

It is rather astonishing to see a literary critic coming to believe that artistic beauty is a snare of the Devil, but they were, after all, unsettling times.

The Metaphysics of Tragedy

The epigraph of the last essay in **Soul and Form**, "The Metaphysics of Tragedy," is from Meister Eckhart and the essay itself shows Lukács definitely immersed in religious questions. It opens with the rather odd statement that "A drama is a play about man and his fate – a play in which God is the spectator" (152). Lukács is equating the modern play with the medieval mysteries, the Athenian tragedies, the Port Royal theater. This tells us at once that he will be using the words "drama" and "play" in this specific, elevated sense. The inner form of this type of drama is to be opposed to the "richness and fulness" of reality: "In drama there is only one person who speaks (his technique being a perfect reflection of his innermost nature) while the other merely answers" (152). This is obviously not a general statement about drama; rather, it is a definition of the particular poetic tragedies that Lukács has chosen to deal with in this essay. This dramatic tradition is one in which its theatrical realizations are highly controlled, in contrast to the "anarchy" of life. Here, "life" is the "chaos" of Simmel's philosophy, the force against which the forms are set for the sake of rationality.

> Men never know life at the point where all the streams of life converge. Where nothing is fulfilled, everything is possible. But the miracle is fulfillment. It snatches from life all its deceptive veils, woven of gleaming moments, and infinitely varied moods. Drawn in hard and ruthless outline, the soul stands naked before the face of life. (153)

This miracle is the drama and, a few lines further on, the face of life is called the face of God. Therefore, it is reasonable for Lukács to write that: "every true tragedy is a mystery play. Its real, central meaning is a revelation of God before the face of God" (154). Lukács's view here parallels that of the Neo-Platonic tradition which believes man and his works to be the expression of a divine monologue. For Lukács, the completely godless and alienated era in which he was living was precisely appropriate for the rebirth of divine tragedy, a tragedy not like that of the Greeks, who placed their gods on the stage, but a tragedy played to a hidden God as spectator: "because nature and fate have never been so terrifyingly soulless as they

---

[100]   Marianne Weber, **Max Weber – Ein Lebensbild** (Heidelberg, 1950).

are today, because men's souls have never walked in such utter loneliness upon deserted paths, because of all this we may again hope for the coming of tragedy. . ." (154).

Lukács finds himself in a world after the death of God, or, perhaps, a world from which God has withdrawn. "It was God's voice that gave life to the whole; but then that life had to go on by itself, alone, and the judging voice fell silent forever" (155). Yet the divine presence is felt the more strongly in its absence. The longing for an absent God is the strongest mystical religious emotion. Thus tragedy, the play of which God is the proper spectator, reaches its ultimate development in the absence of God, which means that the tragic consciousness of this period "begins at the moment when enigmatic forces have distilled the essence from a man, have forced him to become essential; and the progress of tragedy consists in his essential, true nature becoming more and more manifest" (155). This is a fruitful way of looking at tragedy. It could be, for instance, the starting point for an interesting interpretation of **Oedipus Rex**. But Lukács is not intent on producing interesting interpretations; he is writing about the "ultimate problems." He sees tragedy as an ontological investigation: "Are there not degrees and gradations of being? Is 'being' a property of all things, or is it a value–judgment passed upon things, a distinction and differentiation between them?" (156) By isolating the essence of human beings, stripping them of life to present them as pure Being, drama reveals the "reality of the soul, the reality of lived experience and faith" (156). Lukács defines lived experience as the outward manifestation of the Idea, and faith as that which affirms the connection between it and the Idea, "and transforms its eternally unprovable possibility into the a priori basis for the whole of existence" (156). This theory of tragedy holds that tragedy is transcendental in the strict sense, that it is not dependent on time and space, that it is precisely the revelation of Being before God. "For lived life, this is not a question of epistemology (as it is in philosophy), but the painfully and immediately experienced reality of the great moments" (156). Epiphany has become ontology.[101]

The next step in Lukács's argument in this essay is the rejection of the reality of history in favor of that of Being. For him, we have in "great moments," "the pure experience of the self." This pure experience is not affected by accidents or occasions, and it is not even affected by the past. "The past, too, is flowing, shimmering and changeable, constantly transformed into something different by new insights" (157). The serious intention behind the statement of this doctrine should not be underestimated. At the end of the nineteenth century (that historically

---

[101]   Lukács in a letter to Paul Ernst in September 1911: "My work on the untragic drama has directed me very much to the question of the boundary between religion and art." Congdon, **The Young Lukács**, p. 81.

minded epoch), Lukács rejects the reality of history itself, claiming that reality is found only in the transcendental experience of the Self. Subjective Idealism could go no further in that direction. This radical subjectivism was to become increasingly popular as the new century developed its character. The moral system associated with this world view is already present in "The Metaphysics of Tragedy." If all that matters is the self, the soul, then social life lies outside the realm of the ethical. There is no inter subjective – i.e., social – ethics. The soul judges itself only on the issue of whether or not it is true to itself:

> No richness or grandeur of the soul's gifts can alter this judgment, and a whole life filled with glorious deeds counts as nothing before it. But it forgets, with radiant clemency, any sin of ordinary life which has not encroached upon the center; even to speak of forgiveness is to exaggerate, for the judge's eye simply passes over such sins without noticing them. (158)

We have, here, what seems almost an aspect of Calvinism or Anabaptism. The deeds of the elect do not count against them at the Last Trump. Therefore – history whispers – do as you will.

Returning to the subject of drama, Lukács can justify the classical unities of time and place by viewing them as images of the timeless and placeless moments of the soul's contemplation of itself. This is the essential subject of tragedy which, for Lukács, "has to express the becoming timeless of time" (158). It is a drama without character development, interaction, or conflict: the static celebration of a great moment of the soul. "The reality of such a world can have nothing in common with that of temporal existence. Realism is bound to destroy all the form-creating and life-maintaining values of tragic drama" (159). It seems clear that Lukács is not concerned with bourgeois realism in the theater. He is concerned with tragedy and with mysticism and with their relationship to one another:

> the mystical and tragic modes of experiencing life touch and supplement one another and mutually exclude one another . . . Surrender is the mystics' way, struggle the tragic man's; the one, at the end of his road, is absorbed into the All, the other shattered against the All . . . Each, separately, means death. . . . (160)

The road of tragedy, of mysticism, perhaps even of longing as taken by the essayist, all of these have the same goal: death. There are moments when a culture turns to death as a relief from intolerable contradictions.

All this writing about ultimate questions has been a propos of the work of Paul Ernst, who is barely mentioned in the first section of the essay. The second part of the essay turns from these general issues to a consideration of the dramatist. (In 1911 Lukács published an article in **Die Schaubühne** entitled "Brunhild (Paul Ernst)," a fitting title for this part of "The

Metaphysics of Tragedy.") Ernst's "Brunhild" is presented as marking the end of the German dramatic tradition, of the effort "to marry Sophocles with Shakespeare" (163). Shakespeare is abandoned. For Lukács, the drama of Ernst "is the tragedie classique reborn: he deepens and interiorizes the aims of Corneille, Racine and Alfieri. It is a genuine return to the great model for all drama that seeks the soul of form – the 'Oedipus of Sophocles'" (164). The play has only three characters, a single set, and takes place between dawn and sunset of a single day. It is "perhaps more Greek than . . . many ancient tragedies." Lukács, in his usual manner of this period, does not so much analyze the play as dream about it: about the play, about death, about the All. We are given a plot summary and a finely worded appreciation of Ernst's skill as a stylist and dramatic architect. "Brunhild" is celebrated as at once the perfect Greek tragedy and the perfect mystical drama. (It is, of course, on the subject of the familiar Germanic myth.)

The third section of the essay introduces some qualifications. Ernst has given up history, the richness and color of history in his search for timeless perfection, and, surprisingly, Lukács does not consider this to be a small sacrifice. "Being-history is a completely pure form of being; one might say it is Being as such" (167). Tragedy tries to find the meaning of history in the everyday in order to read fate, as it were, in the dirt of the street. But historical drama attempts to combine lived experience with the essential life of the soul. Ernst's historical dramas record the transformations of the souls of their protagonists by history as a projection of conflict. These dramas, like his tragedies, end in death, but here death does not bring salvation; it is merely the end of life. Ernst's heroes lose their souls in triumph, they exchange essences in conflict, they find death in victory.

The concluding section of the essay, and of the book as we now know it, begins with the final words of the preceding section, "Form is the highest judge of life" (173), and goes on to claim that "form-giving is a judging force, an ethic; there is a value-judgment in everything that has been given form" (173). In Ernst's play "Ninon de L'Enclos" he considers a character whom both he and Lukács see as not worthy of tragedy: a woman who wants to be free.

> She is the highest of an inferior species: this is the verdict which the dramatic form passes upon the value of her life. She wanted to obtain the highest for herself, and has attained it – the highest, which is freedom; but her freedom is simply liberation from all bonds, not, in the last analysis, a freedom organically born out of her inner most self, identical with the highest necessity – not the completion of her life. Her freedom is the freedom of harlots. (173)

Again, one cannot help thinking of Lukács's relationship with Irma Seidler and the tragedy of that woman's suicide. Yet Lukács claims that tragedy is undemocratic, that it cannot be concerned with "the poor in spirit" or with women. He asks: "Can freedom become a real value in a woman's life?" (174). The answer implicit in this rhetorical question is, of course, no.

Ernst places this perfect and rounded higher world as a warning, a call to action, a light and a goal upon the path of men, but is not concerned with their actual becoming-real. The validity and strength of an ethic does not depend on whether or not the ethic is applied. Therefore only a form which has been purified until it has become ethical can, without becoming blind and poverty-stricken as a result of it, forget the existence of everything problematic and banish it forever from its realm. (174)

With the last two essays of **Soul and Form** Lukács had become a moralist without losing his Impressionism. What is "the precisely appropriate consciousness" that Lukács has been attempting to create in this essay on Paul Ernst? Is it not that consciousness of being-toward-death which is the peculiar gift of Central European mystical philosophy to our time? The ethical purity of Ernst's drama, so "perfect and rounded," stands at the end of **Soul and Form** as a landmark and a warning. Impressionism carries one this far and no further. It has reached that goal for which it has been striving, a point outside history. "Therefore only a form which has been purified until it has become ethical can, without becoming blind and poverty-stricken as a result of it, forget the existence of everything problematic and banish it forever from its realm," concludes Lukács. Pure form, and the appreciation of pure form as a "road" leading to great moments, say, is a way to reach ethical consciousness which knows nothing problematic, nothing of the world. This variety of form is the type of a mental state with which we are familiar: fantasy, illusion, delusion. Beyond this, Impressionism as a mode for the study of literature becomes itself an ideology, one which uses literature to provide a vocabulary and structure for its rhetoric, and little more. The literary essay becomes, in earnest, "thoughts occasioned by" literature. It is finally neither literature nor scholarship.

To recapitulate: **Soul and Form** is a collection of essays mostly written for Hungarian journals in the period 1908 to 1910, for the most part on the subject of German language literature.[102] Having read the reflections "On the Romantic Philosophy of Life," one could then turn to the poems of

---

[102] "Lukács conceived the idea of publishing his **Nyugat** essays, along with three new writings, early in 1909. . . . 'Sequence. I think this must be the order. Novalis (death), Beer-Hofmann (Death as foreignness and the symbol of separation), Kierkegaard (foreignness and separation in life), George (the poetry of foreignness and separation). [Laurence] Sterne (satire on both kinds of foreignness: in content and in form).'" Congdon, **The Young Lukacs,** pp. 48-9.

Novalis and find in them that Romantic world view which Lukács had indicated, one quite sympathetic for a member of an isolated intelligentsia struggling to create a new culture, whether that of Jena in the early nineteenth century or that of Lukács's Budapest. The essay on Kassner creates the impression that each critic is suited to a particular poet or type, that the most visionary of critics, like Kassner, are best suited to write about visionary poets. Lukács also attempts in the essay on George to create in his readers "the precisely appropriate consciousness" for the reading of the text at hand. That point of view is not one that approaches the poet, much less the poetry, in a critical manner. It is an attitude that accepts the poet's interpretation of his role and status. Instead of helping us to understand this poetry Lukács cooperates with the poet to intoxicate us into giving up yet more of our knowledge and ability to reason about human creations. In Lukács's essay on Beer-Hofmann his critical method changes from the Impressionism of the essays on Novalis, George, and Kassner to a loose meditation on literary themes as a basis for religious speculation. This change is accompanied by a parallel change in his use of the word "form." In the earlier essays its meaning is usually "world view," while in the essay on Beer-Hofmann it is most often that which leads "to a great moment of silence," although both are occasionally replaced by an Aristotelian terminology of a hierarchy of genres, each with its fit subject matter. Lukács analyzes Kierkegaard's abandonment of Regine Olsen in the terms of the stages of the soul's journey to God, seeing it as necessary for Kierkegaard's spiritual development and seeing it as having very little to do with the woman in question.

Lukács's placing of Storm in his social and historical context, the derivation from that situation of the particular qualities of Storm's work, and the clear discussion of form as genre result in a brilliant and orderly discussion of bourgeois realism in general and specifically of the short stories and lyrics of Storm. Lukács had, for the moment, put aside most of his Neo-Kantian and mystical concerns, concentrating on giving his readers not an approach to the appreciation of Storm, but a path to the understanding of that author's enterprise. "On the Nature and Form of the Essay," on the other hand, shows that, by late-1910, Lukács had become something of a mystic. However, the new conclusion of "On the Nature and Form of the Essay," written for a German audience, sticks more closely to literary critical considerations than had the Hungarian original, thus serving to introduce Lukács himself to his new audience in a more familiar guise. The essay on Charles-Louis Philippe succeeds in the Impressionist task of preparing the reader to properly appreciate literary works of art, and this distracts us from the main thing, the discourse on longing and love. But, of course, that is exactly the point, the essayist is an ironist. The Paul Ernst piece is as close as Lukács comes in **Soul and Form** to devoting an entire essay to his religious and moral concerns, still, though, on the occasion of literature.

Once more: Lukács was an Impressionist book reviewer, working in an intellectual tradition much influenced by Dilthey and Simmel, when he began the series of essays collected in **Soul and Form.** By the time that he had finished the last of them he was "moved by eschatological hopes of a new emissary of the transcendent God, and [he] saw the basis of salvation in a socialist social order created by a brotherhood." He was to retain such hopes for quite some time.

On Poverty of Spirit: A Conversation and Letter

Soul and Form was dedicated to Irma Seidler. Lukács's emotional relationship with her was summarized in his essay on Kierkegaard and Regine Olsen in **Soul and Form.** After it became clear that Lukács was unwilling or unable to discover a way in which they might remain together, she married another suitor. Shortly thereafter Seidler became the lover of Béla Balázs, one of Lukács's closest collaborators in this period. It is possible that the relationships among these three were even more complex than that. Balázs seems to have had a powerfully unsettling emotional influence. Just as Lukács was turning from aestheticism to mysticism, his personal life was shaken by Seidler's suicide, in reaction to the end of her affair with Balázs – ended by the latter.

To put matters rather schematically, Lukács's situation in 1910–11 was one of alienation and loneliness on a number of levels: he was a member of the urban middle class in a largely rural and feudal society; he was a Jew in an era of anti–Semitism; he was a person who, like many others in Central Europe at that time, felt that the social effects of the industrialization of the modern world were unacceptable; and he was a person who, greatly valuing intimate relationships, found that his intimate life, too, was disintegrating. It was under these circumstances that his thought veered ever more sharply from academic philosophy to a preoccupation with the most radical path available to him leading away from these circumstances: the volitional mysticism of Kierkegaard and Meister Eckhart.

Many documents have been published over the last few years that throw light on the mystical orientation of Lukacs's milieu. The diaries of Béla Balázs, for instance, include passages such as the following:

Gyuri's new philosophy. Messianism. The homogeneous world as the redemptive goal. Art the Luciferean "better made." The vision of the world become homogeneous before the actual process of transformation. The immorality of art. Gyuri's big turn toward ethics.

This will be the center of his life and work.[103]

Balázs's reflections on Seidler's suicide probably were shared by Lukács: "This is my first sin, in the most weighty sense of the word. Strange that before this I felt my life and heart to be pure . . . Since Irma's death religious questions have come to me as well as the compelling thirst to meet my God."[104] The primary text for Lukács's state of mind at this time is the dialogue "On Poverty of Spirit: A Conversation and a Letter."[105] The story was published in Balázs's Hungarian translation in **A Szellem** in 1911 and in the original German in 1912. That Lukács published it in both German and Hungarian is a significant fact in itself. It is not a private confession, but a public document speaking to the concerns of many sensitive Central Europeans in the midst of their cultural crisis. The piece is given the form of a letter from a woman ("Martha") just returned from Italy where she had gone to rest after her sister's suicide. (Lukács himself had been in Florence during this period.) The letter is addressed to another woman and describes a conversation with that woman's son. The young man in question had been involved in some way with Martha's sister's suicide. The letter is an account of a conversation between the young man and Martha concerning his feelings about that tragedy, feelings that lead to his own suicide two days later.

"Martha" traditionally signifies the active life in opposition to the contemplative life as signified by "Mary." The dialogue is explicitly one between the religious ideas of service to and within society and withdrawal into the self in order to search for God. The young man begins the discussion by saying that he has achieved "clarity"; he knows that he was the cause of the suicide of Martha's sister. Martha denies this and attributes her sister's action to some other cause, which is only alluded to mysteriously. If these have specific analogues in the social world, then one might say that Lukács is claiming for himself the responsibility for Seidler's suicide, while knowing, perhaps, that the immediate cause was Balázs's having broken off their love affair. There is not much point in pursuing these specific circumstances too far since the dialogue is an expression of a general situation for a general public. If its overdetermined origin included the uncertain relations among Lukács, Balázs, and Seidler, it also included many other circumstances with which large numbers of people were

---

103 Béla Balázs, "Notes from a Diary," quoted in Lee Congdon, **Beyond the "Hungarian Wasteland"** (Dissertation: Northern Illinois University, 1973), p. 151.

104 Congdon, **Beyond the "Hungarian Wasteland,"** p. 147.

105 "On Poverty of Spirit: A Conversation and a Letter," trans. John T. Sanders, **Philosophical Forum**, III, 3–4 (Spring–Summer 1972). Subsequent citations in the text are from this translation.

familiar in their own lives: anomie, social disintegration, the collapse of organized religion. Private sorrows are often also the particular manifestation of a general social malaise. The fact of the publication of "On the Poverty of the Spirit" indicates that it was not just Lukács's private tragedy that was at issue, but also the themes of ethical and social responsibility as focussed for him by that tragedy.

The practical nature of the internalized response to ethical problems is set up when the male protagonist claims that his guilt for Martha's sister's death is definite because although she knew that she could have asked him for help she did not do so. Left publicly innocent (after all he would have aided her if she had only asked), he became implicitly more guilty for having in effect demanded the public expression of sorrow that was being actively expressed by silence. "To the loud, crying-for-help voice of her silence I turned a deaf ear" (373). Martha's worldly charity is defeated at the start by this dialectic: it is the absence of the cry for help that must be heard. He blames himself for lacking goodness, grace. "Human knowledge is an interpretation of statements and signs. . . ." But for one who is Good "the private thoughts of others become manifest . . . he is the other" (373). As such goodness had been possible for Francis of Assisi, it must also be a demand for him "as long as I don't want to cut myself off from other men" (373). Martha interprets this statement as an impious demand for grace; but he holds that since it has happened once, that a man was Good, it is always possible, and that Goodness is not something that one needs to demand, but, on the contrary something that must be refused. He has sinned by refusing grace and Goodness.

As in **Soul and Form,** Lukács distinguishes here between two kinds of life. They are the worldly life and the inner life, or that of Martha and that of Mary. The lives of most people "are merely social, merely interpersonal; you see: they could be satisfied with duties and their fulfillment" (373). This sounds like a simple condemnation but it is followed immediately by the formulation of a peculiar social ethic. "The fulfillment of duties is, for them, the only possible exaltation of their lives" (373–4). It is an ideal of commitment for the masses, but it is not the ideal that he holds for himself. An ethic is a form, he says, following Simmel, and has its own existence. This existence is "a bridge that separates." People who live in this way never break out of their own particularity; they are bound by their duties. If he lived in this way, alone within the social forms, he would be innocent, but he has other ambitions. "The living life lies beyond the forms, whereas the everyday life lies on this side of them and goodness amounts to being given the grace to break through the forms" (374).

Martha objects that there is no such thing as Goodness, fearing that if he believes that such a state exists, and that he has refused it, he would see himself as trapped in the forms, in the solipsistic universe of the follower. He, in reply, attributes her denial of Goodness, at first, to her knowledge of this danger for him, and therefore to her Goodness, exalting her, deprecating himself, ironically, as it turns out. The ironic operations here, as a matter of fact, are so dense as to be virtually impenetrable. At one moment Goodness is attributed to the merely pious Martha, at the next it is so exalted as to be unreachable by humanity. "Do you believe, then, that if Goodness could still work we would still be human?" he asks. Lukács's concerns here are defined by his moving the epistemology of Simmel into religious categories. Where Simmel taught that the chaos of the world was formed by the mind into knowledge, Lukács makes this an ethical principle.

> Do you believe, then, that if Goodness could still work we would still be human? That this world of the impure, unliving life could still persist? Here, indeed, is our boundary, the principle of our humanity. You remember that I always said: we are mere humans, because we can build spiritual islands in the middle of the unspiritual chaos, and in the grubby (schmatzigen) flux of life. (374-5)

True Goodness, on the other hand, "juts out of life"; it is embodied by Sonya, Prince Myshkin, the whole Dostoevskian ideal. They break through the world of forms, "they are the Gnostics of the deed" (375). For them, "subject and object collapse into one another," they are the other, they are, to use the obvious phrase, beyond good and evil. For these personalities "Goodness is not an ethical category." Having transcended the merely human, "Goodness . . . is the return to real life, man's true discovery of his home." It is the golden age, the utopia of nostalgia that Lukács will establish as the touchstone of reality in **The Theory of the Novel.** (This link between the past and future ideals was well expressed by Paul de Lagarde's declaration: "I live with every breath in a past that never was and which is the only future I crave.")[106]

As in Dostoevsky's work itself, this ideal wavers oddly between the revolutionary, the mystic, and the criminal. Too often those who try to rise above the human condition fall below it. Martha takes this line of criticism: "your Goodness is nothing more than a very elegant and refined frivolity, a gift of ecstasy, obtained without a struggle or - for you] - a cheap renunciation of life . . . It appears to me that you want to leap over the most important stages, to reach the goal without (using) the path" (376-7). Martha is presented here as agreeing with the position taken earlier by Lukacs in "The Essay on the Essay," that it is the path that is important, that the path is the goal. The male in the dialogue replies that he has gone beyond such a position, that "God's claim on us is absolute and unsatisfiable: we are to leap the bounds of interpersonal forms of understanding" (377). He begins a speech reminiscent, in retrospect, of Naphta himself.

---

106 Fritz Stern, **The Politics of Cultural Despair** (Berkeley and Los Angeles: University of California Press, 1961), p. 57.

Goodness is madness, it is not mild, not refined, and not quietistic; it is wild, terrible, blind and adventurous. The soul of the good man has become empty of all psychological content, of grounds and consequences; it has become a pure white slate, upon which fate writes its absurd command, and this command will be followed blindly, rashly and fiercely to the end. That this impossibility becomes fact, this blindness becomes clear-sightedness, this fierceness becomes Goodness – that is the miracle, the grace. (377)

(Thomas Mann was not alone in noting Lukács's often curious union of Jesuit and terrorist, blindness and . . . clear-sightedness.) Speaking of his relationship to the dead woman, Lukács's protagonist continues in the same tone:

But one is not permitted . . . to want to be good, and above all, one is never permitted to want to be good in relation to someone else. One must want to save someone; then one is good. One wants to save another and behaves badly, fiercely, tyrannically, and every act might be a sin. But in such a case even sin itself is no antithesis to Goodness; it is neither more nor less a necessary dissonance in the harmony . . . I wanted to lead a pure life, in which everything was handled with only cautious and frightfully clean-kept hands] this way of living is, however, the application to life of a false category. The Work which is separated from life must be pure. Life, however, can neither become nor be pure . . . And the grand life – the life of Goodness – no longer needs such a purity; it has another purity – a higher one. (378)

The conclusion of this speech befits its Nietzschean drift: "I am withdrawing from life. Because just as it is only the genius, who may play a role in the philosophy of art, so it is only the man graced with Goodness, who may play a role in life" (379). He finds himself made fit for such a role by the suicide of his friend: "her death is, for me, a divine judgment. She had to die, so that my work could be completed – so that nothing remains in the world for me except my work" (379). The woman, even in death, is purely instrumental to his aims, for according to him, "everything has its cause, and motive, but it also has a meaning, and divine judgment can only reside in meaning" (379). By knowing the divine judgment, then, he takes over her death, with its personal causes and motives, into his own life. "Because she was, for me, everything that life could ever be – for that reason, her death and my inability to help, which caused her death – was the judgment of God" (380). Divorced of causes and motivations, removed from the interpersonal, meaning becomes solipsistic and ideal.

Martha accuses him of wishing to be a monk and so taking the easy way out: "Doesn't your asceticism just make things easier for you? Won't your Work, which you want to save, in that you give it human blood as its foundation, become truly bloodless and unprincipled?" (380-1). He replies condescendingly that she is just a woman and "Never will a woman understand with all her senses that life is only a word. . ." (381). Furthermore, "No woman has ever entered the world beyond pleasure and pain unless she was deformed." That this is virtually Lukács himself speaking can be ascertained by comparing these to other similar remarks in **Soul and Form**. Women are pure, unthinking, soulless instruments for the purposes of men. "Even Catherine of Siena was no clear and conscious ascetic, but rather the betrothed of Christ" (381). Men, on the other hand, can achieve the "poverty of spirit," the liberation from personal psychological limitations. "We are only a vague bundle of wish and fear, of desire and suffering; something that at every moment perishes in its own reality. What if we <u>wanted</u> this destruction?" (382). This is the masochism of the soul.

If the death instinct is not in itself sufficient to sustain an ethic, there is a path pointed out by Dostoevsky (and later by Jean Genet) that leads to a solution. "The solution . . . is the great paradox: the unification of temptation with tempted, fate with soul, the devil with the divine part of man . . . only the wildest temptation will be appealing" (382). The young man has, evidently, been reading **The Brothers Karamazov**. He has found there a "negative ethic," a philosophy of self-abasement and nihilism, which becomes a worship of abstract values, of death.

> We must live in this way: our life is worthless, without significance, and we would be ready at any moment to hand it over to death; indeed, at every moment we await only permission to throw it away. But, to be sure, we must live intensely; we must live with all our powers and senses. (383)

He asserts that while the masses should adhere to an ethic of duty and obedience, the few should live entirely without rules, wedded to their destiny. Taken somewhat aback by this, Martha replies: "If I understand you correctly, you want to establish new foundations for the castes. In your eyes, there is only one sin: the mixing of castes." And he replies: "You have understood me marvelously well" (384). The piece ends with a Biblical quotation: "I know your Works, that you are neither cold nor warm; oh, if only you were cold or warm. Because you are lukewarm, however, and are neither cold nor warm, I will spit you out of my mouth" (385).

The young man of this interesting story, wishing to be either cold or hot, but not lukewarm, commits suicide. His creator, convinced of the futility of all forms, aesthetic as well as ethical, convinced of the preeminence of the will, of the necessity for personal salvation, went on to write **The Theory of the Novel,** a devotional text.

The Philosophical Background

The universities of south-west Germany at the end of the nineteenth and the beginning of the twentieth century had an aura of Latin rationality and humanism about them that was often contrasted, in contemporary accounts, with the instrumental and state service orientation of the University of Berlin. The south-west German states of the Reich constituted a kind of internal cultural opposition to the Prussianism that became dominant elsewhere after 1866 and 1870. This opposition was fostered by distant memories of Roman and less distant memories of French occupation, perhaps heightened also by the Catholicism of much of the region, which, in combination with the Reich sponsored Protestanism of official life, led to a certain atmosphere of tolerance not found in other areas of Germany at the time. The questions which were discussed with what one might be tempted to call desperation by the philosophers of Berlin became, in the gentler and more rational atmosphere of Freiburg and Heidelberg, questions of logic and methodology.

After writing **Soul and Form,** that essentially autobiographical and provincial work of a young man torn between poetry and philosophy, Lukács took the decisive step of going to Heidelberg to study with one of the formative intelligences of the twentieth century: Max Weber. Weber appears to us as a major contributor to modern thought, a social thinker whose importance is such as to be comparable only to that set of originators of modes of thought who have not so much defined as shaped our world: Hegel, Marx, Freud. If he was not quite of their rank, if he was, to extend the military image, a Lee rather than a Napoleon, this serves merely to underline his exemplary value. Where, for instance, Freud, in his nearly inhuman grandeur, observed the final crisis of nineteenth-century European civilization from the point of view of the gods, Weber lived that crisis, attempting to hold together in his own personality the contradictions of an entire civilization that was hurtling to destruction. The story of his life seems to us to be an intellectual tragedy of the first order, inspiring the Aristotelian emotions of pity and fear, the anguished identification with the terror of a noble parricide. For many observers Weber "was a champion fighting in a world which was crumbling around him and within him."[107] He gazed steadily at the forces of irrationalism that were overwhelming his

---

[107] Carlo Antoni, **From History to Sociology,** trans. Hayden V. White (Detroit: Wayne State University Press, 1959), p. 121.

world, and if, in the end, they overwhelmed him too, it was a clean defeat, uncomplicated by inner surrender. He claimed, with Wittgenstein (whose thought bears striking similarities to his own) that: "We can keep on asking science: What must we do? How should we live? Science will give us no reply, for science is theory. Each one of us must look within himself."[108]

Max Weber

That aspect of Weber's thought which concerns us here, his epistemology and theory of the methodology of the human sciences, begins with the shared assumption of his time, familiar from the first chapter of this study, "that empirical reality is extensively and intensively infinite."

> This means, first of all, that reality surpasses our power of understanding, so that we can never come to the end of our exploration of events and of their variations in space and time or act on them all; next, that it is impossible to describe even the smallest segment of reality completely or to take into account all the data, all the elements and all the possible consequences at the moment of taking action.[109]

Many of Weber's contemporaries, including, as we have seen, Simmel and Rickert, thought of knowledge as being the representation of facts that might or might not be "out there." This theory brought them to the conclusion that, given the infinite nature of the world and the finite nature of the human mind, complete knowledge, or truth, is impossible. Weber side-steps this impasse by bracketing the problematic nature of the non-human world. Reality is not the world as it really in fact is, or would be if there were no minds to contemplate it. Instead, as we cannot escape the fact that we exist, "Weber says that the things and processes constituting empirical reality are 'given in our consciousness.'"[110] According to Weber, it literally does not make sense to attempt to think of the world outside of the framework of our consciousness of it, and this allows us, once we begin to think of the world as it is "given in our consciousness" to construct rules and methods for its study. This is typical of Weber's thought, to avoid the befuddlement consequent upon much abstract speculation by a

---

108 Julian Freund, **The Sociology of Max Weber**, trans. Mary Ilford (New York: Pantheon, 1968), p. 86.

109 Freund, p. 7.

110 Thomas Burger, **Max Weber's Theory of Concept Formation** (Durham, North Carolina: Duke University Press, 1976), p. 61.

consideration of exactly what it is that we do – or can – know, and how we might go about extending its domain. Here, at the basis of Weber's conception of the task of scientific thought, we have an existential qualification: we are to proceed as if we could accomplish our research goals, even while knowing that in principle attaining them is impossible. This perhaps self-conscious "heroic" stance is in marked contrast to the general surrender of his contemporaries to despair and irrationalism. Since that negative attitude was rooted as much in social conditions as in valid philosophical analysis, Weber's achievement appears as remarkable as it was valuable. Even though he accepted the ideologically-tinged presuppositions of the epistemology of his time – "neither any one science nor all sciences taken together can give us perfect knowledge because the mind is not capable of reproducing or copying reality, but only of reconstructing it with the aid of concepts. And there is an infinite distance between the real and the conceptual,"[111]
– he continued to reject the practical implications of this position.

This achievement came slowly, through a continuous shifting in emphasis of propositions not in themselves radically different from those of Dilthey, Simmel, and Rickert. Weber's definition of scientific knowledge as an "ordering in thought of empirical reality,"[112] was much as Simmel, for instance, had used. But where for Simmel the emphasis was on the artificiality of this ordering, in the forming of reality by the soul, Weber underlined the rationality of the process itself and the fact that this was the nature of all scientific knowledge within the natural sciences as well as the human sciences. This in itself was an important breakthrough (if it only had been heeded), showing that it is not necessary for the human sciences to copy the methodologies of mathematics or physics in order to be rigorous. Nor is it necessary to abandon rigor for Nacherleben. If all scientific knowledge is "an ordering in thought of empirical reality," the choice of the mode of that ordering, as we shall see, is determined by the relative fruitfulness of the system in question. Now Weber held that in all cases this ordering of empirical reality operates through the manipulation of concepts. He "was satisfied to show that for understanding to be empirical knowledge it has to be in the form of concepts,"[113] as, given the then prevalent theory of knowledge, understanding had to be understanding of mental events. In holding this he was, once again, quite close to Simmel and Rickert. "The transformation of sensations into facts, and the organization of facts into scientific accounts of the empirical world, i.e., scientific knowledge, are seen by Weber as processes of giving form to

---

[111]   Freund, p. 8.

[112]   Burger, p. 61.

[113]   Burger, p. 9.

contents, namely sensations and facts, respectively."[114] But for Weber this process was instrumental and not arbitrary.

Weber differentiates the objective world from the thinking subject by means of the organization of concepts: "through the category of causality the 'world' as a 'perceived complex of facts' becomes an 'object.'"[115] The problem then is how to order this objective world of facts. Dilthey had approached it through his theory of world views with their conventional validity. Simmel had held that order was introduced through the arbitrary mechanisms of forms and world forms. Weber took an approach that was at once similar to and different from these. Like Rickert, he ordered the objective world of facts with reference to value: "in each case only a part' of individual reality is interesting and significant to us, because it alone is related to the cultural value-ideas with which we approach reality. Only certain sides of the infinitely complex individual phenomena . . . are, therefore, worthwhile knowing."[116] Rickert had written of facts which everyone wanted to know; Weber realized that is not the way to go about developing a useful methodology for scientific research. He held that "scientific truth is only what claims validity for all those who want the truth."[117] Perhaps Weber's involvement in politics had made him realize that there are some people who do not want the truth.

Having limited both the object and the audience for scientific knowledge, Weber goes on to attempt to establish rules for its intersubjectivity, its objectivity.

> The "objectivity" of social-scientific knowledge depends rather on the fact that the empirical data are always related to those value-ideas which alone make them worth knowing, and that their significance is understood on the basis of those values, but that nevertheless they are never made the basis for the empirically impossible proof of the validity of those values.[118]

The concept of value, which is the foundation of this system of scientific objectivity, is, in a move reminiscent of phenomenological bracketing, removed from consideration. It is not, for instance, Dilthey's concept of value derived from poetic insight. We will see later that the concept of

---

[114]   Burger, p. 63.

[115]   Burger, p. 63.

[116]   Burger, p. 79.

[117]   Burger, p. 64.

[118]   Burger, p. 81.

value is not as subjective for Weber as it might seem at first glance. For the moment, though, let us work through the implications of there being certain facts which are worth knowing.

> A fact is worth knowing when its inclusion in an account of empirical reality is a step toward reaching one of the two formal goals of knowledge, depending on which one has been adopted in a particular instance. The standards of selection state under what conditions this is the case. If the goal is knowledge of the general laws governing all empirical phenomena, only those elements of reality are worth knowing which are common to all phenomena, i.e., generic . . . features. If the goal is knowledge of the uniqueness of concrete phenomena, then only those things are worth knowing in which the "individual particularity" of the phenomenon in question manifests itself, those parts which are "characteristic," or "historically essential," or "significant" for scientific researchers.[119]

These two formal goals of knowlege are what Rickert took to be the definitions of the natural and the human sciences. However, Weber's use of Rickert's phraseology did not imply Rickert's conclusions. "While Weber accepted the distinction between generalizing and individualizing methods, he rejected Windelband's and Rickert's conclusions, notably their classification of the sciences on the basis of differences of method . . . He maintained that every science uses each method in turn."[120]

As we move through this argument for the fourth time, we can see that although Weber follows the general line of reasoning taken by Dilthey, Simmel, and Rickert, everywhere he transforms it from abstract speculation to immediately useful precepts for the methodology of science. There is an enormous difference between observations that are fundamentally uncommitted, no matter how brilliant they may be, and research that allows specific controversies to be resolved. Even "correct" assertions about the world are sterile if they are made in the framework of pure speculation: witness the Lucretian atomic theory. Even if Dilthey or Simmel, on the one hand, or Windelband and Rickert on the other, had been right about their definitions of, say, the division between the natural and the human sciences, it would not have mattered, because their definitions would not have opened the way to further research. These were Idealist dead ends. As H. Stuart Hughes has pointed out,

> The great quarrel that had separated Dilthey from Windelband – and later from Rickert – over whether the cultural sciences were distinguished from the natural sciences by the object they investigated,

---

119   Burger, p. 67.

120   Freund, p. 39.

or rather by the method they pursued, Weber found to be irrelevant. In practice, he argued, the object of investigation defined itself through the very method that was directed toward it.[121]

Leaving aside the general considerations of scientific knowledge, we can now follow out Weber's treatment of the specific methodology of research in the human sciences. First, he defines history as a science "whose object, formulated in the terminology of the philosophy of history, represents 'the embodiment of values in concrete phenomena' and which treats 'the human individuals' who themselves 'value' always as 'carriers' of that process."[122] This, then, is a move in the tradition of Dilthey, defining the science of history by its objects. But he at once reconciles this with Rickert's position by defining a mode of selection for the cultural sciences. "'Culture' is a finite segment of the meaningless infinity of the world process, a segment which from the point of view of human beings has meaning and significance conferred upon it."[123] This definition must be compared with the more general criteria outlined earlier concerning that which is worth knowing for those interested in the truth. Culture, defined as that which is meaningful and significant for human beings, is a field of selection for the operation of that earlier standard. Weber contrasts this approach to the historical, cultural, world from the point of view of values and significance with that of the vulgar positivist:

> If the opinion that those viewpoints could be "taken from the material itself" continually recurs, this is due to the naive self-deception of the specialist who is unaware that due to the value-ideas with which he unconsciously has approached his subject matter, a priori he has selected from an absolute infinity a tiny portion as that part with whose study alone he concerns himself.[124]

As Weber refined Rickert's criteria of ideas that are interesting for everyone by adding that they must be interesting to those who are interested in the truth, so he transforms the concept of point of view held by Dilthey and Simmel into a methodological principle:

---

[121]   H. Stuart Hughes, **Consciousness and Society** (New York: Alfred A. Knopf, 1958), pp. 309–10.

[122]   Burger, p. 78.

[123]   Burger, p. 80.

[124]   Burger, pp. 84–5.

Those phenomena which interest us as cultural phenomena are interesting to us with respect to very different kinds of evaluative ideas to which we relate them. In as much as the "points of view" from which they can become significant for us are very diverse, the most varied criteria can be applied to the selection of traits which are to enter into the construction of an ideal–typical view of a particular culture.[125]

Simmel's concept of point of view was nihilistic; Weber turned it into a scientific instrument.

Weber further clarifies the objective possibilities for the human sciences of the seemingly subjective concepts of point of view and values, or interest, with the following illustration:

Between the "historical" interest in a family chronicle and that in the development of the greatest conceivable cultural phenomena which were or are common to a nation or to mankind over long epochs, there exists an infinite gradation of "significance" arranged into an order which differs for each of us. And they are, naturally, historically variable in accordance with the character of the cultures and the ideas which rule men's minds. But it obviously does not follow from this that research in the cultural sciences can only have results which are "subjective" in the sense that they are valid for one person and not for others. Only the degree to which they interest different persons varies. In other words, the choice of the object of investigation and the extent or depth to which this investigation attempts to penetrate into the infinite causal web are determined by the value–ideas which dominate the investigator and his age.[126]

Here, once again, Weber does not seek merely to make definitional or emotional statements about the sciences. He does not, for instance, throw up his hands in despair over the infinite nature of the "causal web." He establishes a procedure which at once provides a definition of his views and an opportunity to test those views while extending the domain of knowledge. Weber's pre-eminence in the line of thinkers that we have been following here was due in part to his determination not only to examine scientific procedures, but to change them, and also to the fact that he was able to accomplish that goal.

---

125   Max Weber, "'Objectivity' in Social Science and Social Policy," in **Max Weber's Ideal Type Theory,** ed. Rolf E. Rogers (New York: Philosophical Library, Inc., 1969), pp. 18-9.

126   Burger, p. 81.

We can know the human world because it was created by humans more or less like ourselves. This line of reasoning would have it that because of this difference between the natural and the human world, the mode of study of the human world must be different from that of natural science. The human world is continually changing; indeed, one of the factors of change in the human world is the process of our study of it. Whereas for Dilthey and Simmel this was a, perhaps the, insurmountable problem for the theory of the human sciences, for Weber it was the point at which those problems could be overcome. If that unknown quantity which is the subjectivity of the historian as observer cannot be predicted, it can be held stable, bracketed in his calculations as value and interest, allowing procedures that would take into account the solution of other variables once that one was held constant. Weber's instrument for this bracketing procedure was his theory of ideal types.[127] Here the situation that necessitated the formulation of Weber's theory is worth examining in some detail. He described it as follows:

> The attempts to determine the "real" and the "true" meaning of historical concepts always reappear and never succeed in reaching their goal. Accordingly the synthetic concepts used by historians are either imperfectly defined or, as soon as the elimination of ambiguity is sought for, the concept becomes an abstract ideal type and reveals itself there-with as a theoretical and hence "one-sided" viewpoint which illuminates the aspect of reality with which it can be related. But these concepts are shown to be obviously inappropriate as schema into which reality could be completely integrated. For none of those systems of ideas, which are absolutely indispensable in the understanding of those segments of reality which are meaningful at a particular moment, can exhaust its infinite richness. They are all attempts, on the basis of the present state of our knowledge and the available conceptual patterns, to bring order into the chaos of those facts which we have drawn into the field circumscribed by our interest. The intellectual apparatus which the past has developed through the analysis, or more truthfully, the analytical rearrangement of the immediately given reality, and through the latter's integration by concepts which correspond to the state of its knowledge and the focus of its interest, is in constant tension with the new knowledge which we can and desire to wrest from reality. The progress of cultural science occurs through this conflict. Its result is the perpetual reconstruction of those concepts through which we seek to comprehend reality. The history of the social sciences is and remains a continuous process

---

127 Carlo Antoni has remarked that: "Weber realized that it was difficult to convey the fluidity and change of the historical world given the rigidity of the terms of orientation and comparison, and he sought to transcend this problem with his logic of the ideal type." Antoni, p. 168.

passing from the attempt to order reality analytically through the construction of concepts – the dissolution of the analytical constructs so constructed through the expansion and shift of the scientific horizon – and the reformulation anew of concepts on the foundations thus transformed. It is not the error of the attempt to construct conceptual systems in general which is shown by this process – every science, even simple descriptive history, operates with this conceptual stock-in-trade of its time. Rather, this process shows that in the cultural sciences concept-construction depends on the setting of the problem, and the latter varies with the content of culture itself.[128]

Weber's theory of historical research, in contrast to those of Rickert and Simmel, for instance, allows the history of the present to be written, as long as we realize that such a history, or such histories, must also embody the values of the present. The subjective nature of historical research (or any research), which to Dilthey and Simmel seemed a barrier to our knowledge of the world, was for Weber an instrument for the acquisition of ever more exact and extensive knowledge of the cultural world. All that had to be given up was the quest for certainty.

Weber's solution to the methodological problems of the human sciences was his theory of ideal types.[129] This theory originated in his consideration of economic research, and is best illustrated by another somewhat lengthy quotation:

---

128   Weber, pp. 32–3.

129   "Weber developed his theory of the ideal type as a consequence of his participation in heated discussions over the nature of social-scientific knowledge which characterized the Methodenstreit of his day. The two poles of the Methodenstreit were represented by subjectivists and positivists, and their dispute, in its simplest terms, can be reduced to an argument over the nature of social-scientific knwowledge. The subjectivists maintained that social-scientific knowledge is inherently subjective – that is, concerned exclusively with human meaning and values – and thus is radically different from the knowledge of the natural sciences. The positivists maintained just the opposite: social-scientific knowledge could be obtained through the same methods as those employed in the natural sciences and thus social-scientific knowledge is just as "scientific" as that of the natural sciences.

"In the broadest terms, Weber's position can be interpreted as an attempt to synthesize the best aspects of both these positions. His intent was to retain the subjective grounding of the social sciences while, at the same time, providing a "scientific" basis for social-scientific research. But Weber's position was profoundly influenced by

We have in abstract economic theory an illustration of those synthetic constructs which have been designated as "ideas" of historical phenomena. It offers us an ideal picture of events on the commodity market under conditions of a society organized on the principles of an exchange economy, free competition and rigorously rational conduct. This conceptual pattern brings together certain relationships and events of historical life into a complex, which is conceived as an internally consistent system. Substantively, this construct in itself is like a utopia which has been arrived at by the analytical accentuation of certain elements of reality. Its relationship to the empirical data consists solely in the fact that where market-conditioned relationships of the type referred to by the abstract construct are discovered or suspected to exist in reality to some extent, we can make the characteristic features of this relationship pragmatically clear and understandable by reference to an ideal-type. This procedure can be indispensable for heuristic as well as expository purposes. The ideal typical concept will help to develop our skill in imputation in research: it is no "hypothesis" but it offers guidance to the construction of hypotheses. It is not a description of reality but it aims to give unambiguous means of expression to such a description . . . An ideal type is formed by the one-sided accentuation of one or more points of view and by the synthesis of a great many diffuse, discrete, more or less present and occasionally absent concrete individual phenomena, which are arranged according to those one-sidedly emphasized viewpoints into a unified analytical construct.[130]

Weber does not claim that ideal typical constructs are true, only that they are useful:

whether we are dealing simply with a conceptual game or with a scientifically fruitful method of conceptualization and theory-construction can never be decided a priori. Here, too, there is only one criterion, namely, that of success in revealing concrete cultural phenomena in their interdependence, their causal conditions and their significance. The construction of ideal-types recommends itself not as an end but as a means.[131]

---

other attempts at synthesis advanced by participants in the Method-enstreit, particularly Rickert and Windelband, as well as by the theories of Emil Lask." Susan J. Hekman, **Weber, the Ideal Type and Contemporary Social Theory** (Notre Dame, Indiana: University of Notre Dame Press, 1983), pp. 19–20.

[130]   Weber, p. 17.

[131]   Weber, p. 19.

After we have completed our ideal typical construction, which is formed from the contemplation of empirical data, we can go back to the data and examine it more carefully in the light of the model. (Thus Weber revived, and demystified, Dilthey's hermeneutical circle.) He refined the theory of knowledge in the human sciences by a methodological consideration, dividing the historical "investigation into two parts: on the one side stands the construction of an ideal and rational activity and on the other the description of the real, concrete activity which, in comparison with the pure schema, will reveal the irrational deviations and the intervening causes which determine them."[132] Weber, unlike some of his critics, was always careful in his methodological writings to emphasize that the ideal typical construct is artificial:

> since value orientation is involved, our ideal typical construct of, say, an epoch or a doctrine, for the purpose of penetrating their meaning, will certainly differ from the concept formed of that epoch by those who lived it, or from the meaning of the doctrine which its proponents attached to it. Depending on the nature of our research, we can construct the ideal type of liberalism on the basis of the values to which its proponents related social conditions, but we can also construct other ideal types by relating liberalism to our own values or to those of an opposing school of thought.[133]

Weber had considered the theories and precepts of his forerunners in the historical sciences. He had little patience with the "past-mindedness" advocated by historians in the tradition of Ranke, whom he characterized as "the modern relativistically educated historian . . . [who] on the one hand seeks to 'understand' the epoch of which he speaks 'in its own terms,' and on the other still seeks to 'judge' it, . .". Weber believed that "the elementary duty of scientific self-control and the only way to avoid serious and foolish blunders requires a sharp precise distinction between the logically comparative analysis of reality by ideal-types in the logical sense and the value-judgment of reality on the basis of ideals."[134] He was able to extend this critique to include those scholars of the pragmatic tradition, those who had opposed all uses of theory in the human sciences. In his usual forceful manner Weber wrote:

----

132   Antoni, p. 171.

133   Freund, p. 64.

134   Weber, p. 26.

If the historian [in the widest sense of the word] rejects an attempt to construct such ideal types as a "theoretical construction," i.e., as useless or dispensable for his concrete heuristic purposes, the inevitable consequence is either that he consciously or unconsciously uses similar concepts without formulating them verbally and elaborating them logically or that he remains stuck in the realm of the vaguely felt.[135]

The realm of intuition and that of the vaguely felt were concepts for which Weber had nothing but scorn: "Let him who wants intuition go to the cinema."[136] Less off-handedly, Julian Freund explicates Weber's derogation of intuitional understanding in this way:

intuition pertains to the realm of feeling and is therefore not a means of scientific cognition, for not only does the latter require the elaboration and construction of concepts, but those concepts must also be precisely defined. Their place can never be taken by experience, which is diffuse, personal, incommunicable and unverifiable. It is an esthetic, and not a scientific approach to reality.[137]

The primary exponent of the use of intuition in the human sciences had been Dilthey, who "had . . . observed that in historical knowledge there was to be found something more than what was contained in naturalistic knowledge. This was what he called 'understanding through reliving.' Weber pointed out that it was not enough to merely relive in order to understand."[138] But Weber took Dilthey seriously enough to make a thorough-going analysis of Dilthey's final appeal to a scientific psychology as the basis for understanding in the human sciences:

Abstract theory purported to be based on psychological axioms and as a result historians have called for an empirical psychology in order to show the invalidity of those axioms and to derive the course of economic events from psychological principles. We do not wish at this point to enter into a detailed criticism of the belief in the significance of a – still to be created – systematic science of "social psychology" as the future foundation of the cultural sciences, and particularly of social economics. Indeed, the partly brilliant attempts which have been made hitherto to interpret economic phenomena psychologically show in any

---

135   Weber, pp. 21–2.

136   Antoni, p. 123.

137   Freund, pp. 44–5.

138   Antoni, p. 170.

case that the procedure does not begin with the analysis of psychological qualities, moving then to the analysis of social institutions, but that, on the contrary, insight into the psychological preconditions and consequences of institutions presupposes a precise knowledge of the latter and the scientific analysis of their structure.[139]

Weber's theory of ideal types was the summation, as well as the solution, of the controversy about the nature of the human sciences that loomed as one of the crucial issues of Central European philosophical thought in the years 1880 to 1920. It can be applied reflexively to that controversy itself in order to demonstrate that Dilthey and Simmel, as well as Rickert and Tönnies, were exponents of various "one-sidedly accentuated models" of knowledge and society. Weber's theory, as set forth in his methodological writings, is the basis for many of our current ideas of how to conduct research not only in the human but also in the natural sciences. It is quite similar to other theories of model building that had their origins in Central Europe at that time: Boltzmann's techniques in physics, for instance, and Wittgenstein's picture theory of meaning, as well as some aspects of Freud's work. Unfortunately, in his practice, especially in **Economy and Society,** Weber was liable to fall into the trap of reifying his models, so that that otherwise impressive book often gives the sense of being merely a parade of two dimensional sketches of social relations. Thus H. Stuart Hughes is at least partially correct in his assessment of Weber's achievement: "In refusing to recognize anything absolute about value-judgments – in abandoning all metaphysical support for ethical or practical norms – Weber had taken his leave of Rickert and come close to the world of twilight relativism in which Dilthey had dwelt."[140] It may be observed that this journey into the twilight had taken place by way of a long detour, a detour which in itself was a solid accomplishment. There is a tremendous difference between the despairing embrace of relativism, arrived at through little more than the pure contemplation of the infinite nature of the empirical world, and the utilization of relativism as a mode of scientific research. Weber's work, rightly understood, can be seen as having pushed back the boundaries of the irrational, giving us more light in the human world. And yet, in the end, Weber arrived at a position even more suspect than that of Dilthey, a position, in some respects, close to that of Simmel. According to Carlo Antoni,

Dilthey had pointed out the modern "anarchy of values." Weber accepted it: "Anyone who lives in the world cannot avoid experiencing within him a struggle between the plurality of values, each of which appears binding when taken by itself. It is necessary to choose which of

---

139   Weber, pp. 15–6.

140   Hughes, p. 310.

these gods one wishes to serve, but regardless of the choice, he will always find himself in conflict with one of the other gods of the world." . . . As in Kierkegaard and the "crisis theologians," faith, for Weber, had become a commitment.[141]

Or perhaps, more exactly, commitment had taken the place of faith.

When he went to Heidelberg to study under Weber, Lukács, then, had been working in an intellectual world dominated by a negatively charged concept of totality: the infinite extension and intension of all possible facts and viewpoints, the alien and alienating world of human culture – bureaucratic, over-populated, disruptive of the dearly held values of community and continuity. The human mind was taken to be engaged in a process of forming its perceptions of this totality, in self-defense, through the imposition of still other points of view or values. For Simmel, Lukács's earlier teacher, these forms had been arbitrary and somewhat desperate; for Weber they were the necessary instruments of the progress of science itself. In the period 1907 to 1916 Lukács was to move from Impressionism to the subjectivist relativism of Simmel to the objectivist relativism of Weber. At that point he parted company with sociology and embarked on voyages of commitment unknown in Heidelberg. His work in **The Theory of the Novel** on a typology of the novel might be taken as an illustration of the consequences of ignoring Weber's warning that the ideal-types are models, not realities. This was a natural consequence of personal and social concerns that had little to do with scholarship, and we shall conclude by indicating that this tendency to privilege the enabling values of research over research itself is one shared by many of those who, in our own day as well as in his, subscribe to an ideology of the spirit.

---

[141]   Antoni, pp. 141–2.

THE THEORY OF THE NOVEL

Soul and Form illustrates Lukács's transition from Impressionism to mysticism by way of Simmel's Neo-Kantianism. **The Theory of the Novel** shows us the result of adding to those already sufficiently composite tendencies Hegelianism and a version of Weber's methodology of ideal forms. The Hegelian influences in **The Theory of the Novel** are well known and have been widely discussed.[142] Yet we should not simply designate the work as "Hegelian" and leave it at that. As in the preceding chapters **Soul and Form** was analyzed as a record of the dynamic resolution of certain early influences on Lukács, we turn now to **The Theory of the Novel** in order to pursue the understanding of that text, also, beyond mere categorizing, Hegelian (or Marxist]) or otherwise. We will find, in particular, the influence of Dilthey, an influence felt as an aestheticization of philosophy, a tendency to use literature for "spiritual" purposes, welling up through the more Apollonian Weberian apparatus.

As there has been much recent "reading" of **The Theory of the Novel** as an idea of a Lukács, rather then as a specific collection of words and ideas, it might be useful to begin with an old fashioned close reading of the work's first paragraph, to ground us, as it were, in its actual meaning and context.

Selig sind die Zeiten, für die der Sternenhimmel die Landkarte der gangbaren und zu gehenden Wege ist und deren Wege das Licht der Sterne erhellt. Alles ist neu für sie und dennoch vertraut, abenteuerlich und dennoch Besitz. Die Welt ist weit und doch wie das eigene Haus, denn das Feuer, das in der Seele brennt, ist von derselben Wesensart wie die Sterne; sie scheiden sich scharf, die Welt und das Ich, das Licht und das Feuer, und werden doch niemals einander für immer fremd; denn Feuer ist die Seele eines jeden Lichts und in Licht kleidet sich ein jedes Feuer. So wird alles Tun der Seele sinvoll und rund in dieser Zweiheit: vollendet in dem Sinn und vollendet für die Sinne; rund, weil die Seele in sich ruht während des Handelns; rund, weil ihre Tat sich

---

142 Martin Jay, **The Dialectical Imagination** (Boston: Little, Brown and Company, 1973), p. 201.

von ihr ablöst und selbstgeworden einen eigenen Mittelpunkt findet und einen geschlossenen Umkreis um sich zieht. "Philosophie ist eigentlich Heimweh," sagt Novalis, "der Trieb, uberall zu Hause zu sein."[143]

"Selig sind die Zeiten. . . ." [Blessed are those Ages . . .], Lukács plunges us at once out of the social disquiet of his early twentieth century into the "sacerdotal" time of the Golden Age, out of history and into the closed loops of a non-spatial reality where individual actions are mere reflections of archetypal actions and are real only insofar as they are faithful to the details of those archetypes.[144] "Selig" does not simply mean happy, but can also mean blissful or blessed, conveying a religious happiness; the word in this sense is traditionally used with reference to the recently dead and so carries with it the promise of salvation. "Zeiten" [Ages] is explicitly an ahistorical signifier, pointing to the geographical-temporal confusion which is characteristic of literature concerning such matters as the Golden Age and the Isles of the Blessed.[145] The opening phrase as a whole, "Selig sind die Zeiten," tells us that Lukács believed, or professed to believe, that there exist certain areas of human being-in-the-world where or when the living, simply by being alive at such a time or in such a place, are in a state of grace similar to that of those who have died and gone to Heaven. Such a beginning would seem to indicate that the mode of thought to be followed in **The Theory of the Novel** is the dialectic of the ideal forms of Platonizing mystics and the Life Philosophers, a mode of thought aimed at the invocation, at least, of the "spiritual" equivalent of the non-alienated community celebrated by Tönnies.

". . . für die der Sternenhimmel die Landkarte der gangbaren und zu gehenden Wege ist. . . ." [when the starry sky is the map of all possible paths. . . .] The starry heaven is the map of all possible paths or roads precisely when the point of view adopted is that of a sacramental universe. Spiritualism and astrology were much in the air at the time that Lukács was writing **The Theory of the Novel.** The Babylonian term for sky is composed of the same "starry heaven" combination as is the German "Sternenhimmel,"

---

143   Georg Lukács, **Die Theorie des Romans** (Neuwied und Berlin: Hermann Luchterhand, 1963), p. 22.

144   In "the 'primitive' ontological conception: an object or an act becomes real only insofar as it imitates or repeats an archetype. Thus, reality is acquired solely through repetition or participation; everything which lacks an exemplary model is 'meaningless,' i.e., it lacks reality." Mircea Eliade, **The Myth of the Eternal Return** (New York: Bollingen Foundation, 1965), p. 34.

145   Arthur O. Lovejoy and George Boas, **Primitivism and Related Ideas in Antiquity** (New York: Octagon Books, 1965).

and this further helps to locate the mode of thought present here as referring to the astrological world view native to that land between the rivers.[146] In the terms of that world view the starry heaven of the universe is actually a map of humanity's path through the world, both for the physical purposes of navigation and for the spiritual mode of navigation by means of horoscopes. The method of anthropocentric astronomy was one common to the Babylonians, the Hellenistic system of Ptolemy, and the Christian Middle Ages. Reference to it is an indicator of an ahistorical system of thought, closed to both random and dynamic historical factors. Within such an imaginative framework Lukács would have been quite justified in asserting that in a Golden Age the stars are a map of all earthly possibilities. This is not to say that Lukács "believed" in astrology. He is simply indicating an association. The myths of the Golden Age presuppose a closed universe: anthropocentric, finite, and safe. It is, as a matter of fact, this closure itself that is the motivation for such forms of thought. The myths of the eternal return are the social projection of the horror of individuals faced with the (Neo-Kantian) endless openness of profane history.[147]

". . . und deren Wege das Licht Der Sterne erhellt." [ages whose paths are illuminated by the light of the stars.] The paths, which in the preceding phrase had been as much spiritual as physical, in this phrase are illuminated by starlight, just as if they were mere nighttime footpaths. Or, at least that would have been the case, except that the ambiguity of "erhellt" brings the double meanings back, so that the stars as light sources illuminate the paths, as roads, and also the stars as heavenly indications of God's Will show us the courses which our lives are to follow. The stars do this, that is, if we live in one of those ages which Lukács wished to believe were blessed by virtue of this situation. The entire first sentence of **the Theory of the Novel** is something of an incantation. Lukács was not using his words as signifiers of any ordinary signified; he was using them to indicate a utopian wish. There are no material referents for such statements: ultimately they refer to the histories of their own forms.

---

146 "Sennacherib has Nineveh built according to the form . . . delineated from distant ages by the writing of the 'heaven-of-stars.' Not only does a model precede terrestial architecture, but the model is also situated in an ideal (celestial) region of eternity." Eliade, p. 8.

147 "We emphasize once again that, from the point of view of anhistorical peoples or classes, 'suffering' is equivalent to 'history.'" "Hence it is more probable that the desire felt by the man of traditional societies to refuse history, and to confine himself to an indefinite repetition of archetypes, testifies to his thirst for the real and his terror of 'losing' himself by letting himself be overwhelmed by the meaninglessness of profane existence." Eliade, p. 97, footnote 2, and p. 92.

"Alles ist neu für sie und dennoch vertraut. . . ." [Everything in such ages is new and yet familiar. . . .] In a Golden Age, in Paradise, out of history, everything is new and yet familiar. When everything is new, we see everything with a particular clarity, our eyes freed of the clouds of habit. Such a vision is said to be "childlike," or "as on the first day of Creation," "made strange," or "defamiliarized." The novelty of the new is that it impresses us with the radical otherness of things. It might be said that we only actually see an object when we see it as if for the first time. ("As if" for the first time, because when we actually perceive something for the first time, we often do not see it at all, being unprepared for perception.) It is, therefore, a further perfection of the Blessed Times that perceptions then are in the condition least likely to cause the agony resulting from the knowledge of the differences between the object, the subject, and the representation. It is only then that novelty can be seen as being "intimate," "familiar," "trusted," and so not so much the outrageous other as it is in less favored times, such as Tönnies's world of societal alienation or Simmel's horror shop of unfamiliar cultural clutter.

". . . abenteuerlich und dennoch Besitz." [. . . full of adventure and yet their own.] The Edenic world is a space of adventure, of venturing out from the known, which, in our world always means going out into the unknown. According to Lukács's first mentor, Georg Simmel:

> the most general form of adventure is its dropping out of the continuity of life . . . while it falls outside the context of life, it falls, with this same movement, as it were, back into that context again . . . it is a foreign body in our existence which is yet somehow connected with the center; the outside, if only by a long and unfamiliar detour, is formally an aspect of the inside . . . the perception of contrast characteristic of adventure is that an action is completely torn out of the inclusive context of life and that simultaneously the whole strength and intensity of life stream into it.[148]

But in the Blessed Ages, adventures only serve to bring the adventurer further into the known familiar. This unusual situation is structured by the great map of the Zodiac, which allows the "blessed," always knowing the way home, to play as much as they care to on a path constantly illuminated through the darkness of the dialectical twin of the Blessed Times, that is, history itself. There are no adventures, in this sense, in history; there are only actions and their consequences. The function of Lukács's Blessed Ages is to act as the utopian denial of history, its agony and its sorrows.

---

[148] Georg Simmel, "The Adventurer," in **Georg Simmel: On Individuality and Social Forms,** ed. D.H. Levine (Chicago: University of Chicago Press, 1971).

"Die Welt ist weit und doch wie das eigene Haus. . . ." [The world is
wide and yet it is like a home . . .] The third set of oppositions in this
paragraph is that which defines the world as being both wide and
homelike.[149] Each of the three oppositions constitutes a pair united by the
sacred character of the Blessed Ages. The world is stated progressively to
be new, full of adventure, and wide, while still remaining familiar, our own,
and like a home. Gesellschaft has been denied. This world is that of
comfortable Gemeinschaft. There is only one place that we all know that
corresponds to these conditions and that place is childhood. This is
conveyed much more forcibly by the expression "Das eigene Haus" than by
the English "like a home." For it is certainly our own house that is the wide
world, new, yet familiar, of childhood. And it is the repeated history in each
individual of the gradual acquaintance of the world of childhood, and its
end, that is projected back into the childhood of the race as the myth of the
Golden Age.

". . . denn das Feuer, Das in der Seele brennt, ist von derselben
Wesensart wie die Sterne . . ." [. . . for the fire that burns in the soul is of
the same essential nature as the stars . . .] The world, at such times, is also
homelike, according to Lukács, because it is known by means of the
internalized essential nature of the stars. The divine spark of the soul is
characterized here as starlight. The stars themselves are the materialized
Will of God, as the Zodiac; so, in the Blessed Ages, the soul is synonymous
with the Will of God.

There can be no religious loneliness in such a world, no loss of faith, no
doubt, none of that distance between subject and object that was the focus
of so much anguish for those first generations who had experienced the
death of God in the passing of Christian Europe after the French and
Industrial Revolutions. Lukács was looking toward an earlier world where
one had no misgivings, because all knowledge of the outside was
internalized. This is the end of the road followed by the essayist. It is a
short circuit of the Kierkegaardian dialectic.

". . . sie scheiden sich scharf, die Welt und das Ich, das Licht und das
Feuer, und werden doch niemals einander für immer fremd. . . ." [. . . the
world and the self, the light and the fire, are sharply distinct, yet they never
become permanent strangers to one another . . .] Here two more sets of
opposites appear: The first involving the world and the self, the second
putting the "light" against "fire." These opposites are said in each case to be
sharply distinguished, but never permanently estranged from one another.
The world is the home which is illuminated by the light from the fire of the

---

149 Weber's influence on the Lukács of this period is evident in this
      relentless use of binary oppositions, among other things. See Fredric
      Jameson's interesting article on Weber, "The Vanishing Mediator," in
      Working Papers in Cultural Studies, 5 (Spring 1974), 111–49.

stars, which also burns in the soul or the self. "Feuer" here is being transmitted from the essential substance of the stars and the soul, into the hearth fire of the intimate home, linked as it is in the parallel statements with the self in opposition to the world. The world, then, is being compared to light, which has a quality of the other, being the messenger of the Will of God, travelling from the stars to the soul.

". . . denn Feuer ist die Seele eines jeden Lichts und in Licht kleidet sich ein jedes Feuer." [. . . for fire is the soul of all light and all fire clothes itself in light.] Light and fire are related to each other, as fire is the essential nature, the soul, of light, and always displays itself by means of an enveloping light. The rhetorical metaphysics of the early Lukács reflects at this point the influence of the ancient Iranian cosmology of light and its descendants through Platonism and various strands of Christian and Kabbalistic thought. As fire and light cannot become "strangers" to each other because fire is the essential nature of light, so, perhaps, in the Blessed Ages the self is the essential part of the great Self of the world, for which reason in those times there is no alienation of the individual from the world. It is characteristic of the various systems of light metaphysics to emphasize the all-pervasive nature of light and the way in which it can extinguish the particularity of the individual soul. Light, then, is symbolic of a celestial Gemeinschaft.

"So wird alles Tun der Seele sinnvoll und rund in dieser Zwiheit . . ." [Thus each action of the soul becomes meaningful and rounded in this duality: . . .] In these Blessed Ages there is a natural perfection embodied in the three pairs of unity of the world noted above, as well as in the fact that each action of the soul becomes rounded and meaningful as a result of those dualities. A rounded perfection of action is apparently more wonderful, as a perfection, than the perfection of stasis. Each action of the soul becomes meaningful and rounded because there is no alienation between the individual and the world: the light which shows the individual soul its path through the world is the Will of God. The emblem of this identity is the conception of roundness, which, from the time of Pythagoras, has been a symbol of divine perfection.

". . . vollendet in dem Sinn und vollendet für die Sinne. . . ." [. . . complete in meaning - in sense - and complete for the senses . . .] All actions of the soul are fulfilled for the mind and they are also fulfilled and complete for the senses. The representation of reality and the perception of reality are in complete agreement as to the perfection of all the actions of the soul, and, if this is true, then there are no doubts as to the reality of either the world of the senses or the world of ideas. In other words, these problems, which have so tormented philosophers, are problems that arise in connection with the Fall, and did not exist before then. (This is part of the meaning of Plato's myth of an Ur-humanity, with four arms and four legs, and their differentiation into the incomplete human beings of the present era.)   Lukács thus resolves the Neo-Kantian subject/object dilemma by means of Neo-Platonic metaphysics.

"... rund, weil die Seele in sicht ruht während des Heandelns. . . ." [. . . rounded because the soul rests within itself even while it acts . . .] "Rund," in Lukács's phrase, has become another name for perfection, rather than simply an attribute of perfect being. The "round actions of the soul" are perfect actions, because action, which usually implies imperfection (if Being is perfect it need not act), is in this case simultaneously action and nonaction, which is, in this system of thought, rest. Thus, the particular type of action that Lukács refers to, the particular type of journeys that are being taken, are not those common to the ages that are not "blessed."

"... rund, weil ihre Tat sich von ihr ablöst und selbstgeworden einen eigenen Mittelpunkt findetund einen geschlossenen Umkreis um sich zieht." [. . . rounded because its action separates itself from it and, having become itself, finds a center of its own and draws a closed circumference around itself.] The actions of the soul are said by Lukács to be rounded because they first separate themselves from the soul, and then return to it, having found a true center and "closed the circle." This action is the type of Neo-Platonic love, action going out, being reflected, and drawing back into the primary center.[150] The soul and the self are their own center as we know they are part of the same fire which is that of the stars and have no need to go yearning after rest in some other totality. Not only is each action of the soul rounded, as it were, in three dimensions, but it is also rounded in the two dimensions of the unmoved "Mittelpunkt." The soul, in the Blessed Ages, does not change, it is at rest, asleep, as it were, in the perfect triple roundness of its own being at one with the world.

"'Philosophie ist eigentlich Heimweh,' sagt Novalis, 'der Trieb, überall zu Hause zu sein.'" ['Philosophy is really homesickness,' says Novalis, 'It is the urge to be at home everywhere.'] Novalis's epigramatic definition of philosophy as homesickness brings Lukács's introductory statement to a conclusion, allowing us to observe that philosophy, in this tradition, is a drive which attempts to dissolve the otherness of the world and to bring the self back to the condition of the Blessed Ages, when it was at one with the world and all was single, rounded, at rest and at home. The first paragraph of **The Theory of the Novel** can be seen as the answer to the problems posed by the last paragraph of the Hungarian "On the Nature and Form of the Essay." The essayist has indeed found a road down which he is "going, going, going . . ." and that road leads to the perfect world of the Golden Age, the Heavenly Jerusalem of revealed faith, which could, therefore, stand shining in the distance, as a measure of the depth to which modern humanity had fallen.

---

150   Edgar Wind, **Pagan Mysteries in the Renaissance** (Harmondsworth: Penguin Books, Ltd., 1967).

Happy are those ages when the starry sky is the map of all possible paths – ages whose paths are illuminated by the light of the stars. Everything in such ages is new and yet familiar, full of adventure and yet their own. The world is wide and yet it is like a home, for the fire that burns in the soul is of the same essential nature as the stars; the world and the self, the light and the fire, are sharply distinct, yet they never become permanent strangers to one another, for fire is the soul of all light and all fire clothes itself in light. Thus each action of the soul becomes meaningful and rounded in this duality: complete in meaning – in sense – and complete for the senses; rounded because the soul rests within itself even while it acts; rounded because its action separates itself from it and, having become itself, finds a centre of its own and draws a closed circumference round itself. 'Philosophy is really homesickness,' says Novalis, 'It is the urge to be at home everywhere.'[151]

A reader, picking up a volume entitled **The Theory of the Novel** and immediately encountering the passage quoted above would be readily forgiven for considering it as pure convention or as ornamentation, an invocation of the Muse to be disregarded in the search for, and analysis of, the scientific "theory" of the novel apparently to be found later in the book. But "interpretation proceeds by steps, and the first step on which everything else depends is the decision to which genre a given work is to be assigned."[152] To decide prematurely that **The Theory of the Novel** belongs to the genre of technical literary criticism, or even to the general category of Lukács's later works **Writer and Critic** or **The Historical Novel,** would be to run the risk of an interpretation so odd as to be useless for understanding. If we have learned nothing else from the last forty years of literary criticism in the United States, we should, at least, have learned to read carefully. A careful reading of the first paragraph of **The Theory of the Novel** cannot but demonstrate the extreme oddity, in our context, of the language and thought used there. That oddity can, to be sure, be simply dismissed as a personal eccentricity on the part of the young Lukács. On the other hand, finding the passage to be exceedingly marvelous,[153] we

151   Georg Lukács, trans. Anna Bostock **The Theory of the Novel** (Cambridge, Mass.: The M.I.T. Press, 1971), p. 29. Further page references in the text are to this edition.

152   E. H. Gombrich, **Symbolic Images** (London: Phaidon Press, 1972), p. 21. See also E. D. Hirsch, Jr., **Validity in Interpretation** (New Haven: Yale University Press, 1967).

153   "The Greeks said that marvel is the beginning of knowledge and where we cease to marvel we may be in danger of ceasing to know." E. H.

may find there a beginning of knowledge, or if not that, at least a beginning of interpretation.

For interpretation, not only context, but the mediations between the context and the literary work are all-important. The context of a paragraph, for instance, is, first of all, the paragraphs around it, and then the work as a whole, and then the other literary works of the author and his or her contemporaries, and so forth until we reach general history. The structural analysis of **The Theory of the Novel** has been performed by Fredric Jameson, so that we can see that: "all of Lukács' analyses of the novel depend on what is a kind of literary nostalgia, on the notion of a golden age or lost Utopia of narration in Greek epic."[154] This "notion," which Jameson derives from the typology of **The Theory of the Novel,** can be found immediately in the language of our paragraph, and thus the stylistic move toward genre classification is confirmed by the structural analysis of the whole. Moving back and forth between the whole and the part in our own hermeneutical circle, we must next move beyond the text.[155]

If the typologies of literary form in **The Theory of the Novel** look forward to those of society in **History and Class Consciousness,** the closest text to the former work, both stylistically and chronologically, is not that volume of Marxist theory, but the Impressionistic **Soul and Form.** We remember that in the opening chapter of that book Lukács asked:

Why, after all, do we read essays? Many are read as a source of instruction, but there are others whose attraction is to something quite different. It is not difficult to identify these. Our view, our appreciation of classical tragedy is quite different today, is it not, from Lessing's in the **Dramaturgy,** Winckelmann's Greeks seem strange, almost incomprehensible to us, and soon we may feel the same about Burckhardt's Renaissance. And yet we read them: why? On the other hand there are critical writings which, like a hypothesis in natural science, like a design for a machine part, lose all their value at the precise moment when a new and better one becomes available. But if − as I hope and expect − someone were to write a new **Dramaturgy,** a

---

Gombrich, **Art and Illusion** (New York: The Bollingen Foundation, Pantheon, Random House, 1961), p. 8.

154 Fredric Jameson, **Marxism and Form** (Princeton: Princeton University Press, 1974), p. 179.

155 Claudio Guillén has observed that "As far as the literary historian is concerned, a [literary] system is operative when no single element can be comprehended or evaluated correctly in isolation from the historical whole . . . of which it is a part." Claudio Guillén, **Literature as System** (Princeton: Princeton University Press, 1971), p. 378.

Dramaturgy in favor of Corneille and against Shakespeare – how could it damage Lessing's? And what did Burckhardt and Pater, Rhode and Nietzsche do to change the effect upon us of Winckelmann's dreams of Greece?[156]

The imagery which assimilates certain types of essayistic writing to that of scientific inquiry or to machinery gives that writing a negative sign, placing it on the inorganic side of the organic/inorganic dichotomy, where, as community is to society and as culture is to civilization, the inorganic signifies the new, the unpleasant, the foreign. We also know a later passage which indicates on which side the Lukács of 1910 felt most comfortable placing himself: "the writings which most resolutely reject the image, which reach out most passionately for what lies behind the image, are the writings of the critics, the Platonists and the mystics."[157]

In order to understand **The Theory of the Novel** it is necessary first to take its language seriously. We cannot regard it merely as a belated example of Impressionism, the work of a Central European follower of Symonds and Pater, carrying with it a critical content that is somehow detachable from its rhetoric. (Such fine writing, like the Art Nouveau itself, achieving a particularly extravagant flowering on the banks of the Danube.) The rhetoric, when closely scrutinized, may be seen as the essential content of the work, a rhetoric, a style of thought, that is typical of the Romantic tradition of German literature, a tradition dating at least from Winckelmann, with its longing for a mythic Greece where the citrons are always blooming, and frequently exemplified by the casting of these Saturnalian longings in the form of books ostensibly about aesthetics, history, or critical theory.[158] **The Theory of the Novel**, like its model, Schiller's **Naive and Sentimental Poetry,** fits quite well into the "Platonist" tradition referred to earlier, a species of Golden Age mythologizing, a genre characterized by longings for spiritual plenitude in a world located with considerable ambiguity as to geography and time, one that definitely could exist only outside of history. Lukács's words, in the 1962 "Preface" to **The Theory of the Novel**, also need to be taken seriously: "the author was not looking for a new literary form but, quite explicitly, for a 'new world.'" (20) That "new world" was as little social as literary, and if it was not as specifically sectarian as that of

---

156   Lukács, **Soul and Form,** p. 2.

157   Lukács, **Soul and Form,** p. 6.

158   Here we might remember Freud's significant experience of the "impossibility" of going to Athens, an Athens located, for that typical cultured Central European, in a Golden Age outside reality. See Sigmund Freud, "A Disturbance of Memory on the Acropolis," in **Collected Papers** (London: The Hogarth Press Ltd. and The Institute of Psycho-Analysis, 1950), V, p. 302.

Lukács's friend Buber, it was most certainly religious.

We can gain some idea of what the Lukacs of **The Theory of the Novel** meant by such puzzling but crucial terms as "roundness" in that first paragraph by consulting a later passage: "In Giotto and Dante, Wolfram von Eschenbach and Pisano, St. Thomas and St. Francis, the world became round once more, a totality capable of being taken in at a glance . . . A new and paradoxical Greece came into being: aesthetics became metaphysics once more" (37-8). If something is round, it is a totality "capable of being taken in at a glance"; its meaning is immanent. Here we are once again in the midst of the triangle of critic, Platonist, and mystic. In order to understand the seriousness of that positive valorization of metaphysics, a valorization that approves of the collapse of analysis into idealism, we must move once more away from the text and into intellectual history.

> Friedrich Schlegel once wrote that the French Revolution, Fichte's doctrine of science and Goethe's **Wilhelm Meister** represented the greatest events of the age. This juxtaposition is characteristic of the tragedy and greatness of the German cultural movement. For Germany, there was only one way to culture: the inner way, the way of revolution of the spirit; no one could seriously envisage a real revolution. Men destined for action had to fall silent and wither away, or else they became mere utopians and played games with bold possibilities in the mind.[159]

We need not move far. The author of the above observation in the essay "On the Romantic Philosophy of Life," which we have referred to more than once, was the slightly earlier Lukács of **Soul and Form**. The retrospective ironies of the passage need no comment; we will simply take its obvious point and note that the "intellectual tendency" of the Central European intelligentsia at the beginning of the twentieth century, as it had been at the beginning of the nineteenth, was to deny the existence of a social order that appeared to be too oppressive to accept and too powerful to change.

Lukács has written that **The Theory of the Novel** was "inspired" by the onset of the First World War.

> At first it was meant to take the form of a series of dialogues: a group of young people withdraw from the war psychosis of their environment, just as the story-tellers of the **Decameron** had withdrawn from the plague; they try to understand themselves and one another by means of conversations which gradually lead to the problems discussed in the book – the outlook on a Dostoevskian world.[160]

---

[159] Lukács, **Soul and Form**, p. 43.

[160] **The Theory of the Novel**, p. 12. For more information about the

This withdrawal into a Florentine tower from which one looks out on the world was a characteristic movement of turn of the century Life Philosophy. Thus, social thought is removed to "higher ground." It was no accident that this school of philosophy arose in the authoritarian states of late-nineteenth-century Central Europe, where a politically powerless middle class, trapped between a landholding ruling class and an increasingly desperate working class, saw many advantages in a world view that had minimal contact with social and historical reality and maximum contact with the world as lived experience, that is, as intimate emotion. Although it will not do to move from an "entire social, economic, or intellectual system" directly to the "single literary work,"[161] any more than it will do to move directly the other way, still, it is not surprising that the typical work of the "Intellectual Sciences" school of thought was written by a member of an ennobled banking family, isolated by language, religion, and class.

> Hofmannsthal in one of his dialogues makes Balzac differentiate between two types of men: the life-capacity of one is crystallized in drama, that of the other in the epic, so that one can imagine men who could live in a play but not in an epic. Perhaps these distinctions could be carried through all literary forms and a scale of life-capacities established according to each.[162]

Although the Lukács of **Soul and Form** was "Impressionist," "Neo-Kantian," and mystical, and the Lukács of **The Theory of the Novel** "mystical," "Hegelian," and Weberian (and the next three Lukácses Marxists of different types), we should not lose sight of the continuity among them. If already in the Hofmannsthal reference from **Soul and Form** we find the beginnings of the categorizing of **The Theory of the Novel**, we find in it, too, the odd evasions of the reality of historical life that characterizes most of the work. (Who are these men who live not in the world but in epics or dramas? What is the point of these categories of possible novels, containing only one or two examples?) There is the continuity, also, of the longing for wholeness throughout the work of all the Lukácses, a longing that remains a central value even after being stripped of its Kierkegaardian mysticism.[163]

---

intellectual atmosphere of the time, see Allan Janik and Stephen Toulmin, **Wittgenstein's Vienna** (New York: Simon and Schuster, 1973).

161 Guillén, pp. 418-9.

162 Lukács, **Soul and Form,** pp. 24-5.

163 I would like to thank John Beverly for first bringing to my attention

We are now ready for that step of interpretation which is "the decision to which genre a given work is to be assigned." As we have seen, **The Theory of the Novel** is of a Platonist lineage. An entire family of texts can be identified, a genre hitherto concealed as uneasy member of others: philosophical, historical, or critical. From Plato to Lessing, Nietzsche, Marcuse, and the Post-Structuralists, they seek (or regret) plenitude and transcendence, sharing a habitual nostalgia indistinguishable from utopianism. Such a philosophy "ist eigentlich Heimweh, der Trieb, uberall zu Hause zu sein." In this family **The Theory of the Novel** finds a true home. This genre is itself close to the prescription of the young Lukács, as influenced by Dilthey, the call for an aesthetics that is very nearly a metaphysics. Such texts are written in response to the intolerable pressures of social systems on individual human beings, and it is no accident that they frequently take the form of essays in aesthetics or aesthetic history, as a society's culture is one of the most sensitive indicators of its underlying health or malaise. The family resemblance of these texts prepares us to read **The Theory of the Novel,** as a wish, as, in a way, a novel or a fantasy, a search through literary history for exactly those lost Blessed Ages, for immanence, for God.

I was then in the process of turning from Kant to Hegel, without, however, changing any aspect of my attitude towards the so-called 'Intellectual Sciences' school, an attitude based essentially on my youthful enthusiasm for the work of Dilthey, Simmel and Max Weber. (12)

We have seen in earlier chapters that Lukács' "youthful enthusiasm" for Dilthey, Simmel, and Weber gave him a special approach to the study of literature, and that his interest in the first two resulted in a subjectivist Idealism as the basis for his work, an epistemological position often wrongly identified with Kant. These ideas lead to the conviction that the human world is a chaos upon which the mind must impose forms, forms which must be arbitrary to some extent. There is, especially under the influence of Hegelianism, an easy misinterpretation of Weber, which would result in similar ideas, misunderstanding the ideal-types as manifestations of Absolute Spirit rather than as heuristic models. As we have seen, Lukács's early literary criticism had been Impressionist, and inasmuch as it was self-consciously so, also based on subjectivist theories of knowledge. These came together in the later essays of **Soul and Form,** and in such individual pieces as "On the Poverty of Spirit," as a belief that writing as such, and in particular essayistic writing, is privileged as a mystic exercise,

---

Lukács's early interest in Kierkegaard.

as a path to God. It was during this period that Lukács impressed even the pious Marianna Weber as being notably possessed of Messianic religious beliefs.

The legacy of the German Romantic tradition, including the aesthetic writings of Hegel and Fichte, combined easily with Simmel's theories and the poetry of Endre Ady to charge literary creation with great spiritual importance. As the successor of the epic, poetry in particular was hardly discriminated from religious utterance and the novel at this time seemed to Lukács to be much more than an art form or craft among others; he conceived of it, in a version of Dilthey's philosophical stance, as a world-forming act, a way of making sense of the world. Keeping this in mind we should not find it unusual that the genesis of **The Theory of the Novel** was an ethical situation, not a literary question. "The immediate motive for writing was supplied by the outbreak of the First World War. . . . [Thus it was] written in a mood of permanent despair over the state of the world" (11-2). For Lukács this was the most direct means of coming to grips with ethical and epistemological problems. The beginning of **The Theory of the Novel** shows that the book's proper end is not the understanding of a few novels, or even of the nature of literary creation as such, but rather how one might best approach the ethical problems of living in an "age of absolute sinfulness." This is not to say that the book is without a true literary dimension. It is, on the contrary, steeped in the literary. It was important for Lukács, as for the other writers of his intellectual school, to bind together literature and ethics, form and spirit. He did this through an emphasis on genre. As a later Lukács observed:

> The author of **The Theory of the Novel** was looking for a general dialectic of literary genres that was based upon the essential nature of aesthetic categories and literary forms, and aspiring to a more intimate connection between category and history than he found in Hegel himself; he strove towards intellectual comprehension of permanence within change and of inner change within the enduring validity of the essence. (16)

If the methodology was now often Weberian, the motives were still those of the philosophers of Absolute Spirit and "Life."

This dialectic of genres is based on "the search for permanence within change" developed in the first part of the book. Although **The Theory of the Novel** has been read a good deal, the first, and by far the longest part, has generally been neglected in favor of the typology of the novel elaborated in the second part. To be properly understood, that typology must be set in the context of the book as a whole, indeed, as has been argued here, in the context of both Lukács's other early works and the intellectual climate of the times. Let us, then, return to our reading of that first part, not, to be sure, on the scale with which we have explicated the book's first paragraph, but at sufficient length to examine the piece's implications for the practice of criticism. This reading will take the form of an extended commentary on those passages of the first part of **The Theory of the Novel** that carry its main argument. This will bring out the unique qualities of Lukács's text, which are neither those of literary theory nor those of literary criticism, but derive from a pre-analytic, post-critical philosophy pressed into the service of a theoretical – rather than practical – negative theology.

The mature Lukács was often a perceptive critic of his earlier work (as well as being a subtle apologist for it, even while seeming to warn us against it). Recalling the composition of **The Theory of the Novel,** he noted that:

> The first, general part of the book is essentially determined by Hegel, e.g. the comparison of modes of totality in epic and dramatic art, the historico-philosophical view of what the epic and the novel have in common and of what differentiates them, etc. But the author of **The Theory of the Novel** was not an exclusive or orthodox Hegelian; Goethe's and Schiller's analyses, certain conceptions of Goethe's later period (e.g. the demonic), the young Friedrich Schlegel's and Solger's aesthetic theories (irony as a modern method of form filling), fill out and concretise the general Hegelian outline. (15)

That which is suppressed here is the heritage of Dilthey and the Neo-Kantians, a heritage the mature Lukács was not eager to acknowledge. The subtitle of the first chapter identifies its subject as "The forms of great epic literature examined in relation to whether the general civilisation of the time is an integrated or a problematic one." The subtitle is Hegelian in its phrasing in terms of epochs, Neo-Kantian and derived from Life Philosophy in that tell-tale word "forms." In this case the epochs are defined by reference to the available immanence of meaning, or the lack of it. Immanence for Lukács is the key to the dialectics of the structure of literary forms. Furthermore, he finds the interest of literary studies in the ethical concerns that concentrate on such Romantically and religiously charged concepts as the spiritual health of a society. This is evident from his definition of philosophy as "a form of life or as that which determines the form and supplies the content of literary creation . . ." (29). If philosophy is a form among forms, and futhermore has as its primary purpose the service of literary creation, then it seems clear that for Lukács, as for Dilthey, the study of literary works leads back directly to philosophical studies, or, at least, cannot be entirely distinguished from them.

We can go further than that, because the task of Lukács's philosophy was to draw an "archetypal map" which, in epic times; showed "how every impulse which springs from the innermost depths is co-ordinated with a form that it is ignorant of, but that has been assigned to it from eternity" (29-30). Literary form, then, is the working out of Absolute Spirit in literary history. Lukács takes the Romantic position that earlier historical periods develop into later periods on the model of childhood leading eventually to maturity. In epic times, "Being and destiny, adventure and accomplishment, life and essence are . . . identical concepts," because "then every action is only a well-fitting garment for the world" (30). These ages are the childhood of humanity.

After making this distinction Lukács turns from this reification of Greek culture to its manifestation in epic writing. (By epic writing Lukács means a general attitude. He hardly cites a work by title.) He believes the epic to be philosophically oriented in a peculiar fashion, namely one which takes philosophy to be the handmaiden of theology.

> The world of the epic answers the question: how can life become essential? But the answer ripened into a question only when the substance had retreated to a far horizon. Only when tragedy had supplied the creative answer to the question: how can essence come alive? did men become aware that life as it was (the notion of life as it should be cancels out life) had lost the immanence of the essence. (35)

In other words, the epic cannot be understood by persons in epic times, it can only be created by them. Just as the song of a bird is beautiful to us, but simply a manifestation of being for the bird, so the epic fullness of life can only be appreciated later, when it is felt as a loss. ("Essence" here has to do with unself-consciousness, the presence of the spiritual, a presence that can only be felt, at a later period, as an absence.) The same is true of tragedy.

> Just as the reality of the essence, as it discharges into life and gives birth to life, betrays the loss of its pure immanence in life, so this problematic basis of tragedy becomes visible, becomes a problem, only in philosophy; only when the essence, having completely divorced itself from life, became the sole and absolute, the transcendent reality, and when the creative act of philosophy had revealed tragic destiny as the cruel and senseless arbitrariness of the empirical, the hero's passion as earth-bound and his self-accomplishment merely as the limitation of the contingent subject, did tragedy's answer to the question of life and essence appear no longer as natural and self-evident but as a miracle, a slender yet firm rainbow bridging bottomless depths. (35-6)

The epic world speaks to the tragic and the tragic to the philosophic. Philosophy is an aesthetic form, if it is placed so, just as much as epic and tragedy. This blurring of categories, which runs both ways, making epic and tragedy as philosophical as Platonism, is at the heart of Lukacs's aesthetic dialectic, the point of his departure from the cooler analyses of Dilthey. Epic, tragedy, philosophy, are all forms of spirituality, possible roads of the soul to Immanence, or God. Which of these roads is open to the individual depends on the nature of the age.

As epic gives way to tragedy and that to philosophy, the loss in each case, in true Hegelian fashion, is also a consummation, a surpassing. For philosophy, "Plato's new man, the wise man with his active cognition and his essence–creating vision, does not merely unmask the tragic hero but also illuminates the dark peril the hero has vanquished; Plato's new wise man, by surpassing the hero, transfigures him" (36). (This is a peculiar interpretation of Plato on two counts. "The new man" is a Christian concept as much, if not more, than a Greek idea and "essence–creating vision" is a Neo–Kantian transformation of this Platonic essence–perceiving vision of the philosopher.) As Hegelian categories, the forms of the epic (or those of literature in general) arise in history, but they are not bound to history. "These stages are the great and timeless paradigmatic forms of world literature: epic, tragedy, philosophy" (35).

They can recur. Each successive civilization goes through them. This cyclical, rather than linear, approach to the philosophy of history is in opposition both to orthodox Christian and to secular historicism. The former is oriented by the three unique events of Creation, Incarnation, and Judgment, the latter recognizes only the first of these, if that, or perhaps only duration and change. The stages of Hegel's (or Vico's) philosophy of history, echoed by Lukács, are reified metaphors, or incompletely deconstructed remnants of an older way of thought. This causes Lukács to overstate his case. Wishing, apparently, to emphasize the religiosity of the Middle Ages as parallel to that of classical Greece, he turns the Meistersingers into Homeric bards. "A new and paradoxical Greece came into being: aesthetics became metaphysics once more." The lumping together of poets, painters, and mystics in order to arrive at a "spirit of the age" was characteristic of the Intellectual Sciences school and is still a favorite device of those seeking an alternative to well–mediated historical narrative. Although this is the dominant tendency in **The Theory of the Novel,** even Lukács saw that at least for his own time it was important to clearly differentiate between art and other modes of knowledge.

Henceforth, any resurrection of the Greek world is a more or less conscious hypostasy of aesthetics into metaphysics – a violence done to the essence of everything that lies outside the sphere of art, and a desire to destroy it; an attempt to forget that art is only one sphere among many, and that the very disintegration and inadequacy of the world is the precondition for the existence of art and its becoming conscious. . . . A totality that can be simply accepted is no longer given to the forms of art: therefore they must either narrow down and volatilise whatever has to be given form to the point where they can encompass it, or else they must show polemically the impossibility of achieving their necessary object and the inner nullity of their own means. And in this case they carry the fragmentary nature of the world's structure into the world of forms. (38–9)

While it might be possible to view such circumstances as beneficial for the arts, Lukács chose to look at them not from the aesthetic, but from the metaphysical vantage point. The freedom of the arts, as the free choice of the Edenic couple, becomes the Fall. In the absence of the proper circumstances for an art of tragedy, history itself becomes tragic.

> Kant's starry firmament now shines only in the dark night of pure cognition, it no longer lights any solitary wanderer's path (for to be a man in the new world is to be solitary). And the inner light affords evidence of security, or its illusion, only to the wanderer's next step. No light radiates any longer from within into the world of events, into its vast complexity to which the soul is a stranger. And who can tell whether the fitness of the action to the essential nature of the subject – the only guide that still remains – really touches upon the essence, when the subject has become a phenomenon, an object unto itself . . . (36)

We ourselves are thrown into that phenomenal world which, as recently as Kant, seemed to be somehow other. Humanity is now one thing among others. In this world grown old there is a complete severing of the aesthetic and the spiritual. The spiritual has departed, leaving us only the aesthetic as a memento and consolation: "Art, the visionary reality of the world made to our measure, has thus become independent: it is no longer a copy, for all the models have gone; it is a created totality, for the natural unity of the metaphysical spheres has been destroyed forever" (37). That aspect of artistic creation which was its glory for Simmel, its ability to create a totality, is a mockery for Lukács, a reminder, like the Wailing Wall, of what we have lost. A reminder and still something of a consolation.

Chapter Two of **The Theory of the Novel** is entitled "The Problems of a Philosophy of the History of Forms." In it Lukács attempts to solve the problem of change in the world of aesthetic forms by referring it to "a historico-philosophical dialectic." He first considers the impact of the disappearance of immanence on artistic forms.

> As a result of such a change in the transcendental points of orientation, art forms become subject to a historico-philosophical dialectic . . . [this] genre-creating principle . . . does not imply any change in mentality; rather, it forces the same mentality to turn towards a new aim which is essentially different from the old one. It means that the old parallelism of the transcendental structure of the form-giving subject and the world of created forms has been destroyed, and the ultimate basis of artistic creation has become homeless. (40-1)

In other words, changing social conditions, including shifting cultural values, do not alter thought processes, but only change the effects of those processes, and those changes, reacting back on the transcendental subject, produce the feeling of homelessness appropriate to an age of metaphysical homelessness. Once this happens, the novel becomes a fit genre for the time, as "the novel form is, like no other, an expression of this transcendental homelessness" (41).

Lukács divides literary forms into two categories: those that are and those that are not intimately connected with the life of the transcendental subject. The former is narrative (at one period the epic, at another the novel). The latter is tragedy, which Lukács takes to be almost independent of historical conditions. But whereas the smallest disturbance of the transcendental correlations must cause the immanence of meaning in life to vanish beyond recovery, an essence that is divorced from life and alien to life can crown itself with its own existence in such a way that this consecration, even after a more violent upheaval, may pale but will never disappear altogether. That is why tragedy, although changed, has nevertheless survived in our time with its essential nature intact, whereas the epic had to disappear and yield its place to an entirely new form: the novel.

There are, in turn, two kinds of tragic drama, that which has some connection with life and that which has very little. The latter Lukács calls modern classicism.

Life is not organically absent from modern drama; at most, it can be banished from it. But the banishment which modern classicists practise implies a recognition . . . of its power . . . life nevertheless rules the bare, calculated severity of the structure based a priori on abstraction, making it narrow or confused, over-explicit or abstruse. (43)

He is probably thinking of such writers as Paul Ernst, whom, nonetheless, he had praised in **Soul and Form**. His discussion of this second type of drama introduces the theme of the problematic hero. Whereas in the older tragedy the hero is one human being among others, the

other kind of tragedy . . . places its heroes on the stage as living human beings in the midst of a mass of only apparently living beings . . . . In this way the condition of the hero has become polemical and problematic; to be a hero is no longer the natural form of existence in the sphere of essence, but the act of raising self above that which is merely human, whether in the surrounding mass or in the hero's own instincts. (43-4).

This drama has become a difficult form in which to write, rather as if it were a metrical scheme that could be easily managed in Greek but not in German. The difficulty has to do with the role of the protagonist, who is no longer an image of community, but is now the image of loneliness, alienation.

> For the Greeks, the fact that life ceased to be the home of meaning merely transferred the mutual closeness, the kinship of human beings, to another sphere, but did not destroy it . . . But when, as in modern drama, the essence can manifest and assert itself only after winning a hierarchical contest with life, when every figure carries this contest within himself as a precondition of his existence or as his motive force, then each of the dramatis personae can be bound to the destiny that gives him birth only by his own thread; then each must rise up from solitude and must, in irremediable solitude, hasten, in the midst of all the other lonely creatures, towards the ultimate, tragic aloneness; then, every tragic work must turn to silence without ever being understood, and no tragic deed can ever find a resonance that will adequately absorb it. (44-5)

The exaltation of the protagonist of the drama to lonely heights, rather like the German Romantics of his essay on Novalis, leaves each of them on his own Alp, as it were, barely within shouting distance of one another. This "historico-philosophical" situation gives rise to an aesthetic.

> But a paradox attaches to loneliness in drama. Loneliness is the very essence of tragedy, for the soul that has attained itself through its destiny can have brothers among the stars, but never an earthly companion; yet the dramatic form of expression – the dialogue – presupposes, if it is to be many-voiced, truly dialogical, dramatic, a high degree of communion among these solitaries. . . . [The] loneliness required by the tragic form, which deals with the relationship to destiny (a relationship in which the actual, living Greek heroes had their being) . . . is also the torment of a creature condemned to solitude and devoured by a longing for community. (45)

Drama cannot portray the life of man in society as it once did. It is now intensely interiorized and has only one theme, that of the loneliness which is its paradoxical essence. The social is the realm of another genre: "Great epic writing gives form to the extensive totality of life, drama to the intensive totality of essence" (46). The familiar terms are those of Neo-Kantian epistemology. What is "the extensive totality of life?" It is the quotidian, everyday experience.

> For the epic, the world at any given moment is an ultimate principle; it is empirical at its deepest, most decisive, all-determining transcendental base; it can sometimes accelerate the rhythm of life, can carry something that was hidden or neglected to a utopian end which was always immanent within it, but it can never, while remaining epic, transcend the breadth and depth, the rounded, sensual, richly ordered nature of life as historically given. (46)

If drama abandons the world, narrative virtually is the world. Narrative is the embodiment of historical existence in art. In contrast to this earthy genre, drama is pure idealism. Taking the vintage of Platonism and distilling it twice, we can produce the fine elixir of utopianism. Lukács's reasoning about drama continues Platonic, reversing, in anticipation, the Sartrean slogan that existence is prior to essence.

> The concept of essence leads to transcendence simply by being posited, and then, in the transcendent, crystallises into a new and higher essence expressing through its form an essence that should be – an essence which, because it is born of form, remains independent of the given content of what merely exists. (47)

This utopianism, this spiritualization of life itself, is, for Lukács, the proper effort of drama. His description of the epic and the novel strongly contrast with this.

> The character created by drama . . . is the intelligible 'I' of man, the character created by the epic is the empirical 'I'. The 'should be' in whose desperate intensity the essence seeks refuge because it has become an outlaw on earth, can objectivise itself in the intelligible 'I' as the hero's normative psychology, but in the empirical 'I' it remains a 'should be'. . . . The 'should be' kills life, and the dramatic hero assumes the symbolic attributes of the sensuous manifestations of life only in order to be able to perform the symbolic ceremony of dying in a sensuously perceptible way, making transcendence visible; yet in the epic men must be alive, or else they destroy or exhaust the very element that carries, surrounds and fills them. (47-8)

Lukács goes on to posit, in a crucial parenthetical statement, the impossibility of the comprehension of "life" by "thought," and the consequence of this impossibility for aesthetics: "The 'should be' kills life, and every concept expresses a 'should-be' of its object; that is why thought can never arrive at a real definition of life, and why, perhaps, the philosophy of art is so much more adequate to tragedy than it is to epic" (48). Concepts express a "should-be" in the Neo-Kantian system because they shape the chaos, and all such forming must have an end in view, if only that of bringing order to thought.

With this Lukács takes leave of drama, his earliest interest, and turns wholeheartedly to the consideration of narrative. He characterizes epics of the classical period by referring to their subject matter:

> Living, empirical man is always the subject of the epic, but his creative, life-mastering arrogance is transformed in the great epics into humility, contemplation, speechless wonder at the luminous meaning which, so unexpectedly, so naturally, has become visible to him, an ordinary human being in the midst of ordinary life. (50)

A "great epic," therefore, can only be written in an age of immanent meaning. At such times the form expresses the totality of life and the natural way in which humanity occupies a place in the world. After the great epic period is over, minor epic forms remain. They exhibit the triumph of art over life: "In the minor epic forms, the subject confronts the object in a more dominant and self-sufficient way. . . . [It] is [the narrator's] own subjectivity that singles out a fragment from the immeasurable infinity of the events of life, . ." (50). An instance of this might be the **Metamorphoses** of Ovid or the pastorals of Theocritus and Virgil. Lacking totality (since they are selected fragments of life), these minor epic forms achieve unity through art itself. "The subject's form-giving, structuring, delimiting act, his sovereign dominance over the created object, is the lyricism of those epic forms which are without totality. Such lyricism is here the last epic unity; . ." (51). This very triumph of the artist is viewed by Lukács as a symptom of decadence. Its efforts necessarily fail to found a lasting form amid the "historico-philolosphical" changes of the world of culture. The Alexandrian unities of the minor epic forms exhibit their brittleness by their artificially stable rules of composition. They break free, as it were, from the human world, and float off out of the reach of a humanity immersed in an ontological crisis.

> But as the objective world breaks down, so the subject, too, becomes a fragment; only the 'I' continues to exist, but its existence is then lost in the insubstantiality of its self-created world of ruins. Such subjectivity wants to give form to everything, and precisely for this reason succeeds only in mirroring a segment of the world. (53)

In a world of fragments, there is no ultimate unity either for the author, the hero, or the tale. Not even the form-creating artistic act can save us from the chaos of the alienating world. We can only look back with nostalgia to that (postulated) earlier condition of bliss expressed by the great epic.

> This is the paradox of the subjectivity of the great epic, its 'throwing away in order to win': creative subjectivity becomes lyrical, but, exceptionally, the subjectivity which simply accepts, which humbly transforms itself into a purely receptive organ of the world, can partake of the grace of having the whole revealed to it. (53)

The proper alignment of essence and life was necessary for the great epic. Without that correspondence, "when the starry sky is the map of all possible paths," the great epic is impossible. The human world changes and art, as objective spirit, must change with it. In the modern world the effort to hold the totality of life moves away from epic, while just those works of art which seem furthest from reality best express essence.

This is not a value judgement but an a priori definition of genre: the totality of life resists any attempt to find a transcendental centre within it, and refuses any of its constituent cells the right to dominate it. Only when a subject, far removed from all life and from the empirical which is necessarily posited together with life, becomes enthroned in the pure heights of essence, when it has become nothing but the carrier of the transcendental synthesis, can it contain all the conditions for totality within its own structure and transform its limitations into the frontiers of the world. But such a subject cannot write an epic: the epic is life, immanence, the empirical. Dante's **Paradiso** is closer to the essence of life than Shakespeare's exuberant richness. (54)

The epic is the form of a world where meaning is present, given, a world where questions are answered before being asked. The novel is a transitional genre, between the world of immanent meaning and one in which the question of meaning, the category of totality, no longer exist: "The novel is the epic of an age in which the extensive totality of life is no longer directly given, in which the immanence of meaning in life has become a problem, yet which still thinks in terms of totality" (56). The novel, then, according to Lukács, is the prose manifestation of an age's worry about absence. It is the literary equivalent of Simmel's lectures about a world grown too full of cultural products to be grasped.

An important step in the change from epic to novel is the emergence of prose as an artistic vehicle. The transition from verse to prose as the medium for narrative can also be accounted for by Lukács's historical and philosophical dialectic. Originally, as a product of free people unworried about absence, epic had been cast in verse. When historical circumstances changed, verse became inappropriate.

The lightness of great epic literature is only the concretely immanent utopia of the historical hour, and the form—giving detachment which verse as a vehicle confers upon whatever it carries must, therefore, rob the epic of its great totality, its subjectlessness, and transform it into an idyll or a piece of playful lyricism. (58)

Verse is necessary for epic narration only while it is appropriate, and appropriate only while necessary. It is impossible, according to Lukács, to use verse for epic narration in problematic ages. The verse form which at one time could convey the whole of life then can carry only part of it, mocking, as it were, the prosaic with a vision of immanent form.

In the world of distances, all epic verse turns into lyric poetry . . . for, in verse, everything hidden becomes manifest, and the swift flight of verse makes the distance over which prose travels with its deliberate pace as it gradually approaches meaning appear naked, mocked, trampled or merely a forgotten dream. (59)

Reading epic verse "in the world of distances," we read it as lyric poetry. It is not that verse was inappropriate for epic in epic times, it is that times change, and as they do that which was once fitting ceases to be so. In problematic times the verse distances the narrative. Verse forms in epic tales of the fallen world are mirages of totality, visions of heaven. In a typically Hegelian move, Lukács shows that while, on the one hand, verse becomes incapable of expressing traditional subject matter, on the other hand it finds a new subject.

> Distance in the ordinary world of life is extended to the point where it cannot be overcome, but beyond that world every lost wanderer finds the home that has awaited him since all eternity; every solitary voice that falls silent on earth is there awaited by a chorus that takes it up, carries it towards harmony and, through it, becomes harmony itself. (59)

Thus the appropriate subject matter for a verse epic after Homeric Greece is not this world, but the other. As Lukács's theory makes the Middle Ages a second Greece, he must find at least one example of a Medieval verse epic. It is **The Divine Comedy**.

> The world of distances lies sprawling and chaotic beneath the radiant celestial rose of sense made sensuous; it is visible and undisguised at every moment. Every inhabitant of that home in the beyond has come from this world, each is bound to it by the indissoluble force of destiny, but each recognises it, sees it in its fragility and heaviness, only when he has travelled to the end of his path thereby made meaningful; every figure sings of its isolated destiny, the isolated event in which its apportioned lot was made manifest: a ballad. And just as the totality of the transcendent world-structure is the pre-determined sense-giving, all-embracing a priori of each individual destiny, so the increasing comprehension of this edifice, its structure and its beauty – the great experience of Dante the traveller – envelops everything in the unity of its meaning, now revealed. Dante's insight transforms the individual into a component of the whole, and so the ballads become epic songs. The meaning of this world becomes distanceless, visible and immanent only in the beyond. (59-60)

The plot of **The Divine Comedy** provides a good illustration of Lukács's philosophy. The situation of each soul Dante the traveller meets is an expression of the life of that soul. Meaning, which was obscured during life, is immanent afterward. The searchers of **Soul and Form** and **The Theory of the Novel** are looking for just such clarity of meaning in their lives. **The Divine Comedy** may be used as a touchstone for the quality of their journeys.

On the other hand, it is difficult to reconcile this idea with any more prosaic view of art. Lukács seems to be saying that the totality of Dante's vision was only made possible by his point of view "being" that of Heaven.

Yet, surely, this is to confuse "Dante the traveller" in the poem with Dante, the author of the poem. If Lukács's position is what it appears to be, the viewpoint of the totality can be achieved in any epoch by any author who believes in the transcendental eye. Be that as it may, once having exempted Dante, Lukács reverts to his stronger line, contending that after Greece verse could not express totality. To this extent, even the Middle Ages were problematic.

> Totality, in this world, is bound to be a fragile or merely a longed-for one: the verse passages in Wolfram von Eschenbach or Gottfried von Strassburg are only lyrical ornaments to their novels, and the ballad quality of the **Song of the Nibelungs** can be disguised by compositional means, but cannot be rounded so that it achieves world-embracing totality. (60)

Therefore, it is prose that is the appropriate medium for the epic of problematic ages. Faced with a world in which both the meaning of life and its totality are hidden, man in problematic ages has a completely different situation to express in narrative than that expressed in the great verse epics. The world appears to be uncertain and meaningless. The novel, the prose epic, can have only one plot: the search for that very absence which makes epic certainty and meaning impossible.

> The epic gives form to a totality of life that is rounded from within; the novel seeks, by giving form, to uncover and construct the concealed totality of life. The given structure of the object (i.e. the search, which is only a way of expressing the subject's recognition that neither objective life nor its relationship to the subject is spontaneously harmonious in itself) supplies an indication of the form-giving intention. All the fissures and rents which are inherent in the historical situation must be drawn into the form-giving process and cannot nor should be disguised by compositional means. Thus the fundamental form-determining intention of the novel is objectivised as the psychology of the novel's heroes: they are seekers. (60)

This is an example of a rhetorical success of the method of the Intellectual Sciences school (echoing with "forms"). As in Newton's **Principia,** the deductive method is a device for presenting results arrived at by other means. Lukács appears to have deduced from his historical and philosophical dialectic the general plot structure of all novels and the character structure of their protagonists. On the other hand, one might see this passage as one which rather severely restricts the definition of the novel, as the early comments had restricted epic. This artificial restriction of the use of the term "novel" becomes more apparent as Lukács adds details to his sketch of the possibilities of the novel. For instance, since the plot of any novel is a search, this necessitates that the novel be about either crime or madness. "For crime and madness are objectivations of transcendental homelessness – the homelessness of an action in the human order of social relations, the homelessness of a soul in the ideal order of a supra-personal system of values" (61-2). The influence of Dostoevsky is traceable here, and, perhaps, that of Nietzsche. "The boundaries which separate crime from acclaimed heroism and madness from life-mastering wisdom are tentative, purely psychological ones, although at the end, when the aberration makes itself terribly manifest and clear, there is no longer any confusion" (61). It is, after all, Alyosha, not Dmitri, to whom we must look as an exemplar. (We will return to Lukács's concern with Dostoevsky at the end of this chapter. For the moment it will suffice to point out that there are works, usually called novels, which are not about either crime or madness. By excluding these from consideration, Lukács's restrictive definition of the novel once more moves the focus of his discussion from literature to world view philosophy.)

The problematic individual has turned within himself. Nature is no longer visible; only the soul is viewed in the contemporary epic, the novel. This leaves lyric poetry as the modern form of a dream utopia, the union of the subject and the object. It alone can still portray nature. The epic forms, the novel, transform even nature itself into an idea within the mind of the subject, while drama treats nature as mere scenery.

> Only in lyric poetry do these direct, sudden flashes of the substance become like lost original manuscripts suddenly made legible; only in lyric poetry is the subject, the vehicle of such experiences, transformed into the sole carrier of meaning, the only true reality. Drama is played out in a sphere that lies beyond such reality, and in the epic forms the subjective experience remains inside the subject: it becomes a mood. And nature, bereft of its 'senseless' autonomous life as well of its meaningful symbolism, becomes a background, a piece of scenery, an accompanying voice; it has lost its independence and is only a sensually perceptible projection of the essential – of interiority. (63)

The problematic individual is either unaware of nature outside himself or sees it sentimentally. This is not an accident. Homeless in the cultural world, the problematic individual cannot even feel comfortable in nature itself. "Estrangement from nature . . . the modern sentimental attitude to nature, is only a projection of man's experience of his self-made environment as a prison instead of a parental home" (64). This is because the world of man-made forms can only be animated by the reawakened souls of the dead that made them. "It is too akin to the soul's aspirations to be treated by the soul as mere raw material for moods, yet too alien to those aspirations ever to become their appropriate and adequate expression" (64). The man-made world of culture is a burden from the past; like an ancestral mansion too pompous for life, it would only be comfortable for the ghosts of those who built it, and yet culture and cultural objects are the true presences for which the state of nature is an inadequate symbol. As Simmel taught, art and culture are a physical sensuous reality formed by the subject and therefore a habitation superior to all others for it. "When the structures made by man for man are really adequate to man, they are his necessary and native home; and he does not know the nostalgia that posits and experiences nature as the object of its own seeking and finding" (64). We are, according to Simmel and Lukács, at a double remove from this. Alienated from nature by our "ancestral mansion," we are also alienated from this cultural habitation that no longer feels like a home. As the epic world-sense collapses, we are less and less concerned with nature until it is fitting that the "epic individual, the hero of the novel, is the product of estrangement from the outside world" (66). But not only is the hero alienated from nature and culture, his representative status is completed by his alienation from all other human beings. "The autonomous life of interiority is possible and necessary only when the distinctions between men have made an unbridgeable chasm; . ." (66).

The novel is "about" emotions and ideas, pure interiority. "The epic hero [by contrast was], strictly speaking, never an individual" (66). Lukács introduces his discussion of the novelistic hero by thus reverting for a moment to his discussion of the character of the epic hero. The epic hero does not worry about interiority; his consciousness is purely external, bound to the community: "the epic hero, as bearer of his destiny, is not lonely, for this destiny connects him by indissoluble threads to the community whose fate is crystallised in his own . . . As for the community, it is an organic – and therefore intrinsically meaningful – concrete totality; . ." (67). Tönnies is invoked here, giving us a clear statement of the dialectic of the epic/organic/intrinsically meaningful community on the one hand, and, by implication, the novelistic/inorganic/meaningless society of modern times on the other. In passages such as this, Lukács's usual stance as a mystic searcher commenting on literature merely as the occasion for leading the reader further along on the journey to God is replaced by that of the typical critical sociologist of his time, Simmel or Tönnies, but the literary and generic material as such counts as little either way; it is at best illustrative of the points to be made. Lukács's ideas about organic community and social totality are part of what Feher has called the "romantic anti-capitalism" of the time. We have seen that the clearest example of this had been Tönnies's **Gemeinschaft und Gesellschaft:** but it was also evident in Weber's and Sombart's work on the origins of capitalism and in the confused anti-business sentiments of lower middle class Vienna which was to provide the basis for Lueger's regime and the example for the fascist movements in Germany and Italy which followed it.

The epic world is linked in many of Lukács's comments with the idea of the organic community, implicitly in contrast to the social organization of contemporary society. Therefore the contrast between the epic and the novel carries all the emotional weight of that nostalgia for pre-capitalist life that was to be one of the primary motive forces of twentieth-century philosophy, literature, and politics. The power of the nostalgia for "the blessed times" in **The Theory of the Novel** does not derive from a wish to actually live in a specific, say Homeric, epic world, but from the typically utopian wish to live in the opposite of the case as it is, in an otherwise unqualified not-modern society, exactly "Nowhere" (Utopia), or to live as one "remembers" having once lived in a carefully fostered illusion of idyllic childhood. Literary utopianism is the artistic manifestation of the social projection of "secondary narcissism," the rejection of the otherness of the world.

The epic, then, is the song of the nursery, while the novel, with all its problems, is the account of adults sadly living out everyday life. For Lukács, the novel is the form suitable to the period following the collapse of an organic community and as such it is an inorganic genre. The difference between the epic and the novel

> is the difference between something that is homogeneously organic and stable and something that is heterogeneously contingent and discrete . . . This aspect is only a symptom of contingency; it merely sheds light upon a state of affairs which is necessarily present at all times and everywhere [in the novel], but which is covered over, by skilfully ironic compositional tact, by a semblance of organic quality which is revealed again and again as illusory. (76-7)

It is an inorganic genre in contrast to the lyric or the epic. Instead of representing the whole by being itself seamless and of a piece, it represents a heterogeneous totality by being an imposed organizational unity. It is a system.

> In a novel, totality can be systematised only in abstract terms, which is why any system that could be established in the novel - a system being, after the final disappearance of the organic, the only possible form of a rounded totality - had to be one of abstract concepts and therefore not directly suitable for aesthetic form-giving. (70)

As a system it exists to highlight the contrast between the subjective and the social. The former is vivid and present, the latter alien, a mere convention.

The novel is the perfect genre for the world of distances, since it focuses on distance alone: "In the created reality of the novel all that becomes visible is the distance separating the systematisation from concrete life: a systematisation which emphasises the conventionality of the objective world and the interiority of the subjective one" (70). For Lukács, a novel has three elements: nostalgia as solipsism, social structures as sheer facticity, and the relationship between these expressed as an account of lived experience. He makes the qualification that these are all abstract.

> The elements of the novel are, in the Hegelian sense, entirely abstract; abstract, the nostalgia of the characters for utopian perfection, a

nostalgia that feels itself and its desires to be the only true reality; abstract, the existence of social structures based only upon their factual presence and their sheer ability to continue; abstract, finally, the form-giving intention which, instead of surmounting the distance between these two abstract groups of elements, allows it to subsist, which does not even attempt to surmount it but renders it sensuous and the lived experience of the novel's characters, uses it as a means of connecting the two groups and so turns it into an instrument of composition. (70-1)

The genre appropriate to the alienated world takes its very principles of composition from the distance between the nostalgic emotion of the protagonist and the sheer facticity of the modern world. Principles of composition or forms, in Neo-Kantian thought, are ways of organizing the world. These, in turn, are defined by the very chaos which they attempt to control. "Every art form is defined by the metaphysical dissonance of life which it accepts and organises as the basis of a totality complete in itself. . ." (71).

Here, Lukács's deductive analysis once more begins to yield details. Plots of novels are "determined" by a certain metaphysical danger. In the effort to construct a unity from the subjectively perceived chaos of the world,

The danger by which the novel is determined is twofold: either the fragility of the world may manifest itself so crudely that it will cancel out the immanence of meaning which the form demands, or else the longing for the dissonance to be resolved, affirmed and absorbed into the work may be so great that it will lead to a premature closing of the circle of the novel's world, causing the form to disintegrate into disparate, heterogeneous parts. (71-2)

The immanence of meaning has migrated from the world into art, but threatens to vanish even from that frail vessel. The form of the novel comes into being under the pressure of the need to conceal the lack of meaning in the world and the need to avoid lyricism, which is concrete utopianism. These dialectically opposed forces are synthesized in the novel through the agency of form. Their resolution is irony.

The irony of the novel is the self-correction of the world's fragility: inadequate relations can transform themselves into a fanciful yet well-ordered round of misunderstandings and cross-purposes, within which everything is seen as many-sided, within which things appear as isolated and yet connected, as full of value and yet totally devoid of it, as abstract fragments and as concrete autonomous life, as flowering and as decaying, as the infliction of suffering and as suffering itself. (75)

Ironically, the novelist projects all the lost values of the organic world into the world of distances, their very absence from the world calling forth their memory in art. This forming is in itself, for Lukács, an ethical act: ethics as part of the realm of artistic forms. "In the novel . . . ethic – the ethical intention – is visible in the creation of every detail and hence is, in its most concrete content, an effective structural element of the work itself" (72). Although convenient, this doctrine can be dangerous. The ethical component of the structure of the novel can masquerade as the ethical content of the lost utopian world:

> where ethic has to carry the structure of a form as a matter of content and not merely as a formal a priori, and where a coincidence, or at least a marked convergence between ethic as an interior factor of life and its substratum of action in the social structures, is not given as it was in the epic ages, there is a danger that, instead of an existent totality, only a subjective aspect of that totality will be given form, obscuring or even destroying the creative intention of acceptance and objectivity which the great epic demands. (74)

One would think that, given the fallen nature of the world of distances, this danger would be inevitable.

Taking leave of these ethical questions, Lukács returns to the consideration of the structure of the novel. He finds that the novel is not, like an epic, a lyric, or a tragedy, a finished work. It is, on the contrary, the paradoxical reification of becoming itself:

> the novel, in contrast to other genres whose existence resides within the finished form, appears as something in process of becoming. . . . As form, the novel establishes a fluctuating yet firm balance between becoming and being; as the idea of becoming, it becomes a state. Thus the novel, by transforming itself into a normative being of becoming, surmounts itself. (72–3)

This is a Hegelian summary of the Romantic aspects of novelistic structure. One could think of various novels which would benefit from being read in this way, **Tristam Shandy**, being one, recalls the argument in **Soul and Form**. Making the observation more concrete, Lukács finds that the solution to this oscillation between being and becoming is the typical structure of the novel as biography. "The fluctuation between a conceptual system which can never completely capture life and a life complex which can never attain completeness because completeness is immanently utopian, can be objectivised only in that organic quality which is the aim of biography" (77). If completeness is "immanently utopian" and the lyric and tragedy are "complete," it would be possible to develop an interesting theory of the utopian function of those genres (which Lukács had partially done in **Soul and Form**). Here, though, Lukács is primarily interested in finding meaning in the form of the novel.

In the biographical form, the unfulfillable, sentimental striving both for the immediate unity of life and for a completely rounded architecture of the system is balanced and brought to rest: it is transformed into being. The central character of a biography is significant only by his relationship to a world of ideals that stands above him: but this world, in turn is realised only through its existence within that individual and his lived experience. Thus in the biographical form the balance of both spheres which are unrealised and unrealisable in isolation produces a new and autonomous life that is, however paradoxically, complete in itself and immanently meaningful: the life of the problematic individual. (77-8)

The life of the problematic individual, as a story, is the instrument by means of which meaning reappears in the world. In contrast to the epic hero, who was part of a community and never existed in isolation, in the novel: "Individuality . . . becomes an aim unto itself because it finds within itself everything that is essential to it and that makes its life autonomous – even if what it finds can never be a firm possession or the basis of its life, but is an object of search" (78). The novelistic hero succeeds in living in a world of immanent meaning, but it is a world of pure interiority, of endless searching. This was, at that moment, Lukács's prescription for the emotional compensation for the loss of meaning in everyday life.

The novelist has a problem in attempting the description of both the world and the interiority of the problematic individual. On the one hand there is

the inability of the outside world, which is a stranger to ideals and an enemy of interiority, to achieve real completeness; an inability to find either the form of totality for itself as a whole, or any form of coherence for its own relationship to its elements and their relationship to one another: in other words, the outside cannot be represented. (79)

There are no forms to express incoherence; as the Neo-Kantians taught Lukács, forms are the mind's ability to shape chaos. On the other hand, in "the subjective world of the soul the ideal is as much at home as the soul's other realities" (78). The solution to this problem is to present it from the point of view of interiority rather than from that of the world, in other words, to do in fiction what Lukács desired to do in fact: abandon the world for the soul and its realities.

At the level of the soul, the ideal by entering lived experience can play, even in its content, a directly positive role; whereas in the outside world the gap between reality and the ideal becomes apparent only by the absence of the ideal, in the immanent self-criticism of mere reality caused by that absence; in the self-revelation of the nothingness of mere reality without an immanent ideal. (78-9)

From Lukács's vantage point at this time, the world was, or at least strongly seemed to be, incomprehensible. Historical circumstances, as represented by social conditions in Central Europe and the War forced thinkers predisposed toward Idealism to consider all things from the more radical edges of that point of view. Thus, for Lukács, it was necessary to discuss the novel as focussed on the soul of the problematic individual.

> The inner form of the novel has been understood as the process of the problematic individual's journeying towards himself, the road from dull captivity within a merely present reality – a reality that is heterogeneous in itself and meaningless to the individual – towards clear self-recognition. After such self-recognition has been attained, the ideal thus formed irradiates the individual's life as its immanent meaning . . . The immanence of meaning which the form of the novel requires lies in the hero's finding out through experience that a mere glimpse of meaning is the highest life has to offer . . . (80)

The meaning which becomes immanent in the novel, and thus constitutes its purpose, is the idea that life is a search for meaning. The novel is the objectivization of spiritual becoming. This concept of life is familiar to us from **Soul and Form**. The novel, like the essay of the final sections of **Soul and Form**, is a road to "meaning," "presence," the "ideal." The problematic hero, like the Neo-Platonic philosopher, travels through the world observing the Real everywhere as the Imaginary, as signifiers of a metaphysical signified.

> The novel is the epic of a world that has been abandoned by God. The novel hero's psychology is demonic; the objectivity of the novel is the mature man's knowledge that meaning can never quite penetrate reality, but that, without meaning, reality would disintegrate into the nothingness of inessentiality. (88)

The notion that the "mature man" has that "without meaning reality would disintegrate" is a Simmelian notion. Meaning is interior to the subject, reality is chaos without concepts to form it. In the absence of immanent meaning, which amounts to the same thing as the absence of God, meaning can be found in the Kierkegaardian activity of the search for meaning. Lukács sought this not necessarily in lived experience, but definitely in art, in writing, in fiction. The division between God and the world finds its parallel in that between meaning and reality, and both these divisions achieve partial resolution in the form of the novel. It is not the sheer facticity of the novel that concerns Lukács; it is the form in which it is cast that matters.

> The composition of the novel is the paradoxical fusion of heterogeneous and discrete components into an organic whole which is then abolished over and over again. The relationships which create

cohesion between the abstract components are abstractly pure and formal, and the ultimate unifying principle therefore has to be the ethic of the creative subjectivity, an ethic which the content reveals. (84)

Putting together, say, the knight and the windmills, Cervantes creates out of these oddly mixed elements a unified object, a story.   But ultimately the unity of the novel cannot be something as banal as plot. The mere narrative of plot produces not a novel but something quite different, what we call the best-seller.

The novel – unlike other genres – has a caricatural twin almost indistinguishable from itself in all inessential formal characteristics: the entertainment novel, which has all the outward features of the novel but which, in essence, is bound to nothing and based on nothing, i.e. is entirely meaningless. (73)

How does one tell one from the other? By spiritual inspection. The true novel is not simply a narrative, it is not merely entertainment. It is an event in the ethical universe. Moreover, the unity of the true novel constitutes in itself an ethical realization.

The novel, as an ethical document, must focus on its representation of the subject, the novelistic hero. Lukács contrasts these alienated protagonists with the youthful heroes of epics. "The heroes of youth are guided by the gods: whether what awaits them at the end of the road are the embers of annihilation or the joys of success, or both at once, they never walk alone, they are always led" (86). The heroes of drama are also unlike those of the novel.

The dramatic hero knows no adventure, for, through the force of his attained soul that is hallowed by destiny, the event which should have been his adventure becomes destiny upon the merest contact with that soul, becomes a simple occasion for him to prove himself, a simple excuse for disclosing what was prefigured in the act of his attaining the soul. (88)

In contrast to the epic hero, the hero of the novel is always alone; his road and its goal are equally uncertain. In contrast to the tragic hero, the events of his story are his adventures; they are not meaningful in themselves, although they may lead to meaning. "The mental attitude of the novel is virile maturity, and the characteristic structure of its matter is discreteness, the separation between interiority and adventure" (88).

The implied values here are a little confused. The novel, as the appropriate genre of a fallen world should not be morally superior to the epic or to tragedy, genres of a world immanently meaningful, yet Lukács repeatedly refers to the novel as exhibiting "virile maturity." Perhaps there is a certain tragic grandeur in the hopeless quest for meaning conducted by the problematic hero, or perhaps this superiority is a manifestation of the Christian world over the pre-Christian world.

Lukács's dialectic of the problematic hero operates between interiority and adventure: "The novel tells of the adventure of interiority; the content of the novel is the story of the soul that goes to find itself, that seeks adventures in order to be proved and tested by them, and, by proving itself, to find its own essence" (88-9). The novel separates adventure from interiority, but it also combines them. Where in the epic the adventure, the event, was a confirmation of meaning, in the novel meaning is interiorized as part of the search for meaning. Interiority itself can be divided further; it is "the product of the antagonistic duality of soul and world, the agonising stance between psyche and soul . . ." (88). Without distance there is no interiority; consciousness, as it were, can only exist as a contrast to the inanimate. The novelistic hero might have to function in the absence of the gods, but, in contrast to the epic hero, he remains nonetheless conscious, mature, more truly human than his more primitive counterpart.

> The novel is the form of mature virility: its author has lost the poet's radiant youthful faith that 'destiny and soul are twin names for a single concept' (Novalis); and the deeper and more painful his need to set this most essential creed of all literature as a demand against life, the more deeply and painfully he must learn to understand that it is only a demand and not an effective reality. (85)

The result of the distance between the soul and the world is that interiority is emphasized, which produces melancholy. This situation is presented by Lukács as part of lived experience not merely as a stage in the history of art and as part of the way in which the development of the individual recapitulates that of humanity.

> The melancholy of the adult state arises from our dual, conflicting experience that, on the one hand, our absolute, youthful confidence in an inner voice has diminished or died, and, on the other hand, that the outside world to which we now devote ourselves in our desire to learn its ways and dominate it will never speak to us in a voice that will clearly tell us our way and determine our goal. (86)

The stage of secondary narcissism is an ordinary period of psychological development. Eventually we abandon its allures, recognize the world as other, and attempt to deal with the world under the sign of the reality principle. This does not prevent us from feeling regret, even nostalgia, for that childhood dream of a world which was not other, but as familiar to us as our own bodies. Projecting similar ideas onto the development of the novel, Lukács finds that only the demonic brings relief from the melancholy of a God-forsaken world. He begins this phase of his discussion by sketching an emotional description of life in the world of distances.

Biological and sociological life has a profound tendency to remain in its own immanence; men want only to live, structures want to remain intact; and because of the remoteness, the absence of an effective God, the indolent self-complacency of this quietly decaying life would be the only power in the world if men did not sometimes fall prey to the power of the demon and overreach themselves in ways that have no reason and cannot be explained by reason, challenging all the psychological or sociological foundations of their existence. (90)

When the "demonic" is injected into this "quietly decaying life" the effect is that of a powerful awakening.

Then, suddenly, the God-forsakenness of the world reveals itself as a lack of substance, as an irrational mixture of density and permeability. What previously seemed to be very solid crumbles like dry clay at the first contact with a man possessed by a demon, and the empty transparence behind which attractive landscapes were previously to be seen is suddenly transformed into a glass wall against which men beat in vain, like bees against a window, incapable of breaking through, incapable of understanding that the way is barred. (90)

We feel the power of this description. Similar feelings went into the composition of Gide's early novels, Hesse's romances, all that world-weary literature of the first two decades of the twentieth century.

Lukács turned to irony, as did many of his contemporaries, as a way of understanding a world seemingly inaccessible as if behind plate glass.

For the novel, irony consists in this freedom of the writer in his relationship to God, the transcendental condition of the objectivity of form-giving. Irony, with intuitive double vision, can see where God is to be found in a world abandoned by God; irony sees the lost, utopian home of the idea that has become an ideal . . . (92)

God is not dead, nor even removed from the world. Yet the divine is hidden and visible only to those who know how to see. The link between religion and irony, such as that established here by Lukács, has been traditional at least since Kierkegaard's work on **The Concept of Irony.** In accord with his theory of the essay as propounded in **Soul and Form,** Lukács in **The Theory of the Novel** uses the novel as the occasion for writing about his religious experiences. This obsession is pursued nearly openly in the section of **The Theory of the Novel** devoted to irony.

The writer's irony is a negative mysticism . . . and in it there is the deep certainty, expressible only by form-giving, that through not-desiring-to-know and not-being-able-to-know he has truly encountered, glimpsed and grasped the ultimate, true substance, the present, non-existent God. That is why irony is the objectivity of the novel. (90)

The writer reaches God through the spiritual exercise of composing ironic novels. When he does so, the matter of the novel becomes transcendent, objective. With this Lukács has reached his conclusion to the first part of **The Theory of the Novel:** narrative, as epic, is an expression of immanence. In fallen times writing becomes a way to find the presence of God in a world that seems to have been abandoned by God. If the writer is a mystic, then writing itself is a religious act.

> A mystic is free when he has renounced himself and is totally dissolved in God . . . Normative man has achieved freedom in his relationship to God because the lofty norms of his actions and of his substantial ethic are rooted in the existence of the all-perfecting God, are rooted in the idea of redemption . . . The detour by way of speech to silence, by way of category to essence, is unavoidable: when the historical categories are not sufficiently developed, the wish to achieve immediate silence must inevitably lead to mere stuttering. But when the form is perfectly achieved, the writer is free in relation to God because in such a form, and only in it, God himself becomes the substratum of form-giving, homogeneous with and equivalent to all the other normatively given elements of form, and is completely embraced by its system of categories. (91)

The quality of art is a religious quality, the study of the forms of art is the study of religion, a path to God. **The Theory of the Novel** is, by the way as it were, a devotional book. It is "about" the novel, rather than, say, drama, only because ours is formally a novelistic and ironic age.

> Irony, the self-surmounting of a subjectivity that has gone as far as it was possible to go, is the highest freedom that can be achieved in a world without God. That is why it is not only the sole possible a priori condition for a true, totality-creating objectivity but also why it makes that totality – the novel – the representative art-form of our age: because the structural categories of the novel constitutively coincide with the world as it is today. (93)

The first part of **The Theory of the Novel** is an apologia, a theoretical justification for the (unfinished) work as a whole. The core of that justification is that the study of the historico-philosophical aspects of the novel form is particularly liable to bring us to religious truth. Lukács's thesis about his own work is that he "happens" to be writing about the novel; he could just as well be writing about drama or horse racing; the important thing is not the occasion for his religious observations but those observations themselves. His theories and comments on the novel are to him what the plots of their romances are to Catholic science fiction writers: decorations on their piety, lace-work on an altar.

The Typology

The second part of **The Theory of the Novel,** the "Attempt at a Typology of the Novel Form," has had much more attention devoted to it than has the first. A well-known essay on the book spends one third of a page on the latter and more than twenty times that amount on the former.[164] Yet the second part of the book is only about half the length of the first and is firmly rooted in the epistemological and religious positions elaborated there. It is perhaps best read as an historical sketch of the background for the unwritten conclusion of the book, the essay on Dostoevsky. The dependence of the second part of the book on the theoretical basis and limitations established earlier is emphasized by its opening, the first sentence of which is virtually a summary of the earlier part of the book.

> The abandonment of the world by God manifests itself in the incommensurability of soul and work, of interiority and adventure – in the absence of a transcendental 'place' allotted to human endeavor. There are, roughly speaking, two types of such incommensurability: either the soul is narrower or it is broader than the outside world assigned to it as the arena and substratum of its actions. (97)

The second sentence of the foregoing is the basis for the Diltheyan typology of the novel that is elaborated in this part of the book. The comparative familiarity of the material and its subordination to that which preceded it and to that which was meant to follow it will allow this commentary to be restricted to the essential lines of the argument.

Lukács deals first with the narrow souls of heroes in the novels of "abstract idealism." The argument is once again presented in deductive fashion. The mentality of abstract idealism is first defined as "demonism."

> The demonism of the narrowing of the soul is the demonism of abstract idealism. It is the mentality which chooses the direct, straight path towards the realisation of the ideal; which, dazzled by the demon, forgets the existence of any distance between ideal and idea, between psyche and soul; which, with the most authentic and unshakeable faith, concludes that the idea, because it should be, necessarily must be, and, because reality does not satisfy this a priori demand, thinks that reality is bewitched by evil demons and that the spell can be broken and reality can be redeemed either by finding a magic password or by courageously fighting the evil forces. (97)

---

[164] David H. Miles, "Portrait of the Marxist as a Young Hegelian: Lukács' **Theory of the Novel, PMLA,** 94(1979), pp. 22-35.

The reasons for this mentality are stated and its implications are set out as
follows:

> The narrowing of the soul of which we speak is brought about by its
> demonic obsession by an existing idea which it posits as the only, the
> most ordinary reality. The content and intensity of the actions which
> follow from this obsession therefore elevate the soul into the most
> genuinely sublime regions whilst at the same time accentuating and
> confirming the grotesque contradictions between the imagined and the
> real. And this is the action of the novel. (98–9)

Now that we know that the action of the novel is restricted to what is
allowed by such humors, we can deduce the nature of the plots of such
novels: "The life of a person with such a soul becomes an uninterrupted
series of adventures which he himself has chosen. He throws himself into
them because life means nothing more to him than the successful passing
of tests . . . He has to be an adventurer" (99). Having worked our way
through this chain of deductive reasoning we find, perhaps not too
surprisingly, that it leads to a specific actual novel of abstract idealism. It is
Don Quixote, of course, which Lukács, with the gesture of a magician
pulling a rabbit out of his hat, produces at just the right moment.
Unfortunately, **"Don Quixote** – like almost any truly great novel – had to
remain the only important objectivisation of its type" (104). One suspects
that the rabbit was already there before the act began, that the whole
elaborate performance of the deductive derivation of the plot of the novel
of abstract idealism from the width of the hero's soul was so much
magician's patter to distract us from watching too closely as Lukács's essay
on negative theology was adjusted so as to better fit the occasion of a
discussion of novelistic typology.

Lukács's purpose in this section of the book is to produce the
appearance of an historical background to his meditations on "the new
man" described by Dostoevsky. That the appearance of an historical
background is all that he thinks necessary is evident from this introduction
of a category with a single member, hardly a convincing demonstration of
the value of his typology. On the other hand, Lukács was not only writing
about God, in passing, as it were, in these early books, he was also writing
some literary criticism.

> Thus the first great novel of world literature stands at the beginning of
> the time when the Christian God began to forsake the world; when man
> became lonely and could find meaning and substance only in his own
> soul, whose home was nowhere; when the world, released from its
> paradoxical anchorage in a beyond that is truly present, was abandoned
> to its immanent meaninglessness; when the power of what is –
> reinforced by the utopian links, now degraded to mere existence – had
> grown to incredible magnitude and was waging a furious, apparently
> aimless struggle against the new forces which were as yet weak and
> incapable of revealing themselves or penetrating the world. (104–5)

As some magicians happen also to be good comedians, Lukács, the Platonist, was also a good literary historian. He produces for us a sketch of those vital links between the individual work of art, the intellectual climate of the times, and general history which are the <u>sine</u> <u>qua</u> <u>non</u> of understanding. Or, if he does not quite bring them out, he indicates their presence somewhere in the wings, avoiding crude Positivism without quite succumbing to either Idealism or formalism.

If **Don Quixote** is the only true instance of type, Lukács believed that **The Human Comedy** represents at least an interesting attempt to reach the ideal by another path:

> Balzac chose a completely different path towards epic immanence. For him the subjective–psychological demonism which is characteristic of his work is an ultimate reality, the principle of all essential action which objectivises itself in heroic deeds; its inadequate relation to the outside world is intensified to the utmost, but this intensification has a purely immanent counterweight: the outside world is a purely human one and is essentially peopled by human beings with similar mental structures, although with completely different orientations and contents. As a result, this demonic inadequacy, this endless series of incidents in which souls are fatally at cross-purposes with one another, becomes the essence of reality, and we obtain that strange, boundless, immeasurable mass of interweaving destinies and lonely souls which is the unique feature of Balzac's novels. (108)

If Lukács had only taken his own comments more seriously, rather than presenting them as disguises for his deductive magic tricks, he might have given us a valuable reading of, say, Balzac, a quarter of a century earlier than he eventually did, but his considerable literary critical powers are confined here in a metaphysical straitjacket, restricted to the occasional brilliant, if seemingly random, observation. Following his bent, then, he eventually simply dismisses Balzac's work with the damning epithet "inorganic." Yet **The Human Comedy** as a whole fails to be an epic;

> none of the parts, seen from the viewpoint of the whole, possesses an organic necessity of existence; if it were not there at all, the whole would not suffer; conversely, any number of new parts might be added and no evidence of inner completeness would prove them superfluous. (109)

Lukács's judgment that **The Human Comedy** is a failure because it is not an epic – and that it is not an epic because it is inorganic (a society, as it were, rather than a community) – is not a commentary on Balzac so much as on the ideology of unity which was at that time beginning to permeate the German-speaking world. The unseriousness of this "problem" for aesthetics (as opposed to ethics) is pointed up by the fact that most of the novels discussed by Lukacs are inorganic in the same way (what could be less unified than **Don Quixote**?), yet it is brought out only in this single case, the judgment being a stage in Lukács's metaphysical argument and not otherwise an aesthetic valuation.

The next type of novel that Lukács discusses is that of romantic disillusionment. This, too, has its origins in the relationship between the size of the soul and that of the world: "In the nineteenth-century novel, the other type of the necessarily inadequate relation between soul and reality became the more important one: the inadequacy that is due to the soul's being wider and larger than the destinies which life has to offer it" (112). Lukács does not bother to tell us how at this particular point in history the soul managed to become so distended. His dialectic continues to operate in the interstellar sphere of pure archetypes. The argument goes that while in the novel of abstract idealism the world does not need the soul, in that of romantic disillusionment the soul has no need of the world. "A life which is capable of producing all its content out of itself can be rounded and perfect even if it never enters into contact with the alien reality outside" (112). ("Rounded" and "perfect" are technical terms familiar, at least, from the opening of **The Theory of the Novel.**) In the Romantic categories operative here, such a life must be pure poetry. This is Goethe's "Confession of a Beautiful Soul" without a trace of irony. The story of a life which "never enters into contact with the alien reality outside" can only be told from within the consciousness of the protagonist. The story is, therefore, shifted inward. There are no longer any adventures, there are only moods. This is "the central problematic of this type of novel: the disappearance of epic symbolisation, the disintegration of form in a nebulous and unstructured sequence of moods and reflections about moods, the replacement of a sensuously meaningful story by psychological analysis" (113). Moods are valued far above the details of everyday life, which in this century have become literally meaningless. This is in accord with Lukács's earlier analysis of the disappearace of meaning from the God-abandoned world of distances. The soul is the only remaining repository of meaning, thus "the outside world which comes into contact with such an interiority has to be completely atomised or amorphous, and in any case must be entirely devoid of meaning" (113). The novel is no longer about marriage or the Balzacian struggle for success in life. The protagonist's only interesting feature is his or her mental state. "A character's profession loses all importance from the point of view of his inner destiny, just as marriage, family and class become immaterial to the relationships between characters" (113).

There is a reason for this radical subjectivization of life: the struggle between the internal and the external has become hopeless. The external has become so absolutely other that there can be no hope of finding meaning there for the soul.

The elevation of interiority to the status of a completely independent world is not only a psychological fact but also a decisive value

> judgment on reality; this self–sufficiency of the subjective self is its
> most desperate self–defense; it is the abandonment of any struggle to
> realise the soul in the outside world, a struggle which is seen a priori
> as hopeless and merely humiliating. (114)

In Germany, or more precisely, in Germany in the age of the French
Revolution and the rise of bourgeois man, all social values were perceived
as lost. Reality was judged inadequate. It was the age of the first internal
emigration of the German intelligentsia.

> The inner importance of the individual has reached its historical apogee:
> the individual is no longer significant as the carrier of transcendent
> worlds, as he was in abstract idealism, he now carries his value
> exclusively within himself; indeed, the values of being seem to draw the
> justification of their validity only from the fact of having been
> subjectively experienced, from their significance to the individual's soul .
> . . The precondition and the price of this immoderate elevation of the
> subject is, however, the abandonment of any claim to participation in
> the shaping of the outside world. (117)

This is familiar as Lukács's typical diagnosis of the world of 1800.
Romanticism, spreading from Germany, flowered in France after the
disillusioning experiences of the early nineteenth century. "In Romanticism,
the literary nature of the a priori status of the soul vis a vis reality becomes
conscious: the self, cut off from transcendence, recognises itself as the
source of the ideal reality, and, as a necessary consequence, as the only
material worthy of self–realisation" (118). Not that this helps much:

> The novel of the romantic sense of life is the novel of disillusionment.
> An interiority denied the possibility of fulfilling itself in action turns
> inwards, yet cannot finally renounce what it has lost forever; even if it
> wanted to do so, life would deny it such a satisfaction; life forces it to
> continue the struggle and to suffer defeats which the artist anticipates
> and the hero apprehends. (118)

In the third chapter of the second part of **The Theory of the Novel,**
Lukács attempts to find a synthesis between the novel of abstract idealism
and that of romantic disillusionment in **Wilhelm Meister:** "Wilhelm Meister
stands aesthetically and historico–philosophically between these two types
of novels. Its theme is the reconciliation of the problematic individual,
guided by his lived experience of the ideal, with concrete social reality"
(132). The forming motif of the novel is appropriate to this task. "The
content and goal of the ideal which animates the personality and
determines his actions is to find responses to the innermost demands of
his soul in the structures of society" (133). This should work, but it fails
due to Goethe's special situation. His

utopian outlook prevents him from stopping at the mere portrayal of the time-given problematic; he cannot be satisfied with a glimpse, a merely subjective experience of an unrealisable meaning; he is forced to posit a purely individual experience, which may, postulatively, have universal validity, as the existent and constitutive meaning of reality. But reality refuses to be forced up to such a level of meaning, and, as with all the decisive problems of great literary forms, no artist's skill is great and masterly enough to bridge the abyss. (142–3)

Lukács has, so far in the second part of the book, galloped along at great speed, producing a deductively derived schema into which various novels are fitted, almost at random, and then dropped after a few comments. The theory is not at the service of literary critical practice; rather, the seemingly practical applications of the theory to literary criticism are little more than chance or rhetorical decorations. Then, in the fourth and last chapter of the section and book as it now stands, Lukács reaches Tolstoy, whom, he claims, was almost successful in writing a prose epic. Tolstoy, it seems, was occasionally able to reintroduce the feeling of immanence into the world. The doors to immanence in Tolstoy's novels are the "great moments" (a concept which Lukács had dealt with at length in **Soul and Form**).

At very rare, great moments – generally they are moments of death – a reality reveals itself to man in which he suddenly glimpses and grasps the essence that rules over him and works within him, the meaning of his life. His whole previous life vanishes into nothingness in the face of his experience; all its conflicts, all the sufferings, torments and confusions caused by them, appear petty and inessential. Meaning has made its appearance and the paths into living life are open to the soul. . . . [But with the return to life] the great moments vanish without a trace. Life goes on in the world of convention, an aimless, inessential life. The paths which the great moments have revealed lose their direction, their reality, as the great moment passes. (149–50)

Life conceals the meaning that the great moment of death reveals. Tolstoy's knowledge of this opens the possibility for a new genre:

in the few overwhelmingly great moments of [Tolstoy's] works – moments which must be seen as subjective and reflexive in respect of each particular work as a whole – he shows a clearly differentiated, concrete and existent world, which, if it could spread out into a totality, would be completely inaccessible to the categories of the novel and would require a new form of artistic creation: the form of the renewed epic. (151–2)

The perfect novel, finally, is that which breaks the novelistic form.

Having, in a few dozen pages, surveyed the history of the novel from the point of view of spiritual matters, Lukács comes to his main, non-aesthetic, point. He is not seeking a new genre at all, but a new world.

> This world is the sphere of pure soul-reality in which man exists as man, neither as a social being nor as an isolated, unique, pure and therefore abstract interiority. If ever this world should come into being as something natural and simply experienced, as the only true reality, a new complete totality could be built out of all its substances and relationships. It would be a world to which our divided reality would be a mere backdrop, a world which would have outstripped our dual world of social reality by as much as we have outstripped the world of nature. But art can never be the agent of such a transformation: the great epic is a form bound to the historical moment, and any attempt to depict the utopian as existent can only end in destroying the form, not in creating reality. The novel is the form of the epoch of absolute sinfulness, as Fichte said, and it must remain the dominant form so long as the world is ruled by the same stars. (152)

As Lukács's search is for a new world, and not for a new novel, the novel does not, ultimately, interest him. And so the book ends on the utopian note (on the occasion of Dostoevsky) that Lukács was to point to nearly half a century later.

> It is in the words of Dostoevsky that this new world, remote from any struggle against what actually exists, is drawn for the first time simply as a seen reality. That is why he, and the form he created, lie outside of the scope of this book. Dostoevsky did not write novels, and the creative vision revealed in his works has nothing to do, either as affirmation or as rejection, with European nineteenth-century Romanticism or with the many, likewise Romantic, reactions against it. He belongs to the new world. Only formal analysis of his works can show whether he is already the Homer or the Dante of that world or whether he merely supplies the songs which, together with the songs of other forerunners, later artists will one day weave into a great unity: whether he is merely a beginning or already a completion. It will then be the task of historico-philosophical interpretation to decide whether we are really about to leave the age of absolute sinfulness or whether the new has no other herald but our hopes: those hopes which are signs of a world to come, still so weak that it can easily be crushed by the sterile power of the merely existent. (152-3)

Whether **The Theory of the Novel** is actually the book which was to be the introduction to the study of Dostoevsky that Lukács was planning during the War years is a question that is open to much fruitless debate. The recent publication of the outline notes for the Dostoevsky project leaves little doubt, though, that if such a book had been written, it would have begun with chapters similar to those which were ultimately gathered together as **The Theory of the Novel**. As the typology of the novel makes little sense as a basis for literary criticism, the proportions of the book as a whole are best explained as those of an introduction to the larger work begun in 1915 as an interruption in the likewise unfinished "Heidelberg Aesthetics."[165] That Lukács himself later denied the identity of the Dostoevsky project and **The Theory of the Novel** does nothing to negate the fact that from the point of view of literary history the three or four projects of those years were all bound together by the same presuppositions and the same goals, that, in a sense, the "Aesthetics," the Dostoevsky book and **The Theory of the Novel** were all manifestations of those same concerns. The accident that resulted in the publication of **The Theory of the Novel** and the suppression of the others has tended to isolate that work, especially when it is read in opposition to Lukács's later criticism and without regard to the essays collected in **Soul and Form**. If reading it as an introduction to a possible Dostoevsky book better enables us to read it clearly, that is, as a continuation of Lukács's ethical and mystical preoccupations and not as an instrument for understanding the novel as an art form in modern terms, then, perhaps, it is best read in that fashion.

The note of hope upon which the book ends reflects a hope for the spiritual regeneration of the social world, such a regeneration as those proposed by Tolstoy and Dostoevsky. It was only after that hope was "crushed by the sterile power of the merely existent" that Lukács literally as well as figuratively left the Spiritual Circle for revolutionary Communism. And yet there is some truth to the analysis of the book offered by the older Lukács:

> **The Theory of the Novel** is not conservative but subversive in nature, even if based on a highly naive and totally unfounded utopianism – the hope that a natural life worthy of man can spring from the disintegration of capitalism and the destruction, seen as identical with that disintegration, of the lifeless and life-denying social and economic categories. The fact that the book culminates in its analysis of Tolstoy, as well as the author's view of Dostoevsky, who, it is claimed, 'did not write novels', clearly indicate that the author was not looking for a new literary form but, quite explicitly, for a 'new world'. We have every right to smile at such primitive utopianism, but it expresses nonetheless an intellectual tendency which was part of the reality of that time. (20)

The book, like much of the "romantic anti-capitalism" of the time, is at once conservative and subversive. God-seekers care as little for big business as do distinguished members of the Central Committee of the Hungarian

---

[165]   Ferenc Feher, "The Last Phase of Romantic Anti-Capitalism: Lukács's Response to the War," **New German Critique,** 10 (1977), pp. 139–54.

Communist Party.

   The essays in **The Theory of the Novel,** like those in **Soul and Form,** discuss literature in the way that a great preacher might discuss any work of art as a metaphor for the devout life. No matter how skillfully it is done, no matter how suggestively he handles the subject, no matter how much learning he brings to bear on it, the work of art is not his central concern. His central concern is the soul.

The Ideology of the Spirit

Lukács began writing in a Central European cultural tradition that was highly self-conscious and beginning to worry that the Self was all that there was available as a field for consciousness. The Life Philosophers' concentration of attention on views of the world as the constituting elements of consciousness had begun, with Dilthey, as an attempt to found a humanistic alternative to the natural sciences. An heir to Romantic philosophy, in attitude if not doctrine, Dilthey popularized an emphasis on the role of the subject in the experience of knowledge, an emphasis that was sharpened further by Simmel's emotional interpretation of the concepts of understanding and world view. Simmel taught Lukács that if there is a world "out there," it can only be experienced as chaos, that ultimately what we know is that which we decide to believe.

These intellectual trends were not occurring in isolation. The industrialization of Central Europe during the two generations preceding Lukács and continuing in his own early years was experienced by much of the Central European population as a catastrophe, a catastrophe expressed by Tönnies as the destruction of Gemeinschaft and the spread of Gesellschaft forms of social organization: the death of traditional Europe. The social result was to separate large numbers of people from their inherited forms of behavior and belief. Both the displaced agricultural workers and craftsmen forced into the new cities and the young middle class intellectuals typified by the German speaking Jews of Budapest, Prague, Vienna, and Berlin felt as if they were now in a strange new world, ominous, disaster prone, seemingly with no place for traditional humane values and relations.

In the essays collected for **Soul and Form** Lukács wrote about literary topics in such a way, following Simmel, as to forge a set of personal beliefs from the materials at hand. Those beliefs were spiritual, approaching the mystical. If nothing is certain, if we can hardly be sure this awful new industrial and commercial world is there at all, all the more reason to search for certainty in religion, in the search for God. By 1910–11 Lukács and many of his friends were, we do not know how seriously, waiting for the Messiah as a solution to the problems of alienation in society and self. Lukács, the book reviewer and philosophy student, was also looking for signs of that solution in art. The artist, the essayist, the poet, were all figures of modes of escape from the intolerable phantasm of modern society into the certainty of the transcendental of which art itself is a figure.

It was at this point that Lukács encountered Max Weber. The transfer of Lukacs's studies from Berlin to Heidelberg, from Simmel to Weber, was a move from a fashionable embrace of irrationality to a despairing and stoical acceptance of the Neo-Kantian conclusions about that irrationality and an effort to think beyond them. Weber had taken the concept of world view from the common stock of ideas of his time, but instead of applying these organizing principles to life, he restricted their use to science, claiming, in true Protestant fashion, that the goals and purpose of life are to be found only within the individual soul, that matters of belief were the basis for interests and were not to be found through scientific investigation. We start thinking from the point of view of values, we do not find values in science, or art. On the other hand, Weber taught that the uncontrollable irrationality of interests and values could be put to scientific use through the theory of ideal types – the deliberate one sided accentuation of models in order to develop and test theories in the human sciences. Weber asks us to declare our emotional imports at the border of scientific inquiry; having made those declarations we can contribute appropriately to the great humanistic effort to understand as much as we can of the world, and not throw ourselves into the embrace of irrationalist world views and ideologies out of despair of understanding everything. Some thought that because man could not be a god, all was permitted. Weber taught that it was sufficiently difficult to be human.

Unfortunately, Lukács, like many others, like Weber himself at moments, forgot that the ideal types were heuristic devices and not Hegelian stages of the Absolute. In **The Theory of the Novel** Lukács reified Weberian categories, producing a typology of the novel, which, by the way, as it were, contained many brilliant insights, but which, ultimately, sought to use literary theory as he had earlier used literary criticism, as a vehicle for spiritual exploration. Where for Weber this development of one-sided models would have been the beginning of an investigation of the data "given in consciousness," literary works themselves, for Lukács it was little more than a rhetorical device, a structure for his mystical explorations. This approach to literary topics was, in its time, a healthy contrast to the well-worn philological Positivism of literary history. More than half a century later Herbert Marcuse, for one, still remembered the excitement created by this opening to philosophy in **The Theory of the Novel** and similar works. The world their grandfathers had made was cracking all around them; what had seemed to be a cage of plate glass was soon to lie shattered at their feet – Positivism had yielded to the excitement of subjectivist forms of Idealism, as Liberalism had yielded to Imperial dreams or their contraries. Soon it would not be necessary to cast about for points of view. History would impose its own.

Not long after publishing **The Theory of the Novel**, Lukács came to the end of what he called his "road to Marx," joining the Party, beginning an unparalleled career as activist, philosopher, literary theorist. Many admirers of the later Lukács have read these earlier books through their knowledge of the way in which he would use the ideas contained in them in other contexts. That is a serious distortion, both of these early works, and of his own example. **The Theory of the Novel** was not a Marxist work. It and **Soul and Form** are much closer to certain later rejections of historical philology and theory in American literary criticism than they are to Lukács's own subsequent writings on the historical novel and critical realism. If he allowed them to be reprinted, what of it? To be unashamed of youthful brilliance is not an uncommon situation, no matter how much opinions have changed with age. Neither is the tolerance of the aged Lukács for his early work a Marxist imprimatur for it. Applying that which we have learned from reading the pre-Marxist Lukács in similar situations, we can be alert to similar uses of literary criticism and theory. Spiritual values can be found in literature, and it is possible for the scholar to devote himself to that quest, but when he does so we should all be aware that he does this not as a scholar, but as a human being with spiritual concerns. "We can keep on asking science: What must we do? How should we live? Science will give us no reply . . ."

This reading of two of Georg Lukács's early literary works has shown us, in particular, that Lukács was neither a conventional literary scholar nor a Marxist when he wrote them, but that situated in an intellectual matrix derived from Life Philosophy and Neo-Kantianism, he was gradually putting this intellectual heritage to use as a way of solving its central problematic, that of values in a "God-forsaken" world. That is a result interesting in itself, particularly now when various scholars attempt on the one hand to claim Lukács's authority for their own spiritual ventures, usually of a nihilistic type, and on the other - even more oddly - some scholars attempt to assert some Marxist point of view for these overtly spiritual essays. In general, our readings can be applied to other, similar books in our own tradition, encouraging us to take seriously what they actually say, as opposed to what we assume they must really mean. For instance, **The Verbal Icon,** a classic work of American literary theory, may now be seen as representative of Lukács's Platonist essay category, a book which appears to be about poetry, when it is "actually" about religious belief.

The central image of **The Verbal Icon** is that of the poem as object, a peculiar object, an icon, which Wimsatt refers to in

A NOTE ON THE TITLE OF THIS BOOK: The term icon used today by semeiotic writers to refer to a verbal sign which somehow shares the properties of, or resembles, the objects which it denotes. The same term in its more usual meaning refers to a visual image and expecially to one which is a religious symbol. The verbal image which most fully realizes its verbal capacities is that which is not merely a bright picture (in the usual modern meaning of the term image) but also an interpretation of reality in its metaphoric and symbolic dimensions. Thus: **The Verbal Icon.**

We expect, then, that the essays so entitled will enlighten us as to how poems, as verbal icons, interpret reality.[166] This is, in fact, what Wimsatt did. He called for such studies and, as a religious man, he asked that the study of poetry result in certain interpretations, those of the religious mind, which reads the great book of the world as a third Testament, a fifth Gospel. One could, perhaps, call it the Wordsworthian heresy.

For Wimsatt, the less we bring our knowledge about the author of a literary work, of a poem, to its reading, the better off we are. A poem is not a "vessel for the spirit" in the Simmelian tradition. It is, oddly enough, something like a pudding.

> Judging a poem is like judging a pudding or a machine. One demands that it work. . . . A poem can be only through its meaning – since its medium is words – yet it is, simply is, in the same way that we have no excuse for inquiring what part is intended or meant. Poetry is a feat of style by which a complex of meaning is handled all at once. (4)

According to Wimsatt, while we are judging our pudding we are relieved of the necessity for considering either the intentions or the knowledge of the cook. The only question at hand, seemingly, is that of taste: Is it a good pudding? For instance, take Coleridge's poem, "Kubla Khan." "Perhaps a person who has read Bartram appreciates the poem more than one who has not. . . . But it would seem to pertain little to the poem to know that Coleridge had read Bartram" (12). We need not even worry whether the cook thought he was making soup instead. If it seems to be a pudding to us, it is a pudding. Only those authorial intentions discernible within the poem need concern us.

Although "we have no excuse for inquiring what part is intended or meant," we must restrict ourselves precisely to meanings. "The critic is . . . a teacher or explicator of meanings" (34). The role of the critic, then, is not, as it at first seems, to discourse exclusively about the formal aspects of poetry. The critic is also concerned with meanings. This reasonable injunction at once gets us into problems. For meanings do not exist by themselves. The world and its parts are meaningless except to a mind. Things have a meaning for someone, they do not simply mean. So far we can follow the Neo-Kantians and Life Philosophers. Many objects, or messages, have meanings because they are meant. This is perhaps the simplest way of considering the matter. If we do not understand something spoken by another person, we can ask: "What do you mean?" But, of course, there are other objects, messages, and events, which have meanings because these are given to them by the person observing the

---

166   William K. Wimsatt, Jr., **The Verbal Icon** (Lexington: University of Kentucky Press, 1954), p. x. Further page references in the text are to this edition.

object or event in question. If we say that a red sky in the morning means stormy weather, we do not intend that the sky is consciously attempting to communicate this information to us. Wimsatt's position becomes understandable, then, only if we realize that he apparently took poems to be objects meaningful in this second sense; that, as he said, they are not messages but exactly verbal icons. The question of meaning, for Wimsatt, is crucially determined by the fact that like painted icons, poems survive their creators. "Though cultures have changed and will change, poems remain and explain" (39). What do they explain? Not the poet's culture or intentions, nor those of her or his culture. If the explanatory power of poetry is transcendental, that which is explained must also be transcendental, ahistorical, uniquely enduring, since all things human change and pass away.

Wimsatt also removed the ordinary reader from the possible field of meaning. These verbal icons, which mean something in spite of not being meant in that way by their originators and without being understood by their readers, have a meaning which is not informative, but moral.

> We inquire now not about origins nor about effects, but about the work so far as it can be considered by itself as a body of meaning. Neither the qualities of the author's mind nor the effects of a poem upon a reader's mind should be confused with the moral quality of the meaning expressed by the poem itself. (87)

As the proper meaning of a Greek Orthodox icon is always religious, not merely aesthetic or historical, so for Wimsatt the crucial interest of poetry was not, as it seems at first, meaning itself, but the "moral quality of the meaning." Wimsatt believed that the interpretation of poetry is a moral gesture. The perfect poet for Wimsatt's purpose in **The Verbal Icon** was indeed Wordsworth. Wimsatt found Wordsworth's world view acceptable despite its heterodoxy:

> As a philosophy it is better than no philosophy, or better, say than dialectical materialism – because it contains much larger elements of truth. As an idea in a poem, a semimetaphoric notion of a spirit pervading a landscape, it need be no more of a philosophy than one chooses to make it. It is one way of being inspired by a landscape, one approach, we may easily say, toward God. (94)

The critic examines the poem, writes about the poem, and finds in it a "philosophy" that is an approach to God. This is the "meaning" of which the critic is the teacher and explicator. We have heard this before.

Wimsatt would have us read poetry, as the early Lukács held that we should write about it, so that by the way, as it were, we can find God. In Wimsatt's case the idea of God in question was fairly strictly defined. He found that: "poems as empirically discovered and tested do tend, within their limits and given the peculiar donnees or presuppositions of each, to point toward the higher integration of dogma" (100). Poetry itself not only leads the way to God, it, iconically, signifies dogma, presumably Catholic dogma. Thus it is not accident that the New Criticism became a privileged domain of the religious scholar:

> There is certainly a broad sense in which Christian thinking ought to be sympathetic to recent literary criticism – a sense arising simply from the fact that recent criticism is criticism; that is, an activity aimed at understanding a kind of value, and a kind which, if not identical with moral and religious values, is very close to these and may even be thought of as a likely ally. (267)

Poetry, for Wimsatt, helps us to approach, means the approach, to God, through "the higher integration of dogma." And literary criticism is the attempt to understand religious values. If Christian thought and the criticism of poetry are related, then it follows that the techniques of Biblical exegesis might be helpful for the literary critic:

> One of the most distinctive features of recent criticism has been its realization of the inherently ambiguous or polysemous nature of verbal discourse, and especially of poetic discourse. But this is something pre-Cartesian and prescientific in spirit, and if it does not immediately derive from, is at least compatible with, an approach to verbal exegesis which persisted from remote antiquity to the Renaissance and has played a not inconspicuous part in the reading of Christian revelation. (268)

This technique of literary criticism, the dwelling on ambiguity and paradox, the search for a personal revelation concerning meaning, does appear similar to a tradition of Biblical exegesis.

There seems, though, something not quite right here. After all, there is a difference between poetry and scripture. Wimsatt himself appeared to recognize this:

> Whereas the modern interpretation of poetry is fully concrete – reading the poet's words not within his limits as intender but in the fullness of his responsibilty as public performer in a complex and treacherous medium – on the other hand the exegesis of Scripture, if I understand its rationale, has been implicitly intentional; because, indeed, it has dealt with inspirations. (269)

This is a problem, but it can be overcome. For Wimsatt, the unknowable mystery of the Divine Intentions was not too different, as a methodological problem, from the unaskable secret of the poet's intentions. In both cases the meaning is to be found in the critic's understanding. Critics, in this view, find themselves methodologically committed to a concern with religious questions.

> Despite the discriminatory efforts of some writers . . . the vocabulary
> and main assumptions of recent criticism have been developing in a
> way that makes it now difficult to speak well of poetry without
> participating in a joint defense of poetry and religion, or at least
> without a considerable involvement in theology. (276)

Wimsatt based his spiritual approach to the study of literature on Christian
dogma itself, in opposition to what he refers to as "totalitarian Marxism," or,
less sensationally, merely in opposition to the older historical scholarship
which took poetry, iconoclastically, as an object for research, not as a tool
for salvation.

Wimsatt meant literally what his book's title implied, that poems are
verbal icons, religious symbols.[167] Literary criticism and literary theory in
the United States since the publication of **The Verbal Icon** have continued
to privilege the concerns of that work.   While many other schools of
criticism have developed or been transplanted here, two important aspects
of the New Criticism have continued to receive respectful consideration:
the moral function of the literary critic and the isolation of literary studies
from other humanistic disciplines, especially from the historical sciences. It
is not that the legacy of the New Criticism has had the effect of excluding
other approaches to literary studies in some direct, programmatic fashion; it
is, rather, that its world view, this ideology of the spirit, has often set the
underlying tone of our work.

The technical side of the New Criticism has virtually faded from view.
Some critics have even lost their concern for the unity of literary works,
substituting an interest in the disunities of the same texts, their
incoherence.   But is the reverse of a proposition so different from the
original? These critics, like Lukács before them, still frequently maintain that
we study literature in search of (or in despair of) values, that the critic or
interpreter ironically dominates both text and author. Wimsatt believed that

---

[167]   The religious basis of the New Criticism is easily discernible in other
books by the founders of the movement.   Brooks and Wimsatt, for
instance, in their **Literary Criticism,** stated that the study of literature
culminates in the Mystery of the Incarnation. (It is not apparent from
the text that anything other than the Catholic doctrine of that name is
intended by this statement.   It is not obviously ambiguous or
metaphorical.) As religious persons do not contemplate a painted icon
exclusively from the point of view of the history of painting styles, so
critics trained or influenced by Wimsatt and the other New Critics
continue to regard the study of literature as a cultural phenomenon to
be subordinated to literature's spiritual role.   Recent attempts to
defend the New Critics against charges of scientism are unnecessary.
The New Critics were always Idealists.

the study of literature is itself an approach to God. Paul de Man, among others, argued that such literary criticism is the product of a crisis: "In periods that are not periods of crisis, or in individuals bent on avoiding crisis at all cost, there can be all kinds of approaches to literature: historical, philological, psychological, etc., but there can be no criticism. For such periods or individuals will never put the act of writing into question by relating it to its specific intent."[168] These critics insist on the desirability of putting the act of writing into question, of defining criticism by this reflexive act. While at first it appears that this is in some sense the opposite of the tradition of Wimsatt, in practice even the most scrupulous nihilism is often nothing but a detour on the high road to faith, is indeed, often exactly the negative moment of the Kirkegaardian dialectic. It is, after all, the contemplation of an absent God, negative theology, which represents the strongest tradition of Western mysticism. This closes a gap in our understanding of current trends in literary criticism, that between those who say they are looking for moral order in literature and those who claim to believe that there is no moral order possible, only a portentous absence.

All these critics – Wimsatt, the nihilists, as well as the tolerant relativists – see literary scholarship as a search for values, and value criticism, or interpretation, equal to or above literature itself. Most of them link this search for values with the search for, or the sorrow at the loss of, religion. Theirs is also the ideology of the spirit, which, like all ideologies, is one way of understanding the world. But the privileging of the interpreter in the act of literary interpretation devalues both literature and religion. There is, after all, a difference between religious mysteries and secular secrets. The former are always, in principle, unfathomable. As David Grossvogel has commented:

> Unable either to grasp or to abandon mystery, [man] resorts to a familiar fraud: he attempts to absorb mystery in speculation; he invents incarnations with which he can cope. Literature plays a part in this process, and most literature is tinctured to some extent with the effects of that concern. An intercessory image is created, similar in its position to that of the initiate, and corresponding to the ritual wherein the initiate demonstrates and secrets his knowledge. But whereas the initiate is eventually absorbed by the mystery he mediates, the image remains wholly within the grasp of man.[169]

---

[168] Paul de Man, **Blindness and Insight** (New York: Oxford University Press, 1971), p. 8.

[169] David Grossvogel, **Mystery and Its Fictions** (Baltimore: The Johns Hopkins University Press, 1979), p. 4.

Literary criticism of the varieties touched upon above has become for many such "an intercessory image." Yet we would do well to remember that, in the words of Weber, "the elementary duty of scientific self-control and the only way to avoid serious and foolish blunders require a sharp precise distinction between . . . analysis of reality . . . and the value-judgment of reality on the basis of ideals."[170] Humanists will probably always be moralists. In many cases we become humanists because we are moralists, because of our concern with moral and ethical issues. Our moral concerns may bring us to the study of literature; they should not prevent us from making that necessary distinction between the "analysis of reality" and "the value-judgment of reality on the basis of ideals."

---

[170] Max Weber, "'Objectivity' in Social Science and Social Policy," in **Max Weber's Ideal Type Theory,** ed. Rolf E. Rogers (New York: Philosophical Library, Inc., 1969), p. 26.

Bibliography

Antoni, Carlo. **From History to Sociology.** Trans. Hayden White. Detroit: Wayne State University Press, 1959.

Arato, Andrew. "Lukács' Path to Marxism." **Telos,** 7 (1971), 128-36.

‒ ‒ ‒ ‒ ‒. "The Neo-Idealist Defense of Subjectivity." **Telos,** 21 (1974), 108-61.

Balázs, Béla. "Notes From a Diary." **New Hungarian Quarterly,** XIII, 47 (1972), 127-8.

Bloch, Ernst. "Schulphilosophen heute." **Durch die Wusste.** Frankfurt, 1964.

Bloom, Harold. "Introduction." **Selected Writings of Walter Pater.** New York: New American Library, 1974.

Breines, Paul. "Bloch Magic." **Continuum,** 7 (Winter 1970), 619-624.

‒ ‒ ‒ ‒ ‒. "Lukács, Revolution and Marxism, 1885-1918: Notes on Lukács' 'Road to Marx.'" **Philosophical Forum,** III, 3-4 (Spring-Summer 1972).

‒ ‒ ‒ ‒ ‒. "Notes on Georg Lukacs' 'The Old Culture and the New Culture.'" **Telos,** 5 (Spring 1970), 1-20.

‒ ‒ ‒ ‒ ‒. "Review of Vacca's **Lukacs O Korsch.**" **Telos,** 5 (1970), 215-20.

Burger, Thomas. **Max Weber's Theory of Concept Formation.** Durham, North Carolina: Duke University Press, 1976.

Congdon, Lee. "The Unexpected Revolutionary: Lukács' Road to Marx." **Survey,** 20 (Spring-Summer 1974), 176-205.

‒ ‒ ‒ ‒ ‒. "Beyond the 'Hungarian Wasteland': A Study in the Ideology of National Regeneration, 1900-1919. Diss., Northern Illinois University, 1973.

‒ ‒ ‒ ‒ ‒. **The Young Lukacs.** Chapel Hill: The University of North Carolina Press, 1983.

Coser, Lewis A. **Georg Simmel.** Englewood Cliffs: Prentice-Hall, 1965.

Dilthey, Wilhelm. **Gesammelte Schriften.** Leipzig, 1914.

Eliade, Mircea. **The Myth of the Eternal Return.** New York: Bollingen Foundation, 1965.

Eliot, Thomas Stearns. "Gerontion." In **The Complete Poems and Plays, 1909–1950.** New York: Harcourt, Brace & World, 1962.

Federici, Silvia. "Notes on Lukács' Aesthetics." **Telos,** 11 (1972), 141–51.

Feenberg, Andrew. "Aesthetics as Social Theory." **Telos,** 15 (Spring 1975), 41–6.

– – – – – . "An Introduction to the Young Lukács." **Alternatives** (Fall 1966), 18–28.

Fehér, Ferenc. "Bloch and Lukács: Two Radical Critics in a 'God-Forsaken' World." **Telos,** 25 (Fall 1975), 155–66.

– – – – – . "Is the Novel Problematic: A Contribution to the Theory of the Novel." **Telos,** 15 (Spring 1973), 47–74.

– – – – – . "The Last Phase of Romantic Anti-Capitalism: Lukács's Response to the War." **New German Critique,** 10 (1977), 139–54.

– – – – – , et al. "Notes on Lukács' Ontology." **Telos,** 29 (Fall 1976), 160–81.

Feher, Zoltan. "Georg Lukács's Role in Dostoevsky's European Reception at the Turn of the Century." Diss. UCLA, 1978.

Frankel, Serge, and Daniel Martin. "The Budapest School." **Telos,** 17 (Fall 1973), 122–33.

Freud, Sigmund. **A General Introduction to Psychoanalysis.** Trans. Joan Riviere. New York: Washington Square Press, 1960.

– – – – – . "A Disturbance of Memory on the Acropolis." In **Collected Papers.** London: Hogarth Press and The Institute of Psycho-Analysis, 1950.

Freund, Julian. **The Sociology of Max Weber.** Trans. Mary Ilford. New York: Pantheon, 1968.

Goldmann, Lucien. **The Hidden God.** Trans. Philip Thody. London: Routledge and Kegan Paul, 1968.

– – – – – . "The Aesthetics of the Young Lukács." **New Hungarian Quarterly,** XIII, 47 (1972), 129–56.

– – – – – . "The Early Writings of Georg Lukács." **TriQuarterly,** 9 (Spring 1967), 165–81.

– – – – – . "Introduction aux Premiers Ecrits de Georges Lukacs." **Les Temps Modernes,** 18 (1962–3), 254–80.

Gombrich, E. H. **Symbolic Images.** London: Phaidon Press, 1972.

– – – – – . **Art and Illusion.** New York: The Bollingen Foundation, Pantheon, Random House, 1961.

Grossvogel, David. **Mystery and Its Fictions.** Baltimore: The Johns Hopkins University Press, 1979.

Guillén, Claudio. **Literature as System.** Princeton: Princeton University Press, 1971.

Hartman, Geoffrey. "Crossing Over: Literary Commentary as Literature." **Comparative Literature,** 28:257–76.

Hauser, Arnold, and György Lukács. "On Youth, Art and Philosophy." **New Hungarian Quarterly,** XVI (Summer 1975), 96–105.

Hekman, Susan J. **Weber, the Ideal Type and Contemporary Social Theory.** Notre Dame, Indiana: University of Notre Dame Press, 1983).

Heller, Agnes. "On the New Adventures of the Dialectic." **Telos,** 31 (1976), 134–42.

– – – – – . "'Von Der Armut Am Geiste,' A Dialogue by the Young Lukács." **Philosophical Forum,** III, 3–4 (Spring–Summer 1972).

Hermand, Jost, and Evelyn Torton Beck. **Interpretive Synthesis.** New York: Frederick Ungar, 1975.

Hirsch, E. D., Jr. **Validity in Interpretation.** New Haven: Yale University Press, 1967.

Hodges, H. A. **The Philosophy of Wilhelm Dilthey.** London: Routledge and Kegan Paul, 1952.

Honigsheim, Paul. **On Max Weber.** Trans. Joan Rytina. New York: The Free Press, 1968.

Hughes, H. Stuart. **Consciousness and Society.** New York: Vintage Books, Random House, 1958.

Isherwood, Christopher. **The Berlin Stories.** New York: New Directions, n.d.

Jay, Martin. **The Dialectical Imagination.** Boston: Little, Brown and Company, 1973.

Jameson, Fredric. **Marxism and Form.** Princeton: Princeton University Press, 1971.

– – – – – . "The Vanishing Mediator." In **Working Papers in Cultural Studies,** 5 (Spring 1974), 111–49.

Janik, Allan, and Stephen Toulmin. **Wittgenstein's Vienna.** New York: Simon and Schuster, 1973.

Kant, Immanuel. **Critique of Practical Reason.** Trans. Lewis White Beck. New York: Bobbs–Merrill, 1956.

– – – – – . **The Critique of Pure Reason.** Trans. Norman Kemp Smith. New York: St. Martin's Press, 1965.

Kermode, Frank. **The Genesis of Secrecy.** Cambridge, Mass.: Harvard University Press, 1979.

Kettler, David. "Culture and Revolution: Lukács in the Hungarian Revolution of 1918/19." **Telos,** 10 (Winter 1971), 35–92.

Kurrik, Maire. "The Novel's Subjectivity: Georg Lukács's **Theory of the Novel."** **Salmagundi,** 28 (Winter 1975), 104–124.

Lichtheim, George. **George Lukacs.** New York: The Viking Press, 1970.

Loewith, Karl. "Max Weber and Karl Marx." In **Max Weber.** Ed. Dennis Wrong. Englewood Cliffs: Prentice–Hall, 1970, 101–122.

Lovejoy, Arthur O. and George Boas. **Primitivism and Related Ideas in Antiquity.** New York: Octagon Books, 1965.

Lord, Albert, and Milman Parry. **The Singer of Tales.** Cambridge, Mass.: Harvard University Press, 1960.

Lukács, Georg. **A lélek és a formák.** Budapest: Franklin, 1910.

– – – – – . **Die Seele und die Formen.** Berlin: Egon Fleischel & Co., 1911.

– – – – – . "Von der Armut am Geiste. Ein Gesprach und ein Brief." **Neue Blatter,** 1912.

– – – – – . "Die Theorie des Romans." **Zeitschrift fur Asthetik und Allgemeine Kunstwissenschaft,** 1916.

– – – – – . "Georg Simmel. Ein Nachruf." **Pester Lloyd,** 1918.

– – – – – . "Emil Lask. Ein Nachruff." **Kant–Studien,** 1918.

– – – – – . **Der Junge Hegel. Uber die Beziehungen von Dialektik und Okonomie.** Zurich & Wein: Europa Verlag, 1948.

– – – – – . **Die Theorie des Romans.** Neuwied und Berlin: Hermann Luchterhand, 1963.

– – – – – . "The Sociology of Modern Drama." **Tulane Drama Review,** 9 (Summer 1965), 146-70.

– – – – – . "The Old Culture and the New Culture." **Telos,** 5 (Spring 1970), 21 ff.

– – – – – . **The Theory of the Novel. A Historico–Philosophical Essay on the Forms of Great Epic Literature.** Trans. Anna Bostock. Cambridge, Mass.: MIT Press, 1971.

– – – – – . "Bela Bartok." **New Hungarian Quarterly,** XII (Spring 1971), 42-55.

– – – – – . "'Preface' The Distinctiveness of the Aesthetic." Quoted in "On Georg Lukács' Unpublished Aesthetics," by György Markus in **Philosophical Forum,** III, 3-4 (Spring–Summer 1972).

– – – – – . "Art and Society." **New Hungarian Quarterly,** XIII, 47 (1972), 44-56.

– – – – – . "Labour as a Model of Social Practice." **New Hungarian Quarterly,** XIII, 47 (1972), 5-44.

– – – – – . "Letters from Lukács to Paul Ernst." **New Hungarian Quarterly,** III, 47 (1972), 88-99.

– – – – – . "On Futurology." **New Hungarian Quarterly,** XIII, 47 (1972), 100-7.

– – – – – . "On the Phenomenology of the Cultural Process." **Philosophical Forum,** III, 3-4 (Spring–Summer 1972), 314-25.

– – – – – . "On Poverty of Spirit, A Conversation and Letter." Trans. John T. Sanders. **Philosophical Forum**, III, 3-4 (Spring–Summer 1972).

– – – – – . "The Philosophy of Art." **New Hungarian Quarterly**, XIII, 47 (1972), 57–87.

– – – – – . **The Soul and the Forms.** Trans. Anna Bostock. Cambridge, Mass.: MIT Press, 1974.

– – – – – . **The Young Hegel.** Trans. Rodney Livingstone. London: Merlin Press, 1975.

Makkreel, Rudolf A. **Dilthey, Philosopher of the Human Studies.** Princeton: Princeton University Press, 1975.

Man, Paul de. **Blindness and Insight.** New York: Oxford University Press, 1971.

Mann, Thomas. **The Magic Mountain.** Trans. H. T. Lowe–Porter. London: Penguin Books, 1960.

– – – – – . **Buddenbrooks.** Trans. H. T. Lowe–Porter. New York: Alfred A. Knopf, 1952.

Mannheim, Karl. "Letters to Lukács, 1910-16." **New Hungarian Quarterly,** XVI (Spring 1965), 93–105.

– – – – – . "A Review of Georg Lukács' **Theory of the Novel.**" **Studies on the Left,** 13, 3 (Summer 1963), 50–3.

Marcuse, Herbert. **Reason and Revolution.** Boston: Beacon Press, 1960.

Markus, György. "The Soul and the Life: The Young Lukács and the Problem of Culture." **Telos,** 32 (1977), 95–115.

Medvedev, P. N., and M. M. Bakhtin. **The Formal Method in Literary Scholarship.** Trans. Albert J. Wehrle. Baltimore: The Johns Hopkins University Press, 1978.

Merleau-Ponty, Maurice. **Adventures of the Dialectic.** Trans. Joseph Bien. Evanston: Northwestern University Press, 1973.

Meszaras, Istvan. **Lukacs' Concept of Dialectic.** London: The Merlin Press, 1972.

Miles, David H. "Portrait of the Marxist as a Young Hegelian: Lukács' **Theory of the Novel.**" **PMLA,** 94 (1979), 22–35.

Parkinson, G. H. R. **Georg Lukacs.** London: Weidenfeld and Nicolson, 1970.

Pater, Walter. **The Renaissance.** New York: New American Library, 1959.

‒ ‒ ‒ ‒ ‒ . "Poems by William Morris." **Westminster Review,** XC (October 1868), 300‒12.

Plantinga, Theodore. **Historical Understanding in the Thought of William Dilthey.** Toronto: University of Toronto Press, 1980.

Plotke, David. "Marxism, Sociology and Crisis: Lukács' Critique of Weber." **Berkeley Journal of Sociology,** 20 (1975‒76), 181‒230.

Radnoti, Sandor. "Bloch and Lukács." **Telos,** 25, 155‒64.

Rickman, H. P. **W. H. Dilthey, Selected Writings.** Cambridge: Cambridge University Press, 1976.

Ringer, Fritz. **The Decline of the German Mandarins.** Cambridge, Mass.: Harvard University Press, 1969.

Sartre, Jean‒Paul. **Critique of Dialectical Reason.** Trans. Alan Sheridan‒Smith. London: NLB, 1976.

Schmidt, James. "The Concrete Totality and Lukács' Concept of Proletarian Bildung." **Telos,** 24 (Summer 1975).

Shell, Marc. **The Economy of Literature.** Baltimore: The Johns Hopkins University Press, 1978.

Simmel, Georg. **Die Probleme der Geschichtsphilosophie. Eine Erkenntnishtheoretische Studie,** 4th ed. München & Leipzig: Duncker & Humblot, 1922.

‒ ‒ ‒ ‒ ‒ . **Lebensanschauung. Vier metaphysische Kapitel.** 2nd ed. München & Leipzig: Duncker & Humblot, 1922.

‒ ‒ ‒ ‒ ‒ . "Die historische Formung." in **Fragmente und Aufsatze aus dem Nachlass und Veroffentlichungen der letzten Jahre.** Ed. Gertrud Kantorowicz. München: Drei Masken, 1923.

‒ ‒ ‒ ‒ ‒ ‒. "Vom Wesen des historischen Verstehens." In **Brucke und Tur. Essays des Philosophen zur Geschichte, Religion, Kunst und Gesellschaft.** Eds. Michael Landmann and Margarete Susman. Stuttgart: Koehler, 1957.

‒ ‒ ‒ ‒ ‒ . "On the Concept and Tragedy of Culture." in **Georg Simmel.** Trans. K. Peter Etzkorn. New York: Teachers College Press, 1968.

─ ─ ─ ─ ─ . "The Adventurer." In **Georg Simmel: On Individuality and Social Forms.** Ed. Donald N. Levine. Chicago: University of Chicago Press, 1971.

─ ─ ─ ─ ─ . **The Problems of the Philosophy of History.** Trans. Gray Oakes. New York: The Free Press, 1977.

Stern, Fritz. **The Politics of Cultural Despair.** Berkeley and Los Angeles: University of California Press, 1961.

Stolper, Gustav, et al. **The German Economy, 1870 to the Present.** Trans. Toni Stolper. New York: Harcourt, Brace & World, 1967.

Thompson, E. P. **William Morris, Romantic to Revolutionary.** London: Lawrence & Wishart, 1955.

Tokes, Rudolf L. **Bela Kun and the Hungarian Soviet Republic.** New York: Frederick A. Praeger, 1967.

Tönnies, Ferdinand. **Community and Society.** Trans. and ed. Charles Loomis. East Lansing: Michigan State University Press, 1957.

Ungvari, Tamas. "The Lost Childhood: The Genesis of Georg Lukács' Concept of Literature." **Cambridge Review,** 93, 2206 (January 1972), 96–100.

Watnick, Morris. "Georg Lukács: Aesthetics or Communism." **Soviet Survey,** 23–4 (1958–59), 60–6; 51–6.

Weber, Marianna. **Max Weber: A Biography.** Trans. and ed. Harry Zohn. New York: John Wiley and Sons, 1975.

Weber, Max. "Objectivity in Social Science and Social Policy." In **Max Weber's Ideal Type Theory.** Ed. Rolf E. Rogers. New York: Philosophical Library, 1969.

Weingartner, Rudolph. **Experience and Culture.** Middletown, Conn.: Wesleyan University Press, 1962.

Wellek, René. **A History of Modern Criticism.** V. 4. New Haven: Yale University Press, 1965.

Wind, Edgar. **Pagan Mysteries in the Renaissance.** Harmondsworth: Penguin Books, 1967.

Wimsatt, William K., Jr., and Monroe C. Beardsley. **The Verbal Icon.** Lexington: University of Kentucky Press, 1954.

Wittgenstein, Ludwig.   **Tractatus Logico-Philosophicus.**   Trans. D. F. Pears and B. F. McGuinness. London: Routledge and Kegan Paul, 1960.

Index